Praise for
maybe it's you

"Lauren Zander has taught me important lessons required to live a life with the most integrity, the most success, and most important—the most fun. My business is killing it, my personal life is the best it's ever been, and my social life is fully loving. Lauren has forced me to face myself over and over again until I am happy."

—Miki Agrawal, founder and chief inventor of TUSHY, THINX, and Wild and author of the best seller *Do Cool Sh*t*

"Lauren and her method have helped me rewrite my inner dialogue, connect deeply to my family, and evolve my excuses so I can be the partner, the mother, the daughter, the sister, and the teacher I've always dreamed I could be."

—Elena Brower, author of *Art of Attention*

"Lauren has changed my life. People say that kind of thing all the time…but this is the real deal. I can flat-out say I have never been happier, more fulfilled, or more certain and excited about the path ahead of me. Nor have I had more FUN! Lauren's method is a gift that is now available to everyone."
—Hugh Jackman

"Lauren Zander is a unique talent with unique insight into the human condition. I have seen her method transform dozens of students over more than a decade of teaching at my university. Now this important work can reach the mass audience it deserves—transforming readers around the world."

—David Mindell, professor, MIT

"Profound and enlightening. Will also make you smile and laugh. And, most important, if taken seriously, it can be transformative. You'll be recommending it to your family and friends who you care about."

—Marc Wais, senior vice president for student affairs,
New York University

"Change takes work! I'm so glad that there is a book that doesn't sugar-coat anything....This book is only for people who are ready for change and to face everything holding them back. You're not alone; I'm on the journey too!"

—Michelle Williams, singer with Destiny's Child

"Practical and inspiring, Zander's [Maybe It's You] shows how owning up to setbacks and shortcomings can turn them into strengths."

—Success magazine

maybe it's you

CUT THE CRAP. FACE YOUR FEARS. LOVE YOUR LIFE.

Lauren Handel Zander

with Marnie Handel Nir

hachette
BOOKS

NEW YORK   BOSTON

Hachette Books
Hachette Book Group
1290 Avenue of the Americas
New York, NY 10104
hachettebooks.com
twitter.com/hachettebooks

Originally published as a hardcover and ebook in 2017 by Hachette Books, Inc.

First trade paperback edition: April 2018

Hachette Books is a division of Hachette Book Group, Inc.

The Hachette Books name and logo are trademarks of Hachette Book Group, Inc.

The publisher is not responsible for websites (or their content) that are not owned by the publisher.

The Hachette Speakers Bureau provides a wide range of authors for speaking events. To find out more, go to www.hachettespeakersbureau.com or call (866) 376-6591.

LCCN: 2016054253
ISBN: 9780316318679

Printed in the United States of America

LSC-C

10 9 8 7 6 5 4 3 2

To my family, born with and bogarted

Man, in his blindness, is quite satisfied with himself, but heartily dislikes the circumstances and situations of his life. He feels this way, not knowing that the cause of his displeasure lies not in the condition nor the person with whom he is displeased, but in the very self he likes so much. Not realizing that "he surrounds himself with the true image of himself" and that "what he is, that only can he see," he is shocked when he discovers that it has always been his own deceitfulness that made him suspicious of others...

—*Neville Goddard*

Contents

Foreword

How to Get Out of Your Own Way

Mark Hyman, MD

Here's the truth about me.

I get in my own way. Chances are, unless you are an enlightened master, you also have blind spots, areas of your life that just don't work—relationships, work situations, your health, finances, your family, etc. How do you deal with them?

If you are like me, you often can see them clearly (or not sometimes!). You find yourself stuck in the same situation over and over again, creating upset and unhappiness. It could be your way of thinking that gets you into trouble, or past traumas and stress, or childhood patterns.

Whatever it is, you have two choices. Live with it and continue to be unhappy, or take a good serious look at yourself in the mirror. The key word here is "mirror." We can't see our blemishes until we have a mirror to reflect them. You can struggle on your own, but the best thing I have ever done is work with Lauren Handel Zander. She is a coach, but far more than that, she understands the human condition—the mental, emotional, and spiritual operating systems that make us who we are.

And she sees how those operating systems get corrupted and mess up our lives, separating us from what we really want, or worse, preventing us from even dreaming of what we want. Lauren and her team have developed The Handel Method, which is a process for debugging your operating system and cleaning up the areas of your beliefs, attitudes, and behaviors that get in the way of your one precious, authentic life. It is a hard process, but it is filled with humor and skillfulness that gets you to laugh at yourself and see the ridiculousness of those beliefs, attitudes, and behaviors that keep you stuck.

I often refer my patients to a coach because they are stuck—even though they know what to do, they just can't do it. In fact, working with Lauren has helped me more than any other thing I have done to learn to communicate, to focus on what is important, to stop worrying and start acting in a way that leads to happiness rather than frustration and stress. It's like a chiropractic adjustment for my mind! Even when it is a little painful and uncomfortable, it hurts good. Like a tight knot in your muscle that needs working out.

Therapy can be helpful, but life coaching is different. For me, it works faster, and is much more focused on change than simply talking. I want someone to get me to stop talking about my problems, and instead to see them in a new light and shift things. It helps me act with integrity, wisdom, clarity, and compassion in everything I do—toward others, but especially toward myself. But I didn't go easily into the process. I resisted it until the suffering was just too much. I hope you don't wait that long!

I first met Lauren Zander at a business meeting in New York. A mutual friend thought we should work together. We shared a cab ride downtown, and very quickly she homed in on the areas of my life that were my biggest challenges, including my marriage and some areas of my career. For the next six months, she gently reached out to me to offer her help. I ran in the other direction, knowing that if I accepted her assistance, I would then have to actually face the areas of my life that were out of integrity. That, in short, I would have to meet the obstacle to an integrated, happy life: me!

The truth was that I didn't want to face the truth. It would mean change, changes in my relationship and work that I didn't want to address. I was caught in a story about my life that took me away from and not toward what mattered to me, and I couldn't actually see it myself. Despite successes in many areas of my life—my kids, my mission and passion in life, my health, my friendships—there were areas of disarray and pain, areas where I kept repeating the same pattern over and over again.

Then when my marriage finally fell apart, I took a deep breath—ready to face what I had not been willing to face—and called Lauren. She drove up and spent a day with me unpacking my life, my beliefs, and the areas of my life that were not thriving. Lauren is an emotional savant. She quickly understood the thinking that was in the way of my happiness and stopping me from achieving my dreams, both personal and professional. For the past five years Lauren has helped me get out of my own way and face difficult challenges with humor and wisdom. She has also supported me in finding peace and happiness, not by avoiding the areas of my life that weren't working but by digging in and fixing them. Recently I had dinner with a friend I hadn't seen in two years. She said that I seemed different, more grounded, centered, happy, and peaceful. And a very big part of that transformation was Lauren's coaching that helped me create a life that is integrated and connected to the truth.

One night a few years ago at a family dinner, her then nine-year-old daughter, Kiya, sat right down next to me and said, "Who are you and what do you do?" Straightforward, honest, but surprising for a little kid. I said, "Well, I help people get to the root of their problems, and why they are suffering." Without skipping a beat she said, "Oh, that's what my mother does."

If you want to get to the root of where your life doesn't rock, or where you feel stuck, or where you are not telling the truth (to yourself or others), then this book is your road map to happiness. More importantly, it's your road map to your own mind, heart, and soul.

Warning Label

Okay. So, not only do I curse, I've been known, on occasion (often), to speak my own Yoda-like language, a combination of wise gibberish, Yiddish, and English. Let's call it Giddish. And though I wish I could tell you many heart-wrenching stories of my own triumph over adversity, I don't really have any. Sure, I dealt with shit. (The likes of which you'll hear more than you possibly bargained for in the pages that follow.) But it's not the deep, dark, and ruthless shit that many of you have. I did not rise from the ashes. I rose from Long Island. My stories are not yours. I know that. What I can tell you, though, is that ever since I was little, I have been on a crusade to heal this world.

As far back as I can remember, I have been up in everybody's faces, a pain in people's asses about their lives and their dreams. I've held my parents to account, inspired my siblings to grow up, and cleaned up every last lie I ever told. I've done every step of this method on myself and have handheld the addicted, the abused, the mean, and the meek—and dared them to do the same. I have helped the lost find their way, and the great to grow.

So, although there is no phoenix here, there is, nonetheless, a fierce, stubborn, wildly insightful, arrogantly honest, crazily committed, and caring human, who will take the heat, the brunt of whatever silver spoon joke you may have, so I can help you have everything you want in your life.

And I mean everything.

(Don't Skip This) Introduction

The Concession Stand

ME, MYSELF, AND WHY

Look. Let's be honest here. If you're looking for niceties, tissues, and sympathy, you've come to the wrong place. I'm not *that* girl. This is not *that* book.

But maybe you're fed up. You're hoping this is the last self-help book your self will ever need. You're more than ready, willing, (a mite masochistic) and able.

You've come to the right place.

Truth is, we're not happy campers, but we so want to be. We're buying all the books. We're watching all the shows. We're on all the diets. But still, lasting change is not happening.

What's up with that?

What I've found is that no one is really asking the right questions. No one is *really* teaching us how to live a life worth living. We are all so busy just reacting to life, so inundated with learning about Christopher Columbus, reading seven hundred books we're going to forget, getting into college, paying off college, and achieving all of our goals that we're not really designing our dream life at all. We're so much greater and more capable than this, except we're not breaking into our own life and discovering our real voice, our real truth, and our real ability to live a life we care so much more about than the one we're seemingly stuck in.

This book is the beginning of *f*ck that* (a technical term).

There truly is a *before* and an *after* to reading this book. Thank you (ridiculously, in advance) for being the type of human who wants a life you believe in, but aren't necessarily in, *yet*. I promise you, if you really dig into this book, read the stories, and do all of the work, your life will never be the same. I will have bitten you.

How'd *I* get bit?

Please take a moment and reread the warning label at the beginning of this book. In particular, see: no hellfires here.

The summer before my second sophomore year of college,* I went to Israel. The big deal of this summer adventure was not so much that I, a Jew, was going to the promised land (we do that), but that I was going there on my own dime, and was, for the first time in my life, going somewhere alone, with zero plans.

I landed in the most gorgeous, most unhip, un-happening kibbutz ever, where there were very few (about two) people who spoke English. The English speaker I befriended was this deep, smart, but overwhelmingly sad man. He was in a relationship with an older woman from the kibbutz who was separated from her city-dwelling husband but was neither planning on divorcing him nor telling him (or many other people in her life) about her new relationship.

See: reason for sad.

He and I were close. I knew every last thing about him and he, me. He was so miserable in his own love story, but had so much compassion for his girlfriend's plight and bought every last one of her excuses that I spent a lot of time arguing with him and fighting harder for his happiness than he. He looked at me like I was a criminal for wanting to change the world, let alone him.

He believed, in no uncertain terms, that you don't get in the world's way.

---

* Now, now, I stepped up and started to care about my education, was transferring to George Washington University, and changed majors, which killed my credits when I transferred. Please note: I could have remembered this less well here.

Meanwhile, I was deeply happy on the kibbutz. I had my routine down and I loved it. I woke up early. Cooked for the entire place. Napped. Read Carlos Castaneda. Listened to my four cassettes: Crosby, Stills, Nash & Young, Rickie Lee Jones, Cat Stevens, and The The. Ran. And pressed repeat.

One day, as I was walking to the volunteer quarters for my nap, I heard something that sounded like, "Look in the bushes, Lauren, right now." And though I certainly heard it—whatever it was (a thought? an internal voice? God/Morgan Freeman?), I, in no uncertain terms, ignored it.

But then I heard "it" again.

And I remember thinking, what the f*ck, Lauren, just listen to yourself. So I did. And in the bushes were two baby birds, without their mother.

I proceeded to wig out.

Not just because of the birding bush moment (and/or the stroke I may have just had), but because I had no idea what to do with the birds. There was no nest. So, I did the only thing I could think of doing—I ran back to the kitchen for help. And whom do I run into? Who else?

The sad, complacent man.

Yes. I asked a fatalist what I should do.

He looked at me like I was the same naive, wide-eyed idealist I always was. "Leave them alone, Lauren. It's fine," he said. Argh. Except, maybe this time he was right. I mean, I knew if I took the birds and they died, I'd feel more responsible for their death than had I left them where I found them.

I went back to my room. I couldn't rest; I was too busy debating with myself. Forty-five minutes passed before I growled, grumbled, and got the eff up to go save the birds. When I got there (and I knew exactly where *there* was), one of the birds was gone, perhaps it had flown away, while the other was gone too (only, in the dead sense).

In that moment, I had my own revelation.

I knew that I would never *ever* call that shot again. I would never let my own fear or worry over an outcome or another person's point of view get in the way of my doing the right thing. I had the capacity in that instance that many other creatures don't—to save another, and I blew it. I chickened out. I made a vow right then and there to live to cause change and never leave anyone behind. If I could do something about it, I should.

The only problem was that I was now in an even bigger quandary.

I was faced with the fact that at home my life was a secret-keeping shit show of examples of things I didn't respect or do anything about, myself included. I went home to New York and blew up everything that needed blowing up: friendships, boyfriends, and, yes, a future divorce. When a dear friend asked me if he should marry my best friend, who I knew was cheating on him, I told him only if he found out what she wasn't telling him.

It went as well as you can imagine.

Reckless of me? Sure. Hey, I was new at this vow. There were bound to be some ruffled feathers, roadkill, and *many* apologies I would owe in my near future. This was the beginning of the end of all the lies in my life, the end of my being fake, and of holding back.

I became me.

I used my transferring to George Washington University as the opportunity it was to abandon ship, start over, and hunt for a whole new community of friends. I was free, happy, and proud in every area of my life, save one.

I couldn't find love (or even get laid) for the life of me.

I was inexplicably benched for the year. Even when it looked like my luck had changed on Halloween, when I was dressed in my best who-gives-a-crap catsuit and hat and got picked up by one of GW's hottest soccer superstars, I got dumped the very next day by him for being Jewish. It was all so odd. Clearly, I was getting dinged for something. I just couldn't figure out for what.

Then I got the memo—my own (and soon, yours).

Unless I designed what I truly and deeply wanted in every area of my life—in this case, my dream when it came to love—I was stuck in a purgatory of sorts; stuck in default, in a reaction to my past, instead of a new and true to my own ideal's design.

The only way out of my purgatory was by breaking into my own life.

I spent the next twenty-five years rewiring myself and creating, evolving, testing, and proving The Handel Method, a step-by-step coaching process that addresses one's entire life and is the basis for this book. The method has changed the lives of tens of thousands of private and corporate clients. It teaches people how to dream, how to realize every last one of their dreams, and how to clean out their closets (literal and figurative), so they can have lives that they're wildly proud of.

In 2005, I met and coached David Mindell, who was not only an esteemed professor at MIT, but was also on the task force assigned to rethink MIT's core curriculum. David was so blown away by his coaching experience that he walked the methodology right into MIT.

A year later, David and I were teaching a three-day pilot course to fifteen students based on The Handel Method. The course, now called "Design Your Life," proved such a success that by 2006, we taught sixty more undergrads, grads, postdocs, alumni, and faculty. Students described the course as "life changing" and "one of the most valuable classes they had ever taken." A full 93.2 percent of them stated that they would recommend the course to others, with many others noting that they wished their family or coworkers could take it as well.

As you can imagine, these MIT students weren't the easiest of "clients," but, without a doubt, were some of the smartest. This is what one chemical engineering student said about the course:

> Before taking "Design Your Life," I always considered myself to be someone who told the truth. I hated lying to people, and prided myself in my ability to be honest. What this class did for me was show me that it is just as important to be honest with *yourself* as it is to other people…I now feel like I am steering the ship, instead of just being along for the ride. The feeling is incredibly empowering, and makes me know that I truly can be active in planning out my life.

Ten years (and more than five hundred MIT students) later, the course is a beloved tradition among the university's students. And we didn't stop with the kids at that one campus—the "Design Your Life" course has been integrated into thirty-five other educational programs, universities, and institutes of learning across the country, including Stanford Graduate School of Business, Stanford University School of Medicine, NYU, Columbia University, Yale School of Drama, Wesleyan University, and the New York City public school system. We are teaching "Design Your Life" in middle schools, high schools, residence halls, and postdoctoral programs, as well as to teachers, faculty members, and administrators all around North America.

How many life coaches can tout that? Not to mention potty-mouthed ones who wear ripped jeans and feathers in their hair?!

I remember thinking forever ago, if I had the gumption to head straight into the schools and teach kids real-life education—how to dream, how to tell the truth, how to be in a relationship, how to forgive their parents and love their siblings, no matter what—wouldn't that make the greatest difference in the world?

Answer: yes.

So here I am. Staying steadfast and true to the promise I made back in the promised land—my, uh, bird calling. I've had maybe one other moment in my life where something came to me and spoke to me that was me. It's a voice I hardly ever get to hear.

But trust me, I now trust me—and listen.

Although I wish I could say that the coaching in this book has never before been spewed, it's not so. However, what I can claim with certainty is that what sets The Handel Method apart is how I, with honesty, balls, and a profound understanding of humanity's predicament, will dig deep to your very core.

The Handel Method works because it's not an idea or a philosophy or a concept or a "way of thinking," like other programs. Instead, The Handel Method is just what it sounds like—a *method*. It has clear, organized steps to follow. The structure and format of *Maybe It's You* is broken down into ten coaching sessions, and at the end of each chapter you will be given written assignments designed to address the areas in your life that matter most to you. Throughout the book, I'll also share four of my clients' inspiring stories of change and assignments they did with me to help you with yours.

Some of the assignments in here are indeed doozies (a military term).

Keep breathing, roll up your sleeves, and yes, feel free to figure out what to secretly name the computer file where you'll stash them. Hell, call it something no one would ever consider opening, like "Dental Records: 1998–2010." Or maybe, you're the old-school type and prefer to handwrite your assignments and would rather buy a bound journal (in the lock-and-key sense) in which to secretly write out your responses, indecipherably. Either way, do what works for you. Just remind yourself, if you're the type that needs an honest but swift kick—your old way of doing things is what got you here.

I'm not going to lie. *Maybe It's You* isn't easy. You and I are going on a ride, a road trip, of sorts. You're going to drive, because who else should, while I call shotgun, bark, and point. Yes, I'm *that* kind of GPS lady. But where I'm taking you, if you're willing to go, is where your happiness resides.

Are you coming?

I dare you. But think about it. I'm not prescribing ten years of therapy to get you there. I'm offering you ten sessions based on twenty years of work I've already done and 22,000 guinea pigs before you.

Hey, it could be worse. You could have been my very first client … *

---

* Hi, Mom!

You Must Be Dreaming

Designing the Life You Want

THE RIDE OF YOUR LIFE

Inside each of us is our ideal life: our true north.

But what happens as we get further along in our journey? We lose sight of where we're going and how we want to get there. We get distracted—by a crazy job, or a health crisis, or a new kid, or a divorce, or a Netflix series, or one of countless other bumps in the road. And slowly, bit by bit, we find ourselves veering off course or never even calling our course.

In *Maybe It's You*, you and I are going to course correct—we're going to ride full throttle toward those ideals. And we're not just racing toward one or two of your deepest desires—we're gunning for *all* of them. Buckle up. I call shotgun. You drive, while I bark* directions at you so doggedly, so much more invested in your dreams than you are, that you can't help but release the autopilot button you didn't even know you pressed long ago.

If we're not the one driving our dreams forward, who is? If we don't figure out how to change jobs, eat healthily, date, fall and stay in love, who will come and save us? No one. But, then again, no one should,

---

* Akin to a small, cute, overzealous, and slightly aggressive terrier.

right? They are, after all, *our* dreams. There's an incredible amount of pride that comes from taking hold of the steering wheel, confronting what's between you and what you deeply wish your life looked like.

Ready?

Before I begin, let's meet some of the clients I've worked with over the years who will be joining us on the ride. Each of them came to me with very different issues, and each has generously agreed to contribute their stories and assignments out of gratitude. Their names and certain specificities have been changed—except for Katie, who, in honor of giving up *ever* hiding in her life again, asked me to use her real name and details.

Donna (age forty-five)—is a loving, stay-at-home Chicago mother of three, disgruntled wife of one, but no one would have known that Donna was actually upset, except her stomach. Donna has irritable bowel syndrome (IBS), a chronic inflammatory bowel disorder. So, although Donna pretended to be completely happy to the outside world, her stomach didn't. With IBS, Donna was full of shit, literally, on the inside too.

Stephanie (age forty)—is a hip, smart, successful businesswoman who had it all—a great career, a good salary, a solid retirement plan, an awesome apartment in Manhattan, a ton of friends and yet, for some reason, she was *still* sad. But what else could Stephanie possibly want or need? How about love, the ovaries of a thirty-year-old, colleagues she didn't loathe, and a different mother.

Ethan (age thirty-five)—is an all-around good guy from Connecticut. You know the kind: kind. He's a great dad, a loyal husband, and a hard worker. Sure, he watches a little porn (but feels really guilty about it) and is a tad self-deprecating. You would be too, if you had a bipolar mom, a biological dad you've never met, a boss from hell, and a hot wife who is cold.

Katie (age thirty-eight)—is a screenwriter from Los Angeles, whose first film, *The Perfect Man*, starred Heather Locklear and Hilary

Duff and premiered in the summer of 2005. Sadly, the film never got as big as Katie. At the premiere, Katie weighed 265 pounds. Her husband said he didn't mind. But that wasn't his only lie. He was gay. Katie was now in the middle of a bitter divorce, hiding out in her sister's guesthouse in Palo Alto, drinking Jägermeister.

Barking direction #1: Find yourself in these great people. They are you. As you read their stories, it might not be easy to fully relate or see your *exact* self in them. Word to the wise: Search out how your life mimics theirs, even if it has a slightly different flavor. The following, for example, may be truer for you:

- You're in a marriage you completely adore, with great kids, but you haven't been in the body you want since your baby was born.

Or maybe,

- You, like Stephanie, are single. And, though you don't live in New York City like she does, you think even the Big Apple sounds like a better dating pool than the dried piece of fruit that represents your state.

Or maybe,

- Like Ethan, you're in a job you don't wholly love, but the salary is good, and you've, oh, I don't know, become kind of dependent on food, your 401(k), and health insurance.

Or maybe,

- Though your spouse is more than likely not gay like Katie's, you cannot remember the last time (six weeks, four days, seven hours) you got any action.

You get the idea. I implore, beg, bark, or whatever works for you to find yourself in one of them or, what the heck, all of them. *Barking direction #2*: Trust me. Over the course of the next several pages, I'm going to walk you through the beginning of this process, showing you how each of these people started to identify what they wanted to change about themselves—and how they began to put that change into action.

Then, at a certain point, I'm going to turn the tables and make you actually tackle some of this same work yourself. Hang in there with me. I'll be there with you, every step of the way.

DREAM ON

The first assignment I give each and every client is to dream.

Are you rolling your eyes *already*? Perhaps this would be a good time to make use of the Lamaze breathing technique none of us ever did and exhale, repeatedly—because this assignment gets worse before it gets better.

I'm going to not only ask you to write down your deepest desires, which most of us are already resistant to doing in the first place, but I will also have you write dreams in twelve different areas of your life—from your body to your love life to your career to areas you possibly haven't thought about in years, like fun, adventure, and spirituality.

Believe me, I get it.

Most of us don't allow ourselves to dream much anymore. Okay. Maybe for a few minutes, after we buy a lottery ticket. But dream and be specific about what we want in twelve different areas? On paper? I mean, how often are we asked this? Answer: never.

We didn't *always* suck at dreaming, right?

If I asked you (and I will) what your dream body looks and feels like, or what your dream community is like, you'd be mystified. More than likely, you'd only be able to tell me what you *don't* want versus what would actually make you giddy. And that's because, at some point, we all stopped dreaming. Either someone told us it was time to get realistic and grow up, or we got hurt or disappointed, put our marbles away, and quit playing. Then, as we got older, we decided it was way smarter to want what we can get rather than what we *deeply* desire.

In other words, we sold out.

But, question for you: What's the order of it? Do you think we stop dreaming and then sell out? Or did we stop dreaming *because* we sold out? Or did we sell out so we didn't have to keep dreaming?

The ease at which we're all tolerating what isn't working in our lives is fairly impressive. But here's the thing: If we stay stuck in the premise that we made our beds and now have to lie in them, do we *ever* have to be fully responsible for causing the change we deeply desire?

What if admitting we have a dream forces us to deal head-on with the gap between what we want and what we currently have?

Dreaming wakes us up to ourselves. It gets us in the right fight. It acts as our own internal GPS, allowing us to see where we want to go, all the while showing us the "traffic" that's in our way. Real happiness comes from knowing that you are giving *all* of yourself and being great in your *whole* life—not just one or two areas in your life where most of us prefer to play, but twelve (see chart on page 14).

Are there areas in this chart where you're feeling great about yourself? Are there areas where you are particularly heartbroken?

Unfortunately, those parts of your life where you feel "less than" will find a way to infiltrate every part of your existence, undermining even the areas of your world that seem to be going just great. If you're not fully proud of your body, doesn't that somehow allow you to date *underqualified* men or women, who are not in the league you wish you were? Does it ever stop you from trying new things or meeting new people? After all, the areas of our lives are all intertwined with one another.

You don't have to be great at math to see that if you sell out in even one area of your life, the average of your *entire* level of happiness diminishes.

But, never fear, I have some good news for you. Each of us *has* made a dream happen at some point in our life, either consciously or unconsciously. We quit smoking. We stopped dating unavailable men or

12 AREAS OF LIFE

SELF — How You Feel About Yourself, Personality Traits & Habits

BODY — Health, Weight & Appearance

LOVE — Dating, Marriage, Sex & Romance

SPIRITUALITY — However You Define Spirituality for Yourself (i.e., God, Church, Temple, Spirit, etc.)

CAREER — Business, Work & School Life

MONEY — Earnings, Savings & Money Management

TIME — Relationship to Time, To-Do's & Time Management

HOME — Where You Live, Your Space

FAMILY — Immediate & Extended Family & Parenting

FRIENDS — Old & New Friends

FUN & ADVENTURE — Indulgent Time, Vacations & Extracurricular Learning

COMMUNITY & CONTRIBUTION — Participation in Your Community

women and found the love of our life. We left that horrible job and got a new one. We ran a marathon. We moved to an exciting new city. We've accomplished amazing things in our lives.

Think about it.

What dream did you make happen? Do you have that dream in your head right now? Well, that particular achievement is proof that you are able to make a dream happen when you want to. The steps you took to realize that dream make up your blueprint for success now. If you can do it in one area, you can in another, and I'm going to show you how.

ASSIGNMENT FOR CHAPTER ONE: **PART ONE**

1. Write down at least three accomplishments you've made happen in your life. Yes, I typed "three."

Notice if the inner voice in your head is trying to tell you that 1) the achievement you just thought of was *actually* no big deal and doesn't really count; 2) you can't think of any at all; 3) it's worse than that, you're pretty darn positive you've accomplished nothing this lifetime; or 4) you are a wild overachiever but you're never impressed with what you've done, always wish you were further along, and can tell me who is.

If you truly can't shut your head up in order to do this, then ask a friend. Our friends, especially our good ones, are much better at copping to our greatness than we are.

How to Dream

The reason we don't know how to even write a dream is because, up until now, we've been living our life not *inside of any* dreams.

Huh?

I know. Look, if you decided that, let's say, your dream in the area of BODY was to run (and finish) the New York City Marathon next year, there would be immediate and obvious actions you'd need to start taking right now. They would include researching training steps, buying the right shoes, eating well, hitting the gym and, uh, running. From here on out, any morning that you'd push the snooze button and make excuses as to why not to run, you couldn't help but feel the breach.

You see, you'd be either living inside of your dream and true to it (with the right actions, e.g., running) or not. And because none of us want to acknowledge the gap between our desires and our actions, we wisely and cowardly avoid admitting our dreams altogether.

Until now...

The following are specific tips for writing all twelve of your dreams. *Barking direction #3*: Don't worry. I will give you enough examples of well-written dreams and not-so-well-written dreams that, I promise, you'll be able to do this yourself.

- **Be specific.** Make sure to be specific and thorough when you paint the picture of your dream. Capture what your dream looks and feels like so that, once you've written it, you can fully visualize it. Your dream should inspire you, give you goose bumps, and even scare you a little. It should be a stretch for you, but not a pipe dream.
- **Write your dream in the present tense.** By writing, I am now doing this, e.g., "I run three miles a day," you are making yourself accountable for it right now, locking yourself in, instead of saying, "I'm going to start running" or "I will run," meaning: I'll get around to it sometime in the future, so I don't have to do anything about it right now. Writing your dream as if it's already happening gives you no choice but to accept your dream as a reality and act accordingly.
- **Be kind.** This is easier said than done. Focus on what you want and not what you don't want. Be positive, but not Glinda the Good Witch goofy. Be sure to keep all negative *digs* out of your dream. What negative digs? Saying things like, oh, I don't know, "my spouse is no longer an asshole" in your LOVE dream, might just qualify as a dig. As opposed to the kinder, gentler (and less asshole-like of you to write), "my spouse is loving, compassionate, and generous."

- **Be honest.** Though this might feel obvious to you already, be *completely* honest here. I mean, your very own dreams are at stake. If you can't admit every last thing you want, how can you get it? If you can't admit what isn't really working, how can you fix it?

- **Breathe.** Note to your snooze-button-pushing, morning-muffin-eating self: Writing down your dreams is not meant to depress you. Truly. It *is*, however, a reality check, an honest measurement of where you are now in comparison to where you want to be. It also reveals what areas in your life are actually working and what areas are not. No matter where you are at this moment, even if it's a hot mess, I swear, this is the beginning of change and discovering your own favorite flavor of bullshit.

Other People's Dreams

Ever notice how much easier, enlightening, and way more fun it is to decipher other people's issues rather than your own? Well then, let's see how **Donna**—our loving mother of three, disgruntled wife of one—did at her first attempt in writing her LOVE dream:

My dream marriage would be one in which we are growing together by being more intimate with each other. I like that we are transparent and I am not hiding or being dishonest. It is so freeing to be honest about who I am. I love learning together and having good conversations. I would love to have a partner who gave me the kind of attention I deserve. Flowers, chocolates, random hugs and kisses. I love surprises—not big ones like parties or expensive gifts, but little things like flowers. I would love a partner who really makes love. I love passion and caressing. I do not like the simple "just have sex and be done with it" stuff. I love all the romance and lingerie, music, oils that go along with a fun sexual experience. I am highly aesthetic and it helps me. I also like it slow and long with lots of kissing and caressing. Loving!

Not so bad, right? Though, let me ask you a couple of questions. Did

Donna follow the tips on how to dream? Is this dream ready to be shared with her husband, her friends, and (if it were rated G) hung on her fridge?

Not so fast, right?

Let's dissect Donna's dream a bit. And, remember *barking direction #1*: Find the Donna in you. Use the work Donna did here, and the mistakes she made, to help you see your own issues lurking within your dream.

The first problem in Donna's LOVE dream is that her dream is written in the conditional tense and not the present, as instructed.

My dream marriage **would be...**

It's hard for us newbies at dreaming to write our dream as if we already have it. No? It's much easier to write it as a someday, one day wish list of a dream. But, remember, you are charged with starting to make it real.

Now let's dig a little deeper or, at the very least, to the end of Donna's first sentence!

My dream marriage would be one in which we are growing **together** by being **more** intimate with each other.

Can you see that both the "together" and "more," though honest, are pointing to some of the issues at hand, versus inspiring Donna?

I am **not hiding** or being **dishonest**.

When Donna says she is "not hiding" or "being dishonest," isn't she sort of (cough, cough) confessing that she's lying to him now?

I would love to have a partner who gave me the kind of attention I **deserve.** Flowers, chocolates, random hugs and kisses.

The "deserve" in that sentence is pretty poignant, no? *Barking direction #4*: Follow me. Can you see how the "deserve" more than likely points to the lens through which Donna is seeing and measuring everything in her life?

Donna clearly knows what she deserves and wants, and every day that she's not getting it, she's measuring how she's being failed. She's neither creating nor designing nor being responsible for her own happiness. She is, in a sense, a lady-in-waiting. And even though she, no doubt, keeps doing "all of the right things" and hoping that one day her husband will get it, do you think Donna asks him directly for what she needs? And even if she did ask him, and he did what she wanted, would it count?

I **would love** a partner who **really makes love**…I do not like the simple "just have sex and be done with it" stuff.

Now, it's sort of hard to inspire yourself about your LOVE dream with your man when, at the very same time, you're kicking him in the groin. And, anyway, isn't sex, um, a team sport?

The poor guy, right? Even if he is as self-centered as Donna dreams he wasn't, Donna is sneakily placing her happiness in his hands, and he's failing her over and over again, without even knowing that he's being tested.

I mean, if we don't ask for what we want in bed, how would our partner know?

I promise you, most first drafts of all of our dreams sound exactly like Donna's. We have no idea how pervasive our current lens and paradigms are and how invested we are in them. A fish doesn't know from "water" until it's no longer in it and, well, by then, it's a little late. Until we start to admit to our dreams, we can't even see the murky water we're swimming in or, at least, have decided we're stuck swimming in. We let our upsets, hurts, disappointments, and judgments trickle into our dreams, so much so that we barely can get ourselves to even write the dream. But, sneaky us, if we don't write our dream, we can't be responsible for the change we actually deeply desire.

After some coaching, here's **Donna**'s rewritten dream:

John and I are so in love. We are like newlyweds. People are in awe of us and find us inspirational as a couple. We are close and intimate. We are transparent and honest. I love that I can be who I am freely. I love that we learn together and have deep, honest conversations about life and philosophy. John and I are so romantic and create magic in the bedroom by lighting candles, massaging each other, giving each other lovely compliments. We show each other how much we love and appreciate each other with little tokens of love like chocolates or small gifts. I get flowers randomly, which I love. We date every weekend and enjoy our sex time together as we slowly caress each other. We grow sexually as we learn more and more about what we enjoy as lovers. We love lingering kisses and connecting through our senses. We are affectionate every chance we get. We are a loving couple who can't get enough of each other.

Now that's something to put on your fridge, be proud of, go to work on, and shave for, right? Sure, Donna's rewritten dream might feel like a stretch to you. But let me ask you something. Isn't going for this new dream a much better sport than the one Donna was engaged with before? And now that Donna is inspired by her dream and has shared it with her husband (yep), the promises that she needs to put in place to realize it are pretty apparent, right? From date nights to deep conversations to hot sex to chocolate kisses, etc.

Don't worry, you and I will get to the Promise Land in Chapter Three.

And what about **Stephanie**'s CAREER dream? Remember, she's our wildly busy but sadly still-single businesswoman in New York City.

My career and what I do contribute to the **greater good** in the world. I work in a very creative and beautiful location (bright, airy, **no** neon lights, natural materials, good views), **with smart, motivated, honest people who get along well**. My work is based in **ethics** and a purpose **larger than dollar signs**. The structure, budgets, roles, and responsibilities **are clearly defined**. The hours are **manageable** and

leave me time to **sustain** a full personal life. My work is challenging **for my mind** and I **contribute** to the whole in **meaningful** ways. I make at least as much money as I make now, and preferably more. There is **flexibility** in my schedule, I am **not micromanaged,** and I am **encouraged to grow** in my area of expertise. My career is an inspiring vehicle—enhancing **my** health, fortitude, mental alertness, and integrity. I go to bed soundly each night, proud and satisfied with my daily accomplishments.

Can you see from Stephanie's first draft of her CAREER dream that much of her dream points to what doesn't work about her current company? Oh, I don't know, like "neon" lit and filled with dimwitted, dishonest, and disinterested people who don't necessarily get along. Right? Remember, you are writing your dream from the perspective that it has *already* happened. If Stephanie is in the job of her dreams, does she really have to specify that the company is ethical? Isn't that a given? Would phrases like, "purpose larger than dollar signs" or "manageable" or "able to sustain" or "not micromanaged" really produce goose bumps (at least, the non–horror film kind)? Doesn't Stephanie's attitude toward her current company feel oddly similar to the cold and inflexible culture she hates about it? Isn't she sort of sneakily wiping the responsibility of her own health, happiness, and sound sleep on them? I mean, if they are indeed the "vehicle" for her well-being, who is actually in charge of holding the steering wheel and driving? Stephanie or the big bad ~~wolf~~ work?

Now let's take a look at **Stephanie's** rewritten CAREER dream:

I am working for the most amazing company. I make more money and actually work less hours! We are known for the contributions we make to the world, and what we give back. My coworkers are brilliant, witty, fun, and generous. We are outspoken, honest, and supportive of each other. We are true teammates, collaborators in pushing each other toward our dreams. I am inspired and excited to go to work. I inspire others and have found my home.

Now, isn't that a dream worth updating your resume for?!

Next, let's look at **Ethan**'s SELF dream. Remember, he's our nice (to everyone but himself) guy who is unhappily stuck with a family of origin that has all the makings of a late-night reality show, a hellish boss, and a nitpicky wife.

> I am kind and fair to myself. I **am able** to motivate myself and let myself off the hook **when** I fail. **I am in control** of my feelings. Even **when** things go bad, I take them in stride and stay positive. My inner voice is my friend and **not a hypercritical ass**. I am proud of myself and my accomplishments. I **do not feel guilty** about my **estrangement** from my family. I feel satisfied that I am a good husband and father. I have self-confidence and I see myself as a strong and positive person. **Failure** or success, action or **inaction** does **not** determine my sense of **worth**. I feel confident in my abilities at work and seek advancement and promotion **without guilt or self-doubt**. I have learned to use my ambition as a resource, rather than **stuff it as an excuse to procrastinate**. I feel that I am **worthy** of success. I **don't** live my life thinking that **I am living below my potential**, but instead living up to exceeding my potential. And I am confident about what I do, what I contribute, and **do not** doubt myself. I treat myself at least as kindly as I treat others. I work as hard on making my life better as I do to make others' lives better.

The poor pup, no? Can you tell from Ethan's first draft of his SELF dream how unimpressed he is with himself? How much he doubts his every move, anticipates his every failure, and how much more invested he is in spotlighting his own "hypercritical ass" than dreaming. Heck, his hypercritical inner voice is not only clearly his BFF, it, in fact, wrote this dream! The more Ethan slips words like "guilty," "failure," "estrangement," "self-doubt," "procrastinate," or "confidence" (three times) into his dream, the more we can feel his current doubt, sadness, and paralysis. And, think about it, if we always doubt ourselves, question our worth, do we EVER have to be wildly brave in our lives (e.g., talk to our estranged family) or are we, in a sense, writing ourselves an indefinite "get out of doing anything we might possibly fail at or be uncomfortable doing" doctor's note?

Let's see how **Ethan** does in his rewritten SELF dream:

> When I walk into a room, people want to know me. I'm that guy. Bold, happy, and unstoppable. I am always looking for the next adventure. I am proud of the contribution I am making to the world. I am decisive, transparent and, did I mention, confident. I am exceeding my every dream and then some. I am a leader everywhere in my life: professionally, socially, and with my family. Yes, even mine! I am a masterful ringmaster, proud of the difference I have made and how open, honest, forthright, and fun I am with everyone. I am deeply happy.

What a difference, right? Now, Ethan, based on this new relationship to the SELF dream he created, could actually have fun (imagine that). As opposed to his first draft, where the smartest (and safest) action would be to feel bad (as good guys do), suffer over his suffering, and never have to get into better (and realer) actions than beating himself up.

And, last but not least, what about our screenwriter, **Katie**'s, BODY dream?

> My body is in the best physical, emotional, and mental state it's ever been in my life. I **finally** look good. I **don't look fat** in jeans. I weigh under 130 pounds. My clothes are feminine and sexy. I am **classy** with my appearance and I like myself when I look in the mirror. When I walk into a room, **people** turn and look at me. I **come across** as hip, together, and intelligent. **People** respect me just by looking at me. My body feels amazing. Mentally, I am free of **past dramas and traumas**. I am **completely** honest and real in my life and do not feel any **burden of lies and deceit** around me. I like **myself** and feel good about **myself** on the inside and the outside. Emotionally I am strong and love **myself** and the people around me. I live a healthy lifestyle from what I put in

my body, to how I treat my body to how my body feels on the inside to how my body looks on the outside. I keep the weight off and stay thin.

Can you tell and even feel from Katie's first draft of her BODY dream with the words she uses, like "finally," "don't look fat," "classy," or "intelligent," how sad and defeated Katie is? That it's not so much what other people think, but actually Katie who doesn't think herself smart or pretty. Do you think that putting "free from past traumas and dramas" in your present dream has you really free from them, or does it let Katie keep the past safely (and somewhat sneakily) right in her pocket?

Let's see how **Katie** did rewriting her BODY dream:

My body is sexy, beautiful, lean, and athletic. I am a size 4/6 and jeans look really hot on me. My stomach has a girly six-pack and I now happily wear bikinis and midriff tops. My legs are sculpted like a dancer's and I love wearing cut-off jean shorts. My arms are toned, and strapless tops look great. My clothes fit so well they look like they've been tailored for me. I am delighted by my new relationship with food and how well I take care of myself. My natural glow inspires others. I am confident and proud in my dream body—loving the way I look and feel.

A world better, no? Can you see how Katie's new dream would indeed inspire her, make her proud and motivated to better her health and body?

You-Turn

Yep. You guessed it. It's time now for YOU to actually do the dreaming part of this assignment. Remember, use the guidelines in this chapter to assist you in writing all twelve of your dreams. Reread my clients' first takes at their dreams and after.

No matter what, all barks aside, this assignment, however arduous (and enormous) as it might be for you, will give you the most awesome road map to your own happiness.

> ### ASSIGNMENT FOR CHAPTER ONE: **PART TWO**
>
> **2. a)** Follow the instructions in this chapter on how to dream, and write your dreams for all twelve areas of your life.
> **b)** Pinpoint the three specific areas you are going to work on for the ten sessions of this book.

Rate Yourself

Once you've written dreams in all twelve of the areas, it's time for you to rate where you are in each area, today. For example, if your dream in the area of LOVE is that you're in an amazing relationship and madly in love and plotting your first trip to Bali together, and, well, you haven't been on a date in four years, six months, two days, and seventeen hours, you most likely would give yourself a low rating in the area.

Use the chart on the next page to help you rate yourself.

Remember, the scale is subjective. What constitutes a 10 or even a 3 for you might not be the same as what it is for your partner. It's important to also pay attention to how you rate yourself. Are you the kind of person who thinks anything remotely close to a horn toot is bragging, so you rate yourself low even when things are pretty darn good? Or, are you the too-lenient Stepford Wife–type who says everything is "great," when, in truth, you're in hell?

> ### ASSIGNMENT FOR CHAPTER ONE: **PART THREE**
>
> **3.** Once you've written your twelve dreams in all of the areas, rate each of the twelve areas on a scale from 1 to 10 (see chart). So, in other words, what would you rate each area today in comparison to the dream you just wrote and love?

RATING SCALE

10	**Sublime**	Moments of sheer bliss, happiness, and pride.
9	**Extraordinary**	The highest sustainable rating for an area.
8	**Happy**	Sustainable, reliable, and consistent state of deep satisfaction. A source of pride.
7	**Pretty Good**	Not a source of pain, but not a source of pride either. Reliable, for the most part...
6	**Fine**	Not intolerable yet, but an area that is actively avoided and its avoidance is often defended.
5	**Lame**	Becoming intolerable and a source of resignation.
4	**Disappointing**	A sad state with moments of indifference and potential hostility.
3	**Bad**	Things are very bad. It is not yet life-threatening or at a point of no return, but getting close.
2	**Acutely Painful**	Virtually unbearable. Things are hopeless.
1	**Excruciating**	Unsustainable level of suffering. Reserved for individual episodes and moments of hell.

Why We Don't Currently Have Our Dreams

Now that you've written (or contemplated writing) all twelve of your dreams, stretched, scared, and rated yourself, it's time for you to describe what's really going on in each area *right now*—in other words, your *current reality*. For example, let's say, in the area of LOVE, these days, you and your partner have sex only about once a month. And, you're hurt that they are no longer initiating it, or even trying to, and it used to be that they wanted you all the time...

In this part of the dreaming assignment, you have the opportunity to describe, in full detail, all of the real struggles and triumphs you've experienced in each of the areas. Being able to see your entire story laid out before you in writing gives you no choice but to see and start to deal with the seemingly insurmountable gap between where you are now and where you want to go.

Also, in this part of the dreaming assignment, I will have you write every last reason you can come up with as to why you gave yourself the rating you did and why you wholeheartedly believe you can't, don't, and may never realize the dreams in your lower-rated areas.

Note to our rationalizing selves: Even though each of us can barely squeeze out five sentences when asked to write out our dreams, when it comes to explaining why we are screwed and cannot possibly attain our dreams, we're magically prolific. The ease with which we confess our "why nots" should have us, at this point, rightfully wondering which team we've actually been playing for all along…

Regardless of it all, this is your opportunity to spew *every* darn thing you need to say about that particular area in your life and the complications that come with it. Leave nothing unsaid. Put all of your doubts, explanations, justifications, finger-pointing, and truths to paper. The more you figuratively "throw up," the better you'll feel. I promise.

Barking direction #5: Go for it. Don't worry. I got you.

ASSIGNMENT FOR CHAPTER ONE: *PARTS FOUR & FIVE*

4. Describe in a few sentences what each area looks like right now. What is your *current reality*?

5. Now, explain why you gave yourself whatever rating you did in each of the twelve areas. Why do you think you don't or can't or haven't been able to realize your dream in that area thus far?

In order to help make this first assignment a tad less daunting, I have summarized it on the next page for you, as well as given you a sample response for parts two through five of it.

CHAPTER ONE: ASSIGNMENT

1. Write down at least three accomplishments you've made happen in your life.

2. **a)** Follow the instructions in this chapter on how to dream and write your dreams for all 12 areas of your life (see below for sample answers to #2 through 5).
   b) Pinpoint the 3 specific areas you are going to work on for the 10 sessions of this book.

3. Once you've written your 12 dreams in all of the areas, rate each of the 12 areas on a scale from 1-10 (see chart on page 26). So, in other words, what would you rate each area today in comparison to the dream you just wrote and love.

4. Describe in a few sentences what each area looks like right now. What is your *current reality*?

5. Now, explain why you gave yourself whatever rating you did in each of the 12 areas. Why do you think you don't or can't or haven't been able to realize your dream in that area thus far?

TIME

The Dream: My life is in balance. I wake up feeling excited to live out a schedule that is an expression of me. My days mirror my priorities. I have ample time to further a career I love, connect deeply with my partner, nourish and exercise my body, and learn and grow as a person. I feel satisfied and full. I move between activities and meetings with grace and ease, arriving on time, efficiently dealing with business at hand (and enjoying it!), and leaving on time for the next engagement. The activities in my day have purpose and meaning, and I focus my attention on each one. I feel powerful and creative in what I take on. I am in command of the things I have to do and want to do. I take time to plan, delegate, and execute. I end my days satisfied, exhilarated, and in love with life.

Rating: 5

Current Reality: My life is horribly out of whack. My work is all consuming. I work until late at night, and come home to find my kids already asleep. I don't have the energy to talk to my wife, and so unwind by watching mindless TV shows until bedtime. And then the day repeats. I used to enjoy reading and exercising and playing cello in a local quartet, but I don't have time for that. At work, I am always in "fire alarm" mode, running between meetings that run late and make me late for the next meeting.

Explanation of current rating: I cannot have my dream because I have a very demanding job. The economy is bad and so we are doing more with less to keep clients. My boss doesn't listen to me and I don't want to look bad by pushing the point. My subordinates are irresponsible and incompetent, and I spend time fixing their mistakes.

Post-Dream-atic Stress

Okay. So, now that all twelve of your dreams are finally written, are you excited and raring to go? Barely breathing? Annoyed and wanting me to shut up already? Quitting?

Wherever you are, it's okay.

All right, that's not entirely true. Wherever you are, *besides* quitting, is okay. Don't quit. Though this first assignment is/was a doozy, please be proud of yourself that you not only cared enough to buy (and read) this book, you've just birthed twelve dreams.

Here are some "morning-after" dreaming hangover tips, reminders, and questions:

1. **Read the dreams** you wrote out loud to yourself. See how they sound and make you feel. Did you carefully follow the instructions on how to write them? Do they excite *and* scare you?

2. Did you **pick the three specific areas** you're going to work on for this book? By now, no surprise here, I recommend that you pick the areas you're least excited to tackle. The areas you've given up on or tried to fix more times than you'd ever admit to. The ones that had you go "ugh" when you saw the cuter-than-they-should-be symbols for them in the chart.

If I haven't rubbed you the wrong way yet, wait until you read this next tip!

3. Once you've picked your three areas, read your dreams to at least three close friends. If possible, in person.

WTF, Lauren?!

I know. But here's the thing. If you've decided, let's say, to rock your BODY, quit gluten, stop smoking weed, and take up Pilates, and yet you tell no one, what's the likelihood you are going to win the battle with your body? Exactly.

Going public with your dream has you accountable for realizing it and ends your right to stay quiet about what matters most to you.

4. Before reading your dreams to your friends and family, make sure that they are going to behave. I'm serious. Some of your friends, God love them, can be as sarcastic and pessimistic as you are/were or they wouldn't be your friends. So, for example, if you're nervous about reading your dreams to them because it's a big deal for you and you're a bit embarrassed, tell them exactly that. If you don't want their advice at this very moment about what you just read them, but instead want them to simply clap for you, you guessed it—tell *them*. Use this momentous occasion to be more honest, vulnerable, and brave with them than you have ever been.

Okay, here's a **POP QUIZ** for you:

If you're worried that your friends have heard this all before, think you have finally lost your marbles and/or this must be a new AA step, you should:

> **A.** say nothing about your fear and let them fail you.
> **B.** text them about it at a more convenient time (i.e., never).
> **C.** tell them.

C (see), you're going to be just fine!

CHAPTER TWO

Maybe It's You

Discovering Your Own Fingerprints on the Crime Scene

TRUE-UP

Have a seat. I've got good news and bad news for you.

Truth is, most of us have already had an inkling about this, but, if not, here goes: The "maybe" in this chapter's title is an out-and-out lie. The only thing in common with every last thing that isn't working in your life *is* you.

There's no maybe about it.

So, how is the fact that your fingerprints are on everything that isn't working in your life even remotely good news? You see, if it's the economy's fault, your mother's fault, your age's fault, or anyone or anything else's fault but your own, then you're just stuck where you're stuck, and there's nothing you can do about any of it. But, if you are the common denominator in all that isn't working in your life, *you* can actually do something about it.

I mean, come on, who else is in charge? Who is putting you in every precarious position and every scenario you're in? Who is the one telling the story of, uh, *your* life? There is no story in your collection without you in it, right? *You* are the key principal. *You* said everything and did everything that got you where you are. Sure, it's not always the prettiest or proudest of tales but, either way, it's the tale we penned, the tale we tell and retell. And most of us don't own that reality. As a matter of fact, we're utterly convinced that nothing is really our fault, especially the bad. After all, we would never do *this*—marry the wrong man, be forty and single, put on one hundred pounds, etc.—to ourselves! Right?

Buzzer.

Worse than wrong, here's what that premise gets you: So long as you don't think you got yourself into the mess you're in, you lose the power to get yourself *out* of the mess.

Barking direction #6: Read that last line again and take a deep breath. Though it's not the easiest pill to swallow, it's a critical one.

When someone actually is the *author* of their own life, they are accountable for every single component of it—from how their life got to where it got, to whom they let into it. Unfortunately, most of us never think that we put ourselves in a bad situation without being the victim of it. But, truth is, when we're the author of our own life, there is no victim except the victim we allowed ourselves to be.

But what do you mean, Lauren? It can't be me. My dad is a lousy communicator, my boss is a narcissist, my mother is a downer, my metabolism is definitely not what it used to be, my kids are total ingrates, my exes are both liars . . .

Listen. I am not saying the list of crimes you have on a person isn't true for you. Of course it is. You have years of evidence to substantiate it. Years. But, given you are the common denominator of all those liars, tyrants, and beasts in your life, as well as the judge *and* jury in their case, isn't there something suspect about all that?

Yes and yay. Okay, the "yay" may be a bit premature at this moment. Hang in there.

Meanwhile, I think it only fair that if I'm coming after you, I rat out myself.

~~MAYBE~~ IT'S ME

This shouldn't come as a huge surprise to you, but, back in the dark ages (my teens), I didn't particularly like my dad* that much. In fact, I would get all beady-eyed just thinking about him, especially when it came to his love of professional sports. He's one of "those" guys. You know the type. The kind that shows very little passion in his own life, but when it comes to watching sports on TV, he becomes another human altogether. He screams at the umps, shouts at the players, and rants like a mad-man. I mean, who screams at a TV? A passionate passionless man, how pathetic! Right? What a hypocrite! And, every time I'd walk past him while he was watching a game, he'd look up and say, "Hey, kiddo" and, in my head, I would be like, *Yeah right, Dad.*

But, one time, I must have humphed by him a little too loud. So much so, he turned off the TV, followed me to my room, and asked me if I was upset about something. In that moment, I decided, what the heck, I'm going to tell him what I *really* think.

Uh-huh.

It came out something like this: "You pick sports over everything, you never do anything but watch sports. Your whole goddamn life is based on sports! You've never been a good dad. You could care less about what is really going on with me."

Gasp.[†]

A bit bewildered, my dad looked at me and said, "Wait a minute. You care? You want to hang out with me? All you had to do was tell me to turn off the TV and I'd turn it off. What do you want to do?"

Now, what do you think my response was? Surprise? Relief? Glee?

Nah.

My real and ever so endearing answer went something like this:

---

* See, Mom, I spread the ~~wealth~~ wrath.

[†] What?! Did you really think I was a *sweet* sixteen?

"Blech. Just kidding! Why would I want to hang out with you? You're boring, you like sports."

Gasp, the sequel.

See, the thing that didn't work about *my* relationship with *my* father was...me. The only difference between the two of us was that I humphed at the TV and he shouted at it.

Ultimately, the sport I was playing (the one so many of us are playing all the time) was assigning blame. We opt to stay sad, mad, and righteous instead of seeing our own fingerprints all over the crime scene. We get to exile people over small infractions and never do anything but grumble.

Sound remotely familiar?

CLOUDY WITH A CHANCE OF DONUTS

Did you ever notice that most of us relate to our lives like we have no control or say over them? Especially in areas where we are *not* particularly proud. We speak about ourselves like we're reporting on the weather, making sweeping generalizations like "I'm bad with money" or "I'm quiet when I meet new people" or "I'm not a morning person." I call that voice of ours the *weather reporter*. It is the voice of passive helplessness. It simply reports on one's life without taking responsibility for any of it, e.g., a snowstorm is hitting the East Coast tomorrow, better bundle up. And, given that a weather reporter has no control over the weather, the best one can do about a storm is describe what's coming, prep for it and, fingers crossed, hope for the best.

And, boy, do we ever believe our own "forecasts." So much so, there is nothing to do about winter storm Katie or winter storm [Insert Your Name Here] except, you know, brace for a 70 percent chance of procrastination with a 30 percent chance of Cheetos if in a bad mood. Can you start to hear the incessant BS we sell ourselves?

Trust me. If, let's say, you've tried to quit eating donuts three times in your life and failed miserably (cough, cough) each time, what do you think would happen if someone on the street came up to you, put a gun to your head, and said, "Eat another donut and you die"?* Do you think you wouldn't or couldn't quit the cruller, for good?

Of course you could and would.

If you can't hear when you are weather reporting about your life as if you have no control over it, saying things like, "I can't help it, It's just how I am, etc.," then you can't get any of your power back. If you can, however, start to hear your own blanket and bullshit statements, you are now in the best of trouble. You are going to have to do something different. Like, really put the donut down, get to the gym, have great sex after twenty years of marriage, learn Italian, ask for that promotion already or, oh, I don't know, how about go hog wild and get up when your alarm goes off.

Uh-oh is right.

Yes. We have *that* much power over ourselves but, conveniently, we don't relate to ourselves as the authors of our own weather. Of course, there are a few times when you truly can't do squat about your "weather," like if you're five feet two inches, a girl, and want to play basketball for the New York Knicks (and get cheered on by my dad). But, besides some obvious examples like that, you are fully in charge and accountable for the direction and description of your life, period.

If you are truly the author of your life and in charge of ALL of it, the good and the bad, then you can roll up your sleeves and get busy doing something about you.

You can change any of it.

HIDE AND SNEAK

Each of us has a little voice in our head that is constantly commentating on everything that is happening in our life. Most of us, however, are

---

* Fine. An unlikely scenario. Unless, of course, you've been to Voodoo Doughnut in Portland and waited in a two-hour line.

so busy or so checked out that we aren't even aware of how this voice is managing our life and making decisions for us. We go through life listening to it without knowing the source of it or the motives behind it. Heck, most of us think this inner voice *is* us.

Good news. It is not.

The voice is critical of you, it squashes your dreams, and it makes excuses for what isn't working in your life. Two of the loudest voices in your head are the *chicken* and the *brat*. Both, without question, already had something less than lovely to say to you about your dream writing abilities in Chapter One. By distinguishing, pinpointing, and naming the voices in our head, it helps us hear them ourselves, understand the negative impact they are having on our life, and even start to have a sense of humor about them.

THE CHICKEN

No surprise here, the chicken is the voice of fear in your head. It's scared and worried. It's not loud in the areas where you are excelling or where you stay in action regardless of your fear, *but* in any area where you are a tad fearful, concerned and/or worried, your chicken hatches a plan to keep you safe. Its job is to always make sure there is an exit route, an escape hatch. It anticipates potential problems. It has collected data throughout your entire life to support its cowardly theories. Though it indeed has a skewed sense of history, your chicken can, at a moment's notice, recount whatever tale it needs to slow you down in the face of anything that might seem hazardous to it—you know, dreadful things like being excited about a date, asking for a raise, telling your mate what you want in bed, etc. It's way more of a doomer than it is dumb. It's accommodating, doesn't want to ruffle feathers, and is willing to watch a dream slip away or start making concessions if there is any risk or discomfort involved. The chicken is conservative, pessimistic, and not the realist it claims to be. Its primary job is to weigh all options and keep you protected in your life, regardless of the fact that a safe life may preclude fun, profound happiness, and pride.

The chicken's myriad excuses seem intelligent, wise, and incredibly reasonable—but in reality, of course, the chicken is, well, just a pussy.

THE BRAT

No surprise here either, the brat is the voice in your head that sounds very much like an annoyed, defiant, and entitled child. It's the adult version of a tantruming four-year-old. The brat is stubborn, manipulative, and always running a scam, either trying to get what it wants or get you out of doing something. The brat's favorite day of the week is tomorrow. It fights harder sometimes for an Oreo than a promotion. Your brat, I swear, even likes a bad day. After all, on a really bad day, you *deserve* that martini, no? Ever notice how on a bad day you never *deserve* a salad? I mean, how long do you think your bad mood would really last if you only fed your brat celery? How many bad days would your brat tolerate if it no longer got rewarded with a drink, a cigarette, or an entire Netflix series on the couch for it?

Exactly.

OTHER PEOPLE'S WEATHER

Just as it's that much easier to hear and dissect other people's issues rather than our own, let's see how a few of my clients fared in parts three and four of their homework from Chapter One.

Let's start with **Katie**, our screenwriter from Los Angeles, in the middle of a nasty divorce, hiding in Palo Alto, stumped as to why she's not losing the last few (eighty) pounds.

In case you've already blacked out the second half of Chapter One's assignment, here's a recap of part four of the assignment, along with

Katie's responses in the area of BODY (health, weight, and appearance), which in part three of the assignment, she had rated herself a 2.

1. **Describe in a few sentences what each area looks like right now. What is your current reality?**

   I have lost a lot of weight and I'm on my way to reaching my goal weight. After that, I'll have surgery to fix all my flaws. Right now, I don't look good in a bathing suit and my wardrobe is awful. I need to get a stylist and redo my entire look. I recently changed my hair color and I'm getting new makeup. I am in the process of transforming my look and presentation but I have a lot of work to do. I need to be more girly and come across as intelligent and feminine. I am currently a work in progress. I look forward to being a 10.

2. **Explain why you gave yourself whatever rating you did in each of the twelve areas. Why do you think you don't or can't or haven't been able to realize your dream in that area thus far?**

   Right now, I'm eighty pounds overweight. After leaving my husband, I cut carbs and didn't eat much and lost fifty-five pounds, which felt good, but I started putting the weight back on. I've been up and down my whole life. I'd lose weight and then put it back on. I can't seem to keep it off or get thin. I don't know what's wrong. I've tried everything. I feel stuck. Also, I have a bad metabolism and I think I have hormone issues. And my mom has had a problem with her weight since her thirties and my dad is a big guy too. The weight issue runs in my family.

Given you've already watched me dissect the first draft of each of my clients' dreams in Chapter One, I imagine you're now a bit wiser to (and warier of) this process.

Great!

No kidding. That's the idea. The more I point out my clients' "weather," the more I need you to see and hear yours. Don't fret if you don't hear your own inner voices straightaway. They don't want to be heard. Why would they? They've spent years making sure you think *it's just how you are* and not simply the chicken feed they've been chucking at you.

Okay. Back to Katie. So, what do *you* think of Katie's responses?

To untrained eyes and ears, Katie's reasoning sounds, you know, reasonable. No one doubts, after losing an impressive fifty-five pounds, that Katie's issues with, for example, her wardrobe, aren't legit. I mean, it has been forever since Katie has given a hoot about herself, it's great that she even cares and cops to the not-so-great state of her hair, makeup, and clothes, right?

Absolutely.

However, if you read Katie's description and explanation of her current reality from the perspective that Katie is actually the author of her own life, the one with the pen in her hand in charge of her own "weather," do you think by what Katie wrote, she truly believes she's at her weather's helm? Or, is she, more so, sneakily predicting a "flood" with a 90 percent chance of inexplicable weight gain?

Let's delve a little deeper and see how Katie did in the second part of the assignment, where she explained why she rated herself a 2 in this area.

I've been up and down my whole life.

Can you start to hear Katie's weather reporter in action? Sure, there is no question that Katie's weight has fluctuated her whole life. That first sentence is a completely accurate accounting. Just as it is accurate that, in winter, it is cold in Alaska. Except where is Katie's hand in her weight fluctuations? Wouldn't a more accurate, honest, and responsible accounting from her read something more like, "sometimes I stick to a diet, sometimes I don't." Can you hear the difference? One has Katie accountable for her weight, and the other has her reporting on her weight gain as if it has nothing to do with *her* hand putting food that is not on her diet into *her* mouth.

How about this one?

I'd lose weight and then put it back on.

Same thing, right? Again, where's Katie's hand in the "cookie jar"? Remember, the weather reporter can do nothing but account and report on what happened or might happen. It snowed eleven inches, it melted, and then it snowed some more. Magically, Katie's part in her own "weather"—*I ate after ten every night and chased whatever I ate down with some Jägermeister*—doesn't make it into her report.

> I can't seem to keep it off or get thin. I don't know what's wrong. I've tried everything. I feel stuck.

Katie, just like the rest of us, has her own philosophies on why her life, her behavior, her personality is the way it is. And, given the way it "is," namely, "stuck," she's doing the best she can. If the weather reporter tells you rain is imminent, you bring an umbrella. Nothing else you can do, right? Even though Katie started every sentence with "I," do you think she thinks she has anything to do with her "rain," with every pound she gained or lost? Answer: not so much.

How do I know? Take a look at the latest breaking news on Katie's storm front:

> Also, I have a bad metabolism and I think I have hormone issues. And my mom has had a problem with her weight for years since her thirties and my dad is a big guy too. The weight issue runs in my family.

Seattle, here we come!

According to weather woman Katie, it sounds like it's going to "rain" for the rest of her life and there's nothing she can do about it but point at her parents, carry a white flag, and surrender to ever losing weight for good.

But, question for you: Doesn't Katie's forecast allow her to keep eating whatever she wants because there is nothing she could do about her weight anyway?

Uh-huh.

That's how sneaky we are. If we can point at anything *but* ourselves as the culprit, we don't have to be accountable for any of it. We can stay brilliantly dumb, report the weather, and waive our rights to our dreams. The minute Katie got to see that it was actually she herself who was getting herself fat—not her mother, not necessarily her hormones, not her ex-husband, but her hand putting the food into her own mouth—her entire world changed. She could lighten up, in every sense of the word.

I'm pretty sure, at this point, some of you might have just gotten mad at me. I promise you, I really *do* know that there are people out there with honest-to-God medical conditions that make losing weight incredibly difficult. Of course there are. Lucky for Katie, she wasn't one of them. In this particular case, Katie's issues with weight and those of a number of her other family members were not medical. They ate unhealthily and barely exercised. It was under her control. And while that was scary to confront at first, it became amazingly liberating once Katie realized *maybe* it was she all along.

Okay, let's see how some of the others did explaining their current reality and rating.

How about **Stephanie**, my career-driven client, who fears she has sacrificed love for success? Here's Stephanie's description of her current reality with her CAREER:

CURRENT REALITY: My current job is **extremely intense and unorganized**. **I am never not working, fifteen hours a day, six days per week**. Leadership in the company is **weak** and the workplace is **fraught with** politics and **instability**. I often feel **marginalized** and **without a voice** (old boys' network) despite the fact that my initiatives and abilities are given the highest praise. **I am not sure how long I will stay**. The business model is **flawed**, and I would like to work somewhere where the organization has a **clearly defined** mission and where the products and services provide **real** value to the company's customers/clients. I hyper-analyze most of the decisions I make and **end up** either finding fault in myself or trying to convince myself the fault is with others. I'm also **worried** about losing time, and that being focused on work **will take away from** my focus on my personal life.

I bet, if you're career-minded like Stephanie, you can hear a lot of yourself in her current reality, yes? I mean, it's pretty apparent why Stephanie is successful (and stress full). None of us would, at this point, necessarily want to work directly with her, but we'd definitely count on her to get the job done.

Let's go investigate the current "weather" in Stephanie's state. Can you tell by Stephanie's description of her current reality: "extremely intense," "unorganized," "never not working," "weak," and "fraught with," how little she is responsible for her own happiness there? Stephanie is reporting the facts as if her hands were tied, leaving her nothing she could do about any of it *but* bitch, stress, and eventually quit.

The minute we fork anything over to the "weather" and shrug the responsibility elsewhere, we no longer have to author something else. Our chicken and brat win. Let's see if we can start to hear Stephanie's chicken clucking and her brat alive and kicking in her reasons why she rated her career a 6.

> **EXPLANATION: If it is possible** to reconstruct my current work environment to be ideal, it would be great to stay there until we know if we are going IPO or not. **I do not have the objectivity at this point** to know if that is possible or not. **If** having my ideal requires I find another job, the reason I have not done this is I have **no idea** what I would do or **even** like to do. **The economy is** poor and I am **fearful** to leave this position without a clear vision for what is next. I also want to **make sure** that my attitude is not the reason why I dislike my current job so much. **I do not feel** I have the **emotional objectivity** to determine which of these is true.

Stephanie's chicken has flown the coop, first line! Can you tell by her "if it is possible," how not so magnanimous her chicken is? She's dying to make a change but is too terrified to do anything about it. And what about the IPO wait? Though I understand it, how long should she *really* give it? And, if she is staying at a company simply so she can cash out and is pointing only at *their* criminal behavior, take another look. That's the brat balking. Just as I had to be willing to see my own temper-tantrum tendencies in my relationship with my dad, see if you can find your equal criminality to whatever (or whomever) *you* are busy pointing at loudly.

Whether Stephanie's company's culture is perfect and fingerprint-free is not the question here. In fact, I'm sure it is not. But, if Stephanie points only at the big bad *them*, she takes the responsibility for causing change totally off of herself. Once Stephanie could catch a glimpse of her own culprit, of her own version of a "girls' club," she could author some new theories about the place and set about to prove them. She could see how bitchy she was actually being about the place, about the boys' club, and how not one of those boys had a chance in hell to work well with her. She could see that if she stopped pointing at "them," she could start plotting instead. She could come up with a plan about what she wanted to see happen at that clubhouse and spearhead the changes. She would be able to start asking for what she wanted, offering up ideas, and see that the more she asked for, the more she was given. Hell, there was nothing they wouldn't do for her. And, now that she was at peace with her company, she magically had much more time with her love life. It seems bitching and bemoaning are a time and energy suck. Who knew?

Uh, your chicken knew . . .

Speaking of finger pointers, let's take a look at part four of **Ethan**'s dreaming assignment:

CURRENT REALITY: I do not believe I am living up to my **potential**. **I believe I have** more to offer and **should be** doing bigger and better things with my life. **I feel very mediocre** not only in how I do things, **but** in the things I decide to do. The **problem is** I do not know what I want, and therefore have even less of an idea how to get there. **I am very rough on myself**. I still beat myself up for things I did wrong as a child. **I get moody**

when I am being cruel to myself and it affects everyone in my family. I am happy with my marriage, **but I** hold back on expressing issues. **I also tend** to not fight fair when the two of us have arguments. **I don't feel very attached** to my parents but our relationship has improved greatly. I would like to be closer to them—physically and emotionally, **but** I am also afraid of them in some ways. **I am** frequently embarrassed of my mom and siblings. **I am** still very suspicious of my in-laws and their intentions. I don't trust them to behave rationally or nicely.

Wow. Rough "weather" in Ethan's neck of the woods, no? It sounds dark and cloudy with strong hurricane-force winds. But where is Ethan doing anything except beating himself up about it with words like "mediocre," "rough on myself," "moody," and "unattached"? As long as Ethan gets to blame his stormy "weather" on his distrust, embarrassment, and moodiness, does he ever have to be responsible for his own happiness?

Let's see how Ethan did on the reasons why he rated himself a 3 in his relationship to SELF. See if you can hear his weather reporter, chicken and/or brat busy at work.

EXPLANATION: I am not there because **I do not know where "there" is** nor do I know how to get "there." It's been ten years, and **I only know what I know**, and if I change fields now, **I will be ten years behind everyone else**. I have a secure financial position with my current efforts. But **I can't** get much higher, even with **a lot of effort**—unless I get **lucky** or something **unexpected** happens. **It is hard** to walk away from a comfort that I know, although what I have gives me **crippling doubts** about what I should be doing and not living up to my potential. Family always has its **challenges**, and **no** family is perfect. I think we just need to do our best to support each other, and **hopefully** everything will be as positive **as possible**.

All righty then. Can you hear how cocky Ethan's chicken actually is about how tied its claws are? If Ethan never claims that the real reason he is "crippled" is because he simply hates to make a decision, does he have to EVER be accountable for making anything great happen in his life? Or does he get to hope for the best, all the while spewing ever so inspiring words like "challenged," "doubts," and "potential"?

Note to all of you smart chickens: There is nothing a chicken likes better than clucking words like "hopefully," "try," "do our best," and "as positive as possible."

Would you put money on someone that "hopes for the best" or on someone that actually does something a tad more productive?

Once Ethan got to see his weather reporter in action (or, actually, not in action at all), he could catch himself in the act; he could see that his self-loathing shtick was a smokescreen. A dense one he used to brilliantly back people away from him. Ethan also got to see that the reason he so loathed himself was not because *he* truly sucked, but because his integrity did. And, once he saw that, Ethan could give his moody, brooding brat a time-out.

Turns out, much to Ethan's sad chicken's dismay, it's hard to beat yourself up when you are actually taking the right actions to forward your dreams.

BELIEVE YOU ME

Other factors that directly impact your inner dialogue are your *beliefs* and *theories*. Good news. Neither your beliefs nor your theories are hardwired. You created them. Both are based on experience, observations, and learning since you were a baby.

A *theory* is when you have an opinion or are speculating about something and, subconsciously, you are collecting evidence to prove it, like "dating after forty is really hard" or "you have to choose between career and family, you can't have both." Clearly, those particular theories influence the actions you take or don't take in the area of love and career. If we ever put our theories under a bright light, we'd have no choice but to see them for what they are—built upon bad logic and grown in manure.

Right?

I mean, let's say for the sake of argument you have a theory that all men want to date younger women, and well, it just so happens that you fit in that other age range—OLD. How's your dating life going to go? Do you even have to get off the couch? And, if you do bother to get up and out, do you even have to care or, for that matter, shower? Do you even have to really like the guy you're going out on the date with? And, if you already can't stand him via text or phone, know it won't turn out anyway, can you, at least, have a drink before you go and, what the hell, read one more e-mail. I mean, it's okay if you're a little late; he's not going to like you anyway. You're old, after all.

Can you see how much a theory, no matter how cockamamie its logic is, informs your entire world? It directs what you think, what you see, what you do and even, in this case, whom you date or don't bother dating.

A *belief*, however, differs from a theory in that it is something that is evidenced over a long period of time, and a done deal for you like "I believe in God." You don't have to explain why you believe in God. It's just the truth for you. After a long time, with enough evidence behind it, a theory will turn into a belief.

But, question for you: Which comes first, the theory/belief or the evidence?

Though it certainly feels like events happen and then the theory or belief is born, try again. We author *everything*. We believe something to be true and *then* prove it, completely disregarding what a bummer it may be to be accurate about something so disempowering like "we can't have it all" or "it's impossible to find love at my age" or "I'll never find a job that will pay me as much as I'm making now," etc.

Can you hear how brilliant those theories are and what they provide?

The "chicken or the egg" joke is even more on us than we know—as we spend much of our life not simply collecting evidence, but manufacturing it to support our sad, less than sweet, cowardly beliefs and theories. Sure, some theories and beliefs are positive. Look in any area of your life where you are successful. You have great beliefs and theories there, I promise. You believed accomplishing your goal (e.g., graduating law school, becoming a CFO, beating cancer, doing a triathlon, getting pregnant regardless of what the fertility experts said, married regardless of what your mother said, etc.) was doable and, voila, you did it. But, in any area where you are flailing, your theories and beliefs not only match it, they provide evidence for your negative results *and* fuel your inner dialogue.

It's why I have you clearly define your dreams in Chapter One. Because, once you can fully and freely see what you want, you are left with a much better and braver question than *What's wrong with the world that I can't have my dream?* You are left with the you-based question: What is the reality you want to author that will allow you to have your dream as its result?

This way, you become fully in charge of your own reality. You also become accountable for having everything you want in your life, and putting yourself into the actions that will fulfill those very dreams. It's all you, all of the time. There's not an iota of *maybe* about it.

If *you* shift, then how you see the world shifts.

Wanna join me?

YOUR GREEN SCREEN

You guessed it. It's that time again: homework time. Did you grunt, groan, or grimace? Did *you* just hear your own brat? If you have kids, did that inner voice happen to sound a lot like they do at five p.m., a.k.a. homework time?

The assignment for Chapter Two is actually, in many ways, much easier than the one you did for Chapter One. I'm not promising this will always be the case but, *barking direction #7:* Enjoy it while you can!

This assignment gives you the opportunity to sniff out some of your own BS. Yes, your very own "weather." What *you* believe to be wholly "true" about yourself. From the "fact" that you're a notorious flake, to always late, to not so great at X and Y. This is your opportunity to start hearing your chicken cluck, your brat tantrum, and how often you spew facts about yourself that have been sneakily (and conveniently) written and evidenced by you. This homework assignment will get you to start seeing the huge pile of "permission slips" you have personally penned to get yourself out of doing something you don't want to do (see: brat) or are too scared to do (see: chicken).

Go to town with this assignment.

ASSIGNMENT FOR CHAPTER TWO

1. Sift through your entire assignment for Chapter One and highlight everywhere you were being a chicken, brat, and weather reporter. Trust me, they are all in there! Mark their favorite words and phrases.

2. Make a list for each voice, compiling everywhere you were a chicken, brat, and weather reporter. That way you can really see the different voices in action: how you cluck, how you tantrum, and how you pontificate like you have no power.

3. List your current not so great theories: your truisms about yourself, others, the world, love, monogamy, etc. In other words, any theories you have in the twelve areas listed in Chapter One where you aren't living true to your ideals, e.g., "my boss is self-centered," "my kids don't appreciate me," "online dating sucks," etc.

4. From the list of theories you just wrote, pick one negative theory from each of three areas you are working on while reading the book, replace each of them with a new theory that aligns with your dream, and start gathering evidence to prove it. So, for example in the area of LOVE, replace "finding love in New York City is difficult" with "so long as I believe that I will find love, I will. If I'm here, so are they."

If you are having difficulty figuring out your negative theories for number three, don't fret. In Chapter Eight, I am going to teach you how to do a *purge*, where you will get to write out all your negative thoughts on a sticky subject (person, situation, area of life, etc.) and hear your theories at play.

A Change in the Weather

Once you have done the assignment for this chapter and found your brat, chicken, and weather reporter, you can now start to catch the three in action as they come out of your mouth. You can start to investigate the weather front you claim you have, and start believing you can shift your current reality.

You, after all, are the one in front of your own green screen. Right? The best way to change the weather is by starting to make promises in areas where you're not particularly proud. Not to worry, I'm coming after your promise-keeping abilities (or lack thereof!) in Chapter Three.

But first, how about another **POP QUIZ**?

If you're slightly offended that I may have just called you a "chicken" or "brat" in the area of, let's say, your CAREER, you should:

A. have a cookie. You know how you get when you're confronted.
B. start hearing all of your trusty truisms about the economy, your profession, your boss, your salary, etc., for the weather report/theories they are, sneakily forecasted by your inner dialogue.
C. commiserate over drinks about it with your BFF, who just so happens to also loathe their latest (ten-year) job.

Yes, **B**, for beliefs.

CHAPTER THREE

The Promise Land

Learning How to Keep a Promise to Yourself

FRIEND OR FAUX

Okay, by now it should be fairly apparent that we all make excuses, cluck, tantrum, weather report, and theorize a ton. But guess what: We've got an even bigger issue. We pretend we're much nicer than we are. Obviously, that's not my particular problem (oh, I have others), but it certainly is much of the planet's.

We're trained early on that when we don't do what we said we'd do (e.g., homework) or when we're caught doing something that is frowned upon (e.g., allegedly cutting up all of your mother's favorite Pucci scarves to make clothes for your Barbie),* so long as we feel terrible, look sad, and say we're sorry (whether we mean it or not), we're decent people.

Even as adults, most of us still think that as long as we feel really guilty, for example, that we didn't call our mother and we have a legitimate enough excuse to go with it, well then, we're doing okay. But, here's a question for you: Does feeling guilty, so long as we have an acceptable excuse, really make us a decent human? Or does it make us, more accurately and simply, well-intended liars?

---

* Hi again, Mom!

PERSONAL INTEGRITY

Did you ever notice that when it comes to keeping a promise to someone else, we're pretty good at it, right? I mean, if we say to our kids, "we'll pick you up at three p.m.," we don't mean "if we feel like it" or "if nothing better comes up"? But, when it comes to a promise to ourselves, e.g., "I'm going to do my physical therapy exercises every day," we are more than willing to excuse ourselves from what we said we'd do, so long as, you guessed it, we beat ourselves up about it.

We're nowhere near as considerate to ourselves as we are to others. We'd never tell our friends that we're going to meet them at the movies and then just not show up. We'll keep a deadline for our boss, because we want to please him or her, but we'll stay at a job we hate, drink a mimosa when we're on a juice cleanse, and date someone with more red flags than a raceway.

The ability to make and keep a promise to ourselves that is a match with our dream is *Personal Integrity*. It is the alignment of your heart (your desires), your mind (your plan), and your body (your actions).

It's where the rubber meets the road with your dreams.

But guess what? No surprise here. See the warning label for humans. Even though most of us suck at keeping promises to ourselves, we walk around like personal integrity is something we have. I mean, how could we not? After all, we're guilt-ridden so very often that we *must* be incredibly good people.

Being able to tell the truth about our own lack of personal integrity has integrity to it. The key to being able to deal with and lighten up about our own humanity is to get wholly honest about our dishonesty.

It's pretty simple. No fairy dust here.

When you can keep a promise to yourself, you become not only proud of yourself, you can trust yourself. Happiness, self-esteem, and personal pride come from knowing you can count on you. Your prescription for profound happiness, pride, and confidence is really simple.

Ready?

Do what you say, and have what you say forward your dreams.

In order to realize your dreams in the three areas you picked to work on in this book, there truly is a set of practices you'll need to follow.

You remember the areas!

They were the ones that made you sad, resigned, and slightly nauseous back in Chapter One. They are the ones that matter most, but the ones you've given up most on. Together, you and I will design the right actions to butcher your chicken and permanently time-out your brat.

Once again, it might be fun (or, at least, certainly more fair) if I introduce you to my own challenged promise keeper.

RUN, LAUREN, RUN!

Back in high school, I was a jock of sorts. I went to a small high school where, yes, everybody made the team. And, if you were not particularly pathetic, you'd make the varsity team. I played varsity soccer, softball, and volleyball. I didn't even realize how much exercise I was doing back then. That is, until freshman year of college, when I did, um, none. And there I was, exactly where many freshmen find themselves, with a fifteen-pound souvenir from their first year of college.

You know when your grandfather on your mother's side (read: not so sweet or subtle in his delivery) tells you that you look "healthy," you should worry. And that's just what I did (and, I mean, *just*). I worried. I got busy blaming. You know, it was my college's meal plan's problem, the work (that I wasn't necessarily doing) load's problem, the no-more-high-school-sports' fault—and then there was, of course, my biggest, most legitimate reason of all: I was a vegetarian. And, well, the options for me to live off the land (in this case, the dorm), were scarce.

Amid all of my confusion as to how I gained the weight, I, like Katie, never once pointed at what I was putting in my mouth (read: bagels). And, not just *a* bagel, two bagels a day. But that was it. No, really. I ate nothing else, save an enormous salad at dinner with garbanzo beans and what have you, cheese (you know, for protein and calcium), and some dressing. None of that balsamic bullshit, a half-cup of full-fat ranch dressing. And, that was it. Oh. Unless, they had baked potatoes, because, you know, we vegetarians particularly need, uh, more carbs. I swear, I thought I was being great. However, eventually and thankfully, I began to hear my own BS, my own convenient confusion, and started to use my own method on myself and did something unheard of.

Ready?

I made a promise to run thirty minutes, five days a week (two days on, one day off). And, when that alarm clock went off in the morning, I got the real joke. I got to hear lazy Lauren. And, boy, was she a piece of work. There were even some days, when I woke up before the alarm went off, and I'd lie there, wide awake, *still* trying to talk myself out of running. And, if that's not ludicrous enough, there were mornings where I'd be in my running clothes, sneakers on and, in the mirror, while brushing my teeth, I could still hear my head trying to talk me back to bed. Yes! Sneakers on. Contact lenses in my eyes. Headphones inches from my ears, and my head still thought it had a chance.

It didn't matter one ounce to the head I call home that running made me happy, healthy, and hot. Not one ounce. It was the first time I fully got how my inner dialogue was working for the wrong team. And guess what happened on any day my head won the round and I didn't run? No longer was I just going to simply beat myself up or bitch about bloat. Now, if I did not go for a run, I had to forfeit my favorite frozen dessert, Tasti D-Lite. And, believe you me, gone were my bagels; f*ck if I was also going to lose my nightly treat.

Uh-uh.

And, there I was, dangling the right carrot before my very own nose to get myself to deal with my less than supportive narrative.

Sure, it's a hokey story. But it's truly how I got to see the need for promises and consequences to harness all our minds, battle our brats, and lock our chickens' coop for good. I got to hear my own blaming and my own brand of bullshit excuses for what they were: my brat holding its breath, doing every last thing to get me back in bed and not deal with my own dream.

EXCUSES

Boy, do we ever have an arsenal of excuses. Many of which, no surprise here, are some variation of our parents' favorite brands of excuses. We use them to explain, justify, and/or self-impose a limitation as to why we can't do something. It's *the* reason we can't get a promotion. *The* reason we can't tell the truth to someone. *The* reason we no longer let ourselves get excited before a first date.

You know how you can tell when you're making an excuse? Do the money test. Ask yourself this: If I gave you one, two, or five million dollars (whatever number works for you), would you be able to get to work on time, drive slower, rage less, be nice to your spawn at witching hour, find a new job, quit sugar, jump your mate happily (and often), etc.?

Duh. Of course, you *could*.

Would you? Well, that's another question (see: brat). You see, all of a sudden, given the right incentive (in this case, money), you could change *anything* in your life. That begets the next question: How come you and your dream aren't worth it?

In any and every area where your results don't match what you say you want, you have to figure out what your favorite brand of excuse is in that area. Once you can start to hear your favorite excuses, you can start to see them for what they truly are: dream decay.

I've found that there are about eight basic brands of excuses. See if any sound familiar.

1. **The Don't-Care Excuse.** You convince yourself that you don't want or need whatever it was anyway, e.g., the new position, it would have been too much work anyway . . .

2. **The Passive Excuse.** Life is happening to you. It's beyond your control, e.g., the TV sucks you in, you don't know where the evening went...

3. **The Genetic Excuse.** You were born this way and can't possibly behave any differently, that's just how your family is, e.g., your father is asocial; your mother is critical.

4. **The Victim Excuse.** Nothing's your fault, you can't help it, e.g., you have to entertain your clients, they drink, so you have to as well; you were late because you were hanging out with friends, etc.

5. **The Everyone Else Excuse.** It's okay because everyone else is doing it or not doing it, e.g., none of your other married friends are having sex anymore either, etc.

6. **The Past-Precedent Excuse.** You've never been able to do it before. You've tried so many times, nothing has worked, why would things change now, e.g., you hate picking up the phone, can't remember birthdays, suck at managing your time, etc.

7. **The How-Things-Are Excuse.** What you want is not possible for you, e.g., you had a screwed-up childhood, you're not getting over it, you'll never be able to have a good life in *that* area, etc.

8. **The Done-Enough Excuse.** No one should ask you for more than you've already done, as if pushing you further might break you, e.g., you've survived twenty-five years of marriage, raised those kids, what else could anyone possibly want from you, etc.

Everyone has their own favorite brand of excuse. In truth, excuses are brilliant. After all, they keep us from having to do something we don't want to do and let us explain why we can't [*fill in the blank*]. Heck, we have permanent no-fault insurance and, best of all, it's the excuses' fault, not ours. Your happiness, self-esteem, and pride, however, pay the premium.

HOW TO MAKE A PROMISE TO YOURSELF

Obviously, we all already know how to make a promise. How to keep one to yourself? Well, that's another story. We'll deal with that shortly. In any case, here are a few basic pointers for making promises. These tips are not so wildly different from the tips on how to dream in Chapter One. Why, you wonder? See the fine print on being human: We are sneaky and, unless specified, we're way too smart to be specific.

1. **Be realistic.** Make sure you are making a promise that you believe can happen. So, for example, promising you are going to win the lottery today might not be the best of promises. Promising to quit smoking cigarettes cold turkey tomorrow when you have smoked for the past thirty years, though awesome, is not so realistic. Promising to incrementally cut down the amount you smoke, given how addictive of a habit it is, and plot the inevitable cease-fire, would make much more sense.

2. **Stretch yourself.** Make sure your promises are a stretch for you. Promising to floss daily (unless you normally don't) is more sleaze than stretch. Right? But, promising to drink X number of glasses of water, make your mammogram appointment, call your brother whom you've been avoiding, finally go and see the apartment your parents just (over a year ago!) bought,* etc., are good promises. Do what you've been putting off. Do the thing that immediately came to mind the minute I started talking about promises. Oh, you know the one (or twelve).

3. **Once again, be specific.** Your promises need to be wiggle-proof. Make sure that when you make a promise, you answer the following questions: How often? How long? By when? How much? Promises, for example, like *I will be nicer to my assistant, hate my commute less, track*

---

* Hi, Mom and Dad. It's beautiful!

my spending more, all have great intent, though what do they really mean? Your promises need to be loophole-free. *I will call my brother by Sunday and speak to him for at least twenty minutes. I will send out five resumes a week, and tell three new people a day about my career dream. I will reach out nightly to three potential dating prospects online that I'm excited about*, etc. You see how slightly different those promises are? They leave very little room for wondering if you kept the promise or not. It's either yes or no.

4. **Use powerful language.** Using sincere but ever so slippery verbs like "hope," "try," and "wish" will not cut it when it comes to making promises that are conducive to keeping. Making a promise like *I will play one entire game of Apples to Apples (or the board game of choice) with my daughter once a week*, for example, is a way different promise from *I'm gonna try to bond with my daughter*.

5. **Manage the external world.** How many of us have blamed the airport or the airlines (back in the day when they fed you) for not keeping to our diet while traveling? Think ahead. If, for example, you know there is a party on Saturday and you have a promise to only eat one dessert a week, wisely save it for the party. We are not a naive species. Stop playing dumb.

6. **Get the joke.** The more you resent having to make and keep a particular promise, the more you need that very promise.

TRUTH AND CONSEQUENCES

In order to start to care, we have to first see how low we've been on our very own list. We actually have to get annoyed with the fact that we can keep promises to everyone *except* ourselves and see what a crime that has been to our own happiness.

That's all fine and dandy, Lauren, but, it's easier said than done. Normally, I can keep a promise to myself for a bit, a New Year's resolution until about mid-February, but then something inevitably happens—you know, life—and I get off track, and the cycle begins again.

At least now you should be able to hear when you are simply weather reporting, right? But here's something else to know about why we fail at keeping promises to ourselves over a period of time: The actual consequence for not keeping a promise to ourselves isn't immediate. For instance, if you are trying to quit smoking, but keep having just one more cigarette, the one more cigarette you have is not going to be the one that kills you. If it were, you wouldn't have it. You wouldn't dare cheat on your diet if you knew you would gain ten pounds overnight, right? And, because the consequences aren't immediate, you ignore them.

Truth is (uh-oh), every time you break a promise to yourself, it does actually kill a part of you, but a less obvious part: your own trust in yourself. The big consequence in life is that every time you sell out on a promise to yourself, your life goes unfulfilled, and on your gravestone they might as well write, "Rest in Peace-ish."

Barking direction #8: Take a moment to locate your sense of humor. You may have left it way back in Chapter Two when I accused you of being your very own problem.

Figuring out the right self-imposed *consequence* is a way for you to get accountable for your own dreams. When you make a promise to yourself and attach a consequence to it, you keep yourself aware of your promise and ultimately aware of your own personal integrity.

Either way, keeping the promise or paying the consequence has integrity. It brings balance back to the promise you made, kept or not kept. It trumps the bullshit of guilt and the need for excuses altogether.

The key is to design the perfect consequence for yourself.

But, Lauren, consequences feel like punishments. I much prefer a reward system. Isn't a consequence going to make me feel worse, when I'm already feeling crappy that I broke the promise in the first place?

Look, you're going to have to trust me here (*barking direction #2?*). Fighting to keep your promise is a much better fight than the one you are in right now. If rewarding yourself worked, it would have. I mean, isn't having the body, health, career, love life, community, and bank account, etc., of your dreams the reward? But has it worked thus far?

Nope.

I've tried the reward system. It just doesn't work. Turns out, we humans do just fine living without the stuff we want. It seems, if we've managed to live okay thus far without that new iPhone 20, that cruise, that dress, that pony, what's another year or decade without it, right?

However, take something *away* from us that we're used to, addicted to, and anticipating—well then, that's a whole other story. Take away that nightly wine, those season tickets, that daily fro-yo, force someone to sleep on the floor for a night, or attend that bachelor party sober!? Well then, watch out. There's almost nothing we wouldn't do to keep our promise.

And that's the point.

That's why the right, self-imposed, funny, outrageous, icky, and irksome consequences work. Consequences should sting enough to make you think twice before you bypass your promise and buy your own brand of excuse. They should have a sense of humor about them and should annoy the crap out of your brat and chicken. So much so that you keep your promise. As sadistic as you may think I am, I promise you I am not out for you to pay your consequence (okay, maybe some of the really funny ones). I'm out for you to do what you said you'd do.

It is, after all, *your* dream we're fighting for.

But, Lauren, don't you think your plan of using a punishment to get us to keep our promise is also a bit too simple to actually work?

The answer to your question is yes. It is. But, now let me ask *you* something. What if it really *is* that simple? What if we're really that predictable and that easily changeable? Wouldn't that be amazing news? Promises and consequences are the keys to the kingdom.

What if getting ourselves out of our own self-imposed jail truly is simple, and the key has always been in our back pocket?

Whew, right?!

Figuring, once again, it's only fair if I'm coming after your consequences, I should cough up more of mine.

HBO AND CHILL

As much as I love my husband, David, if left to my own devices, nineteen years later, three kids under the age of fourteen, and a ton of good television on (hell, who am I kidding, I love bad television), how often would I really initiate jumping him? Not because sex isn't awesome, but, because, once again (see the fine print in the being human manual), when we're not busy blaming, cowering, excusing, feeling guilty, and bullshitting, we're lazy and stingy.

So, in order to tighten the leash on my very own less than generous brat, I have a promise in place to have sex with my husband, twice.

No, not a month. A week!

And, yes, he knows about the promise! I always love when clients ask me if David knows about my promise. Do you know why? It points to the fact that they'd never tell *their* partner. And, no, it's not because it's embarrassing. It's so their partners can't use it against them (or hold them to it).

And, what's my consequence should I not keep that promise?

If I don't have sex with David twice a week, I force myself to forfeit an episode of whatever show I'm currently addicted to on HBO. Permanently. That's right. No *On Demand*. No *HBO GO*. No *YouTube*. Gone for good.

You get the picture: I don't.

Guess who is happier? Sure, David is. But guess what? So am I. And not just because I'm guiltless *and* getting laid, but because I am fighting the right fight with my brat and winning. And, even if I don't win and I don't keep the promise during the week, my higher self *still* wins. You know why? Because my television-preferring stingy brat* loses the likes of *Game of Thrones*, rightfully.

But, Lauren, don't your husband's feelings get hurt that you need to make a promise to have sex with him? Shouldn't you just want to?

---

* I trust you are not missing the irony of like father, like daughter here. Oh, don't you worry, we'll get to *your* parent traits too in Chapter Five.

Sure, it would be great if our species were automatically generous, loving, selfless, and self-regulating. But have you met us? It doesn't matter if each and every time I go for a run outside, I have a spiritual experience and connect with God and nature—do I go for a run daily and automatically?

Yeah, right.

Or, do I sometimes put on my running clothes in the morning, spend a whole day coaching clients and painting, and quite possibly never end up on a run?

Uh-huh.

My sex promise perfectly locks me into being the person and partner I want to be. Where my physical integrity (my actions, i.e., jumping my man) matches my emotional integrity (how I feel, i.e., loving) and my spiritual integrity (my thoughts, i.e., deeply connected).

Finding the right promise, then keeping it or paying up, *is* the secret sauce to happiness.

OTHER PEOPLE'S PROMISES

Let's see how **Donna, Ethan, Stephanie,** and **Katie** did with their promises and consequences.

Remember Donna, our Chicago housewife and martyr of three? In order to realize her dream of having a more intimate marriage, she made promises to herself (and to me) about initiating sex with her husband and about communicating with him daily instead of mumbling about him under her breath. What do you think a good consequence would be for Donna if she doesn't initiate sex once a week?

Since it turns out that Donna likes a good (and secretive) shopping splurge, we picked a consequence that would certainly hit where it hurts: her closet. If Donna didn't keep her promise to initiate sex, she would have to give one of her beloved handbags (of her husband's choice) to a consignment shop.

You still there?

And, no, she can't buy it back. Much like my *Game of Thrones*, there is no return of Ned Stark and, now, of Donna's Louis Vuitton either.

Gone is gone.

Let's take a look at **Donna**'s full *promise sheet*. The promise sheet helps you keep your promises (and consequences) in front of your face rather than leaving it to your head to remember what, I promise, your brat and chicken will want to forget.

DONNA'S PROMISE SHEET

PROMISE	M	T	W	T	F	S	S	EXCUSE	CONSE-QUENCE	KEPT
Initiate sex 1 time a week.				K				N/A	Give hand-bag to Goodwill.	N/A
No spending on anything we don't need, clear any extraneous purchases with John.	K	K	K	K	K	NK	K	Shoes I've been coveting forever went on sale, couldn't resist, needed them.	Return Purchase	Yes
No quiet resent-ing, grumbling. Must clear all grumbles within 5 minutes.	K	NK	K	K	K	K		John came home from work cranky, saw shopping bag, assumed it was something I wasn't allowed to buy. He may have been right, but didn't have to be a jerk about it.	Blow Job	Yes!

K = Kept; NK = Not Kept

Yes, you read *that* last consequence correctly. Sure, I may have suggested it. But, when I heard Donna's silence on the other end of the phone, we both immediately knew that it was the right consequence for her. The key, once again, is *not* to have to pay your consequence, but to fight yourself to keep your promise. If you are left simply appalled that Donna has to be intimate with her husband as a consequence for his bad mood, you are missing the point.

Don't fret, most do.

Donna did not promise to have to service a man she doesn't like. She promised to be responsible for liking *her* man. She promised to clear any grumbles she has with him within five minutes, to find her heart, to speak up, to get clear about something unresolved. Right? Her brat has been challenged. Donna is no longer allowed to walk away pissed and lying about her pissed-off-ness. She is not allowed to swallow an upset.

Yes, I typed that.

And guess what happened when Donna started speaking up and getting responsible for intimacy, romance, and communication in her marriage? Yep. It got HOT! No longer in the heated sense of the word, but in the sexy one.

Speaking of speaking up (*and* changing the touchy subject), let's take a look at what actions/promises **Ethan** put in to help him realize his dream of liking himself and being less of a moody brood.

ETHAN'S PROMISE SHEET

PROMISE	M	T	W	T	F	S	S	EXCUSE	CONSE-QUENCE	KEPT
No being sarcastic or snapping when I'm busy.	K	K	NK	K	K	K	K	Mother-in-law standing in my way when I was carrying a heavy chair.	5-minute foot rub (with cream) to family member.	YES!
No getting mean and then pouty about how mean I got ("Mopey Dick").	K	K	K	K	K	K	K	N/A	Play one full board game of child's choice and have fun playing.	N/A
3 work-related bold actions a day M–F.	K	K	K	K	K			N/A	Must paint totem poles (yes) w/ mother-in-law.	N/A

K = Kept; NK = Not Kept

I swear, it's really not hard to change yourself. You just have to be willing to lighten up about your dark side. Just imagine what the world would be like if all of our parents and their parents and their parents' parents owned up to their own jerkiness within minutes of being a jerk and paid a funny consequence?

You may have grimaced at the peculiarity of Ethan's foot rub consequence. However, it was the perfect consequence for Ethan because he happens to be repulsed by feet. It only took *one* five-minute foot rub to kill Ethan's right to ever be snippy again with his mother-in-law, to ever not have to be accountable for his own actions and reactions.

Finding the right, hilariously heinous consequence for yourself that you'll keep is key. No matter how creative you normally are by day, your brat and chicken will get wisely dumb about figuring this out.

You will have to be willing to *really* hear what your head is trying to sell you. What it has to say to you about you, about me, about the stupid promise you made, about how it doesn't matter anyway. You will have to get to the other side of seeing what it feels like to be that in charge of your own mind, that accountable to your own dream, and that onto your own fraud when it comes to keeping a promise to yourself.

And what about **Stephanie**'s promises? Given it is Stephanie's deepest desire to be in love, I had her not only make promises about her career, but also around dating and even, take a seat, about investigating freezing her eggs.

What do you think happened when Stephanie started to get into better actions than bitching about dating in Manhattan? How many karaoke nights do you think she attended? Uh. TWO (remember, she's a tough cookie!). And, though singing Journey's "Don't Stop Believin'" was both horrific and hilarious, Stephanie started to wisely use her promises to muzzle her own bitch, to kill her own right to be mad at "them"—men, coworkers, her sister, and her mother. She noticed there were a lot of "them" against her in *her* life. She got to stop wondering why no great men were showing, when she was acting far from great herself, and to get in charge of her own social life, instead of her chicken.

STEPHANIE'S PROMISE SHEET

PROMISE	M	T	W	T	F	S	S	EXCUSE	CONSE-QUENCE	KEPT
Rejoin Match .com, tweak pro-file (by Monday) to match the revised LOVE dream I wrote.	K							N/A	If not done by Monday, sign up for speed-dating event that week and go.	N/A
Spend at least 3 hours a week on Match, happily reading profiles.		K		K		K		N/A	Pick one per-son I don't like at work, take them to lunch and have a good time.	N/A
Go out on 1 date a week I am excited about.	NK	NK	NK	NK	NK	NK	NK	I didn't hear back from the two men I sent e-mails to on Match.	Go to a karaoke bar and sing 1 love song per missed date.	Ugh
Read LOVE dream every morning.	K	K	K	K	K	K	K	N/A	No cream in coffee next day.	N/A
No complaining about online dating.	K	K	K	NK	K	K	K	Couldn't help it. They must not read the profile or don't care about age range I say.	$5 per com-plaint to the person to whom I com-plained, with an explanation.	YES
Research about freezing my eggs, costs involved, doctors, etc. and make a decision by end of next month.							K	N/A. Not only did I research it, I made an appoint-ment to freeze my eggs. But I'm not telling my mother about it.	Ask MY mother her opinion about it and hear her out in its entirety, happily.	N/A

K = Kept; NK = Not Kept

Speaking of chicken (roasted and inner), what about **Katie**'s promises and consequences regarding her BODY dream?

Clearly, Katie needed a tight leash on her food, exercise, and alcohol promises. As you can tell from both her promises and consequences, Katie's brat is a bit lazy. The best and only way to deal with Katie, and those of you that can relate to Katie and her need for a "choke collar," is to not only have clear and measurable promises, but also to dangle her own vices before her. That's right, use her caffeine, her diet Red Bull, her sleep, like the carrots they are.

KATIE'S PROMISE SHEET

PROMISE	M	T	W	T	F	S	S	EXCUSE	CONSE-QUENCE	KEPT
Keep DIET (no bread / pasta / rice or sugar, or fried food).	K	K	K	K	K	K	K	N/A	Walk the dog at 6 a.m.	N/A
Log my daily food intake and e-mail to Lauren before bed every night.	K	K	K	K	K	K	NK	Went to a party and got home late. Forgot to send log to Lauren.	Add extra workout for every log I miss.	Ugh
Exercise 3x a week, 40 minutes cardio (running, bike, treadmill, or elliptical) at level 8.	K			K		K		N/A	Lose 2 days of any TV watching.	N/A
3 meals a day from diet food plan (breakfast by 10 a.m. / lunch by 2 p.m. / dinner by 8 p.m.)	3	3	3	2	3	3	3	I was on a business call that ran long on Thursday. Skipped lunch.	If skip meal or late, owe an extra 30 minutes to a workout that week (for each offense).	Yes
5 alcoholic drinks a week.	1	0	0	0	2	1	0	N/A	If I cheat, I lose 14 days of drinking.	N/A

K = Kept; NK = Not Kept

Is it a bummer that we need to dangle our vices and not our dreams before our noses to get us to move? Sure. But so be it. Most of us would fight for our weed, our TV, our wine more than a juicy sex life, so why not use our bad for good?

Turns out, no surprise here, the more Katie kept her promises, the prouder she was of herself. Hell, even when Katie fumbled and broke a promise, she felt proud after keeping her consequence. After all, she was now in the right battle with her brat, and out to butcher her chicken that was swallowing a ton instead of speaking up.

ROAD MAP TO THE PROMISE LAND

It's that time again: yours.

Time for *you* to design promises in the three areas you are working on and come up with the right consequences that will keep your chicken and brat in the right coop and time-out chair. I promise you, you know, or at least can feel, what you're not doing. You really do. If your chicken has you utterly convinced that you don't know what promises would be good for you to make (and keep), you can use your *phone a friend*. Your friends and family will have no problem telling you what they think you should do.

That reminds me. Also and immediately, find an *accountability buddy*. This is different than a drinking buddy. This is someone whom you trust to hold you to your promise. Until you start to notice how great it feels to count on yourself to keep your own promises or pay the consequences, you're not ready to be trusted alone with them.

Barking direction #9: Please proceed with caution. This warning is similar to the one back in the first chapter, when I advised you to tread carefully when reading your old friends your new dreams. You see, many of our friends are actually our friends *because* we have similar beliefs, theories, traits, excuses, and inner dialogue as they do. So now, when suddenly you, let's say, start being responsible for how many drinks you have in a night, do you think your Napa-loving, throw-back-a-few-bottles-with-you buddy will be bubbly and supportive about your new promise? Or will they, in order to not have to deal with themselves, judge the heck out of the "new" you?

Sad, but so.

Look. Finding out who your true friends are is, without question, sobering but, at the same time, it's wholly necessary in order to realize your own dreams—and even to realize your dream in the area of COMMUNITY (whether you knew you were working on it or not).

ASSIGNMENT FOR CHAPTER THREE

1. What's your brand of excuses? Write down three of your favorite excuses you use on a regular basis that keep you from doing what you know you should be doing in the three specific areas you are working on as you read the book.
2. Create a promise sheet for yourself. It should include the three areas you're working on, a kept/not kept column for each day of the week, an excuses column (a wide one!), and a consequence column.
3. Come up with at least two specific promises for each of the three areas you are working on.
4. Come up with an awesome irksome consequence for each of your promises.
5. Find an accountability buddy and share your promise sheet (the filled-out one) with them. Set up a time to review your promises with them daily or weekly, depending on how tight a leash you know you will need when it comes to keeping promises. Obviously, it depends on the person. Katie, for example, needed a daily check-in with me.

Emotional Feng Shui

Keeping promises and paying consequences is not meant to feel like a bigger list of to-dos than you already have (or are already avoiding). If they do, tell your two-faced brat and chicken to flock off. You are the one with the dream. You are the one designing your promises and consequences. I didn't tell you to promise to run when you prefer rowing or to put off the dentist until a root canal is imminent. Designing promises, keeping them, or paying the consequence is a new muscle. The likelihood that this will suck royally for you at first is high. It may take a month or more to get the hang of it and not simply want me hanged.

How I like to prep new clients for this initial suckage is, no shit, by explaining Newton's first law of motion. Newton's law states that every object at rest tends to stay at rest, and an object in a state of motion tends to remain in that state of motion unless an external force is applied to it.

So, let's just say, for the sake of argument, *you* are the object that is currently in a state of rest or inaction, specifically in the areas you are taking on for the book.* What you and I are doing now is applying force—in this case, adding promises to your current state—and it's going to take some real force to get you from a state of rest to a state of motion. Once in motion—in this case, once making and keeping promises—the action of keeping those promises (or paying the consequences) will get easier. It takes a bit to get you to move. If it didn't, you would have already done it yourself. The desire was there, the actions were not.

Is there resistance at first?

Of course. But what you will find on the other side of keeping the promise or paying the consequence is personal pride, confidence, happiness, and self-esteem.

Turns out, even when you break the promise (and you will), but keep the consequence, you *still* end up proud. You see, even though you didn't keep the promise and your brat or chicken won that particular round, they still got dinged for it.

There's still a new sheriff in town: you.

---

* For the offended, please note, I've called you worse.

In case my clients' sample consequences weren't enough examples for you, here are some more awesomely awful ones:

1. Annoying Consequences
- Throwing money to the ground or flushing it down the toilet.
- No chocolate (not even dark).
- No wine (or your favorite libation).
- No coffee (or cream in it). Yes, a latte counts as coffee.
- No Internet.
- No TV or favorite show.
- Donating money (anonymously) to a political candidate that you sorta abhor. Though obviously a particularly awful consequence, a particularly potent one.
- No cell phone, laptop, etc.
- No manicures.

2. Scary/Embarrassing Consequences
- Saying hi to X number of strangers.
- Randomly complimenting X number of strangers.
- Buying coffee or a subway ticket for the person behind you in line, and explaining why.
- Doing an open mic.
- Singing a song on a street corner.

3. Truth-Telling Consequences
- Confessing a broken promise to someone whom you'd prefer not to tell.

4. Relational Consequences
- Calling in-laws or other family members whom you don't particularly like to speak to.*
- Asking your spouse/partner for a good consequence for you.
- Giving a timed massage to husband/wife/partner.
- Babysitting for free.

---

* Hi, Nana! JK.

5. Cross-Purpose Consequences

- Doing push-ups.
- Adding fifteen more minutes of cardio/weights to your gym promise.
- Running up/down a flight of stairs ten times.
- Running outside instead of going to the gym.
- Cleaning out a sock or hardware drawer, whichever is worse.
- Vacuuming out your car.

Okay, I think you have more than enough information to figure out how to head into the battlefield and fight for the right team. And, never fear (or, of course, go ahead), we'll deal more with your head noise in the next chapter.

But, until then, how about another **POP QUIZ**?

If, admittedly, you're a notorious criminal when it comes to doing what you say you were going to do for yourself, you should:

A. make a bunch of never-before-done promises, the more the merrier and, while you're at it, quit a bunch of highly addictive things cold turkey.

B. tell no one about the slew of promises you just made, because you wouldn't want them to feel as guilty as you're gonna feel when you don't keep them.

C. tell someone close to you that knows you (and your liar) about your promises and your consequences. Ask them nicely to be your accountability buddy.

D. have a cookie. You know how you get after over-committing.

C for courageous (not cookie).

CHAPTER FOUR

Change Your Mind

Getting Your Head Under New Management

TALKING HEADS

Ever notice how we are constantly talking to ourselves in our heads? We not only profess to know what others are thinking, but also what their responses will be—and even what they *really* meant by what they said.

Apparently, we are all mind readers, without much proven psychic ability.

Whether we realize it or not, our thoughts profoundly impact us. We spend our entire lives having thoughts, and because no one can hear them or sense them, we think they are fairly inconsequential unless we act upon them.

But is that true?

When it comes to fully understanding the voices in our head or knowing what's *really* happening in our heads, we actually plead ignorant. Like, "Huh, me? I'm talking to myself? Really?"

Sure, there's a level to which we'll admit that we know we're in our heads a bunch, but are we really that attuned to the smack we say to ourselves when we look in the mirror? When we are lying next to our mate? When we're driving to work? When we're attempting to brush our already reluctant kid's hair and she's got a huge (and I mean HUGE) knot in the back of her* head?

No way.

There's this illusion (delusion?) that nothing important is really going on in that dark nightclub where all our thoughts, theories, and inner dialogues dance. But, the truth is, we've all done such a lousy job as a bouncer in that club, it's kind of amazing.

When I start to work with a client about their thoughts, most don't even know what I'm talking about. They've never named it, never caught it, never really understood how much that inner dialogue is running their life. But how could it *not* matter? We are listening to it all the time. It's like a radio or television that is always on that we've gotten so used to, we can barely hear it anymore. No one has ever called a time-out on our mind, blown a whistle on it, and seen its cycle for what it is.

There is a whole level of consciousness that we are not tapped into, and worse, we are not tapped into *on purpose*. Where our brat, our chicken, our weather reporter, along with our traits and theories remain unknown to us.

This entire book is about getting you in there. Getting you in charge of your own mind and narrative. Getting you curating everything that is going on in your brain—so you can change it if you want to.

Our mind can be mean. It holds grudges. It exaggerates. It's mad. It's lazy. It lies. It's irrational. It's hypersensitive. It's hypocritical. It's cynical. It's two-faced. It's sad. It's an addict, a pervert, a racist, a drunk, an attorney, a comic, a psychic, a nutritionist, a gaydar, a personal trainer (a fat, lazy one), a policeman (as it's pretty darn positive that your speed is the fair speed). And, well, it's the CEO of anything and everything, as it certainly thinks it can do everyone's job better.

Clearly, I could go on and on. Our mind has a mind of its own. The only part that we don't admit is that we're not the boss of it. I mean, no

---

* Okay, *my* kid. Hi, Daisy!

wonder we haven't been able to dream in certain areas. We're currently not the one in charge.

That is, until now.

Mastery over your mind comes from the learned ability to choose what is best for yourself to think and feel. To not bullshit yourself, but to align your mind with your desires. To get your own hands back on your life's remote control and press mute when your mind messes with what matters most to you.

Heading in *is* your way out.

Truth is, in areas where you *are* succeeding, you *have* harnessed your mind. If you have a great career, a hot and healthy body, an awesome family, you have indeed figured out how to tell your chicken and brat to bugger off. You have figured out how to smell the fresh bread at a fancy restaurant, hand back the bread basket to the waiter, and order and eat the kale.* You can be powerful in a meeting, even if you are premenstrual (or your partner is). You know how to harness your mind and tell it to stop talking smack to you. Heck, you have even figured out that if you don't listen to that inner voice of yours, it shuts up.

But, in every other area of your life, where you are not winning (yet), you haven't dealt with this. You haven't separated yourself from your inner dialogue, your thoughts, and your theories. Who is catching them?

Answer: no one.

Except now you *are* going to start separating yourself from them. You are going to invent a higher self and start distinguishing yourself from your thoughts, from your lower self. Your higher self is now going to witness your thoughts, evaluate them, nickname them, and yes, curate them. You are going to stop and giggle as you notice what your head says about your husband, your wife, your partner, your boss, your body, the driver next to you. Your higher self is going to ask your lower self, "Is that really me? What am I really like?"

And, you will see that the very minute you start to ask yourself what *you* are really like, *you* have a say over it.

---

* The state bird of California.

THOUGHTS GONE WILD

If we actually really stopped and paid attention to our minds, we'd realize what insidious and incessant hogwash our inner voices say to us. I promise, we wouldn't let our head talk to our kids the way we let it talk to us. The only way to stop your mind from running amok is to catch it in the act. The only way to catch it in the act is to actually put the act of catching it on your to-do list and literally write down what you are saying to yourself daily in a *thought log*.

The ability to press your own mute button is up to you. You have to start hearing those negative inner conversations in action. If you can hear them, you can stop them. We each have endless positive and negative thoughts. Obviously, positive ones are when we champion ourselves and say things to ourselves like, *I'm so excited to go on that vacation, hear what my boss has to say about the huge account I just landed*, etc. Anything that makes us feel good when we think about it is a positive thought.

A negative thought sounds more like, *Oh no! What if my boss is unhappy with my report? What if I don't have a good time on vacation? What if [fill in the blank]?* When you have a series of rampant negative thoughts, I call that a *negative thought train*.

We *all* take a ride now and again. Whether it's an express train or not, whether we can get off at an earlier stop, is up to us. Our thoughts work against our dreams. Yet, we treat these negative thoughts as true, as if they come from our innermost self. We think that because we think these thoughts, and think them often enough, they *must be* valid, rational, and carry some significance.

But do they?

If we think our thoughts to be true and the real us, do we ever have to shut the negative ones down? Be accountable for them? Deal with them?

Nope.

The longer our negative thoughts stay bottled up and are allowed to run relentlessly in our minds, the more evidence they collect and the more "true" they become.

When you recognize your inner dialogue as a negative thought train and call it out for what it is, the choice of believing it, of getting on or off that particular loco-motive is now back in your hands. I promise you that you have more control over your ride than you think.

Once again, let's put money where your mind is. If I offered you a thousand bucks to stop a thought train, you could and would do it.

Why isn't your happiness incentive enough?

Much of whatever is plaguing a person is located in their inner dialogue. A good place to start hearing yourself think is on your commute, in the bathroom, in the shower, or looking in the mirror. Places where your head isn't necessarily just going through a list of regular things to do, but where you can eke out your attitude.

A thought log is really the only way to force yourself into a state of consciousness about your inner dialogue and to find out exactly how you talk to yourself, how you are entertained in the car, what you think about when you sing songs, etc. Does a song take you back to a bad time? To old fights? What you do with your idle time in that mind of yours is something to face, address, and rewire.

Truth is, the minute you have the right promises (and consequences) in place, you can bet that your inner dialogue is going to get rambunctious. Anything that scares the crap out of you in pursuit of your dream, your head will try to talk you out of. Your head runs the scenarios. It tries to get you to run the other way, advises you to not pick up the phone, and commands you to put this book down and ship me back to Long Island from whence I came. In order to pull your thought train's emergency brake, you will have to be willing to see how your inner dialogue manipulates the bejesus out of you.

You'll also start to see that you have consistent patterns in your inner dialogue. We spend an inordinate amount of time thinking the same few unoriginal thoughts over and over again. These *thought patterns* can tell you volumes about you and where you are directing large amounts of your energy. Most often, these thought patterns come from the same source. Ready? It's not particularly groundbreaking or original, but more so, biblically predictable—the seven deadly sins: pride, greed, lust, envy, gluttony, wrath, and sloth.

Since I'm coming after your head's noise, it's only fair that I show you my own mind's preferred train line.

HEAD OF MY HOUSE

Who knew, but when I used to walk down the street in New York City where I lived, I styled people. In my mind, I'd cut their hair, help them lose weight, disapprove of their color choices, and just retool them overall. My mind had a full-time job—apparently, Tim Gunn's! I'm not really sure how I didn't trip on something. My mind was so busy, judgmental, and arrogant. Except one day, I noticed it. I stopped and questioned my behavior. And, at that moment, I could hear it. I realized how incredibly embarrassing, let alone shallow, it was of me. It woke me up to how much was going on in my mind that I wasn't conducting.

In that less than impressive moment with myself, in the realization of how much time I've wasted doing this—namely, most of my life—I knew I needed to take over the narrative and get my mind to do what I wanted it to do. And in that moment, I decided that I was never going to allow my mind to run amok like that again. I was not going to let myself walk down the street Tim Gunn–ing a person up and down. Instead, if my mind needed something to do on that walk, then let *me* give it something better to do. From then on out, whenever I walked the streets of New York, I let myself only think about my business, my clients, new ideas, and where and what I wanted to teach. I used my time and mind for value and fun, period.

When you start to figure out what you're doing with that mind of yours or, better yet, what it is doing with you, you can have a choice about what *you* actually want to do with it, hopefully something more useful and inspiring than what you're doing with it now.

Sure, this notion of just giving your mind something better to think about may sound a bit trite to your dubious doubter, but, however duh-mb it may seem, it's not. Stopping yourself long enough to hear yourself, to figure out how to tell yourself to shut up, and to replace those very thoughts with whatever you want to be thinking about is truly life-altering. Most of us walk around like it's "just our personality," when really we have so much say over our own character and over our everyday narratives.

In fact, we have *everything* to do with it.

YOUR HEAD'S CURRENT TALENT AGENCY

There are two other competing and constant forces with whom we contend in our head when it comes to going for our dreams—the *agent* and the *double agent*. Your agent has good intentions—it fights for your dream—but it spends most of its time fighting your double agent. Your double agent (a BFF of your chicken) works against your dream, though with the guise of protecting it. It speculates. It's even wise to your worries, and is out to make sure you cover your own ass.

The double agent believes it is protecting you from getting hurt, trying to lessen the shame should things not turn out as you wish. So, if you've just started dating someone, it advises you to qualify how excited you are about him or her. It adds phrases like "so far, so good," it likes to knock on wood, cross fingers, and hope for the best, but is it really hoping for the best or cushioning the fall? Actually, it's doing both. Sure, it's protecting you from getting hurt, but that very defense mechanism is also preventing you from learning what you need to learn. It prevents you from risking what you need to risk in the name of your dreams. It leaves you thinking that you are doing your very best, when really, at best, you're doing your second best.

Your double agent, wise as it may be, strives for the silver medal.

But can you see the managing of the potential failure, the just-in-casing, however reasonable and even wise, is also the very reason you can't fully connect to your deepest desires? Not because you can't have what you want, but because your own double agent is betting against you, doubting your success, and telling you to watch out, to double back, just in case it doesn't happen.

Why hedge your bet?

It's genius, really. You're increasing your odds. Even though you are betting against yourself. It's betting that you're right that you were wrong. Worse comes to worst, you either realize your dreams *or* you were right that you didn't. Worse comes to worst, you knew better than to give your whole heart to your dream. You survived the whole experience without ever being too disappointed. You can always say that at least you tried to achieve your dreams. You know, you had good intentions...

Look, your double agent isn't dumb—and that is its very issue. This kind of "fear speculation" also leads to some beneficial behavior: We bring umbrellas, we buy expensive health insurance, we leave for the airport earlier than our inner brat wants to. Sure, some of this *is* quite wise and helpful, but, sadly, your double agent is never truly fighting for your greatness. If you ever even question its wisdom, the double agent can pull out examples of where you've been hurt before, proving how its point of view is accurate. It has a skewed sense of history and logic to support all of its findings and best practices.

It does, after all, have a huge job in your life: running your security.

The minute you started listening to your inner dialogue—in this case, your double agent—your big dream never had a chance. It was screwed the minute you started betting against it. The only way to make a dream happen is to believe 100 percent in it.

Uh-oh.

You have to want your dream so bad that you refuse to give up on it. No matter what anyone says, even (especially) your own head! You will go to the ends of the earth for it. You will slay the ~~dragon~~ double agent. Because it is that very dynamic—the right to hedge your own bet against yourself—that *is* destroying your dream. With the double agent out of the picture, your *true self*, the voice that is true to you, can emerge and fight as one voice for one common purpose—to achieve your dream.

A MUFFLER FOR YOUR MIND

In order to take over your mind and sanction your own inner mutiny, you have to first really parse what *your* mind has been doing for a living. You have to start to hear what that inner dialogue of yours is actually saying to you. It's giving you advice. It's telling you what to do. It's telling you what not to do. It's telling you what mood you are in. It's telling your lactose-intolerant self to eat rocky road.

It's directing everything you are doing and yet *you*, its maestro, can barely hear it.

You and I are going to start to design your inner dialogue. You're going to learn how to quiet those negative voices and amplify the affirming ones. You can do it. But, most of all, you *need* to do it. After all, negative thoughts can't but yield negative results, and positive thoughts can't but yield positive results.

You can start to see how this works, right?

You're in charge of what you're listening to in your mind. You're the only one in there with yourself. You're the one in action or not. Your actions have clear and specific results. Your mind has been the bandleader of your actions and inactions for a long time in any area where you've been happy *and* unhappy in your life

You and I are out to interrupt the negative dialogue that you're spewing and replace it with what *you* want to be thinking and what *you* want to be doing so that *you* can attain the dreams you wrote in Chapter One.

Look at any area where you have realized your dreams. Where you handled your head and you got into the right actions. Where the promises you made to yourself mattered. Where you did what you said you would. Whatever it took. Whatever reasonable, protective, or sensible bullshit your head tried to sell you, sure you heard, but you didn't buy it. It didn't matter. You forged forward, regardless. And, voila, you got what you said you wanted. In any area of your life where you are suffering, struggling, and stuck, your thoughts match your results, period.

Here are five basic steps to reclaim, uh, *your* mind. Don't knock it until you try it, and try it until you master it.

1. **Observe it.** The first thing you are going to do is start paying attention to your thoughts. You're going to start to use a thought log and write down what you're thinking in the language in which you are actually speaking to yourself. Let's say one of the areas you are working on in this book, like Katie, is your BODY. You are now going to make sure when you hear yourself talking to yourself about your body, particularly when you're looking in a mirror, when you're getting dressed, when you're shopping or avoiding shopping, when you are looking at a menu, what do you say to yourself? Listen and write it down.

2. **Name it.** Decide which thought patterns you want to eliminate. You'll start to see that you are constantly talking to yourself about one particular thing, and it's negative, and it makes you feel bad. Find your negative thought patterns that are not aligned with your dreams, and name that thought pattern (e.g., Tim Gunn–ing). Make sure you figure out the right name of that negative thought train you get on and the pattern, so that you can hear it the minute it leaves the station.

3. **Stop it.** The minute you hear that particular thought pattern, you're going to roll up your sleeves and deal with stopping it. You're going to figure out that you can, trite as it may seem, actually tell yourself to think about something else. Because you have let your inner dialogue run wild in certain areas of your life, you have no idea that if all of a sudden you no longer tolerated its tantrum, you could put your foot down and change it. You can stop its rant, decide the game of chicken is over, and call the shots. It is that simple. I dare you to do it. Your dream implores you. The best ways to stop your negative thoughts are to either 1) confess them to someone out loud; and/or 2) make a consequence for yourself for engaging in those thoughts.

If, however, you find yourself in a thought pattern that is way too complicated to just turn off, not to worry, we'll deal with those in Chapter Eight.

4. **Replace it.** Decide which thoughts you actually want to cultivate instead of your current ones, making sure they align with your dreams. As simple as this too may sound to your skeptic, I promise it works. You are in charge of what you want to be thinking about, you just haven't been. You sublet your mind to your brat, chicken, and weather reporter. The worst tenants *ever*. And, just like it takes time and patience to kick bad tenants out, this too is going to take some time. The three squatters have been living there for years, so hire your dreams a good attorney (your higher self)!

5. **Implement it.** Direct your new thought patterns, ensuring that you are thinking—hello!—about what *you* want to be thinking. So, let's say your dream is to fall madly in love and find your soul's mate. Instead of entertaining negative thoughts in your mind about how "dry" your city is, or how unlucky you are, or how you missed the (nonexistent) boat, start instead imagining your trip together to Bali, his or her hand in yours, the ring on your finger, etc. Start getting your mind to quiet down and do what *you* want it to, replacing the bratty, cowardly, and self-sabotaging old thoughts with new, bold, and dreamy ones.

If you follow the five steps above, you *will* take back your mind. Not to worry; I have examples (of course I do). By the time we get to the assignment itself at the end of this chapter, you will have read more samples of people's thoughts than a Vulcan.

THE THOUGHT-FULL-NESS OF OTHERS

You made it. The section where, for a few fleeting moments, I stop pointing at you, at humanity in general, and focus instead on Donna, Ethan, Stephanie, and Katie.

Let's see what **Donna**, our at-home mother of three, sufferer of two (stomach and husband), chatters about full-time in her head. Here are some of the thoughts that landed in her log:

- I feel like I am cornered into going on those meds. It's a serious drug and it scares me long-term. Why can't I try something else? I feel trapped by my own doctor.
- My thighs look thick.
- What the hell is she wearing? I hate when women dress like teens. I hope I don't look like that.
- Why can't the two of them [husband and teen son] just get along.
- Is that how all kids eat at the table? God, they're not just ingrates, they're pigs.
- I should have been more organized for the tutors.
- Who left these dishes in the sink?! Clearly, they don't respect me and all I do. This is the worst pro bono gig EVER.
- Why does he have to bring up the fact that I have totally overspent the last few years at eleven at night while we are lying in bed? I was all ready for a romantic evening and now he brings this up and keeps saying, "What were you thinking?" What a jerk.
- Didn't we just have sex the other day? Does a hand job count?

Can you see how Donna's thoughts circulate, understandably and primarily, between health, self-image, and family? She sounds like so many of us. Particularly, the brave stay-at-home variety of us who are trying to raise a family without losing ourselves. How healthy could nitpicking and swallowing these types of thoughts be on your body? Let alone your digestive tract?

Question for you: If you are nice on the outside, but mean on the inside, whether to yourself or others, aren't you *still* mean? Truth is, it's not actually *nicer* to be quietly mean; it's just more fake. If Donna points only at her husband's outright agitation, she misses her own inner irritation. On purpose.

Let's see how **Stephanie**, our Manhattan single lady, did capturing her thoughts:

- Why didn't I get cramps this time with my period? That's odd. Maybe it's not really a period.
- Maybe it's menopause. Maybe I'm hemorrhaging.
- My mom just said, "Watch out for crazy drivers." She's manifesting danger.
- She's so dramatic. And judgmental. What an angry bitch.
- What did he just say? How arrogant. He's such a pompous ass. If only he knew what everyone at the office really thinks of him. It's not just me.
- What would they do without me? Do they know how much I do?
- My throat hurts. I'll have a cough drop. These have sugar. Shit, my teeth are rotting.
- No wonder I'm single. I'm falling apart. I'm damaged goods. I got my mom's genes. Great . . . but even she's married.

No matter how successful we are on the outside, look what our head does on the inside all day long if left to its own devices. I mean, Stephanie truly wonders why she's not so happy. She thinks it's solely about her work environment, about being single, about how her mother talks to her—but look at how she incessantly speaks to herself.

It's a wonder any of us get anything else done during the day!

Now, do you think anyone else in Stephanie's family sounds like this? Of course. Personality traits, like Stephanie's "Woody Ellen" neurotic cycling here, are cultural, familial, and hardwired.

I think Stephanie might want to give her hypochondriac head a good, long, permanent case of laryngitis, no?

And, what about **Ethan**? His outward thoughts were impressively negative already; let's see what his inner dialogue sounds like. Hell, he's even figured out how to use this coaching to beat himself up some more. Take heed: Your smart head will want to take whatever ride you normally take to get out of doing something different and a tad scary or off-putting.

- My skin is in total eruption; I just want it to go away.
- I'm so disorganized.
- I have no skills; it's all smoke and mirrors.
- I can't introduce myself to hundreds and thousands of people for the rest of my life.
- Holy shit, it's my mom's birthday. I don't want to call but I have to. She is going to be weird on the phone, maybe even passive-aggressive. I should put it off, but then she'll be even more passive-aggressive. I am being passive-aggressive by not calling... Shit!
- I will never get any better at golf. I should not have wasted the money.
- Reg [wife] is going out again. I can't talk to her about it or she will be pissed. All day shopping and then out with friends in the evening. It must be nice.
- I'm not a present father, my home is going to shit.
- I hate my job now; I suck at it, and I hate being bad at anything, but I am not willing to take the failure.
- I am choking on the failure. I am going to my grave, asphyxiating on this.

Ouch, right?

I guess it might not come as a huge surprise to you that both Ethan's biological dad and stepdad weren't so verbally kind. Guess who isn't either? Ethan has a hard time finding a nice word to say to himself, out loud or inwardly. No accident, but his wife, Regina, might not be all that warm and fuzzy herself. Sure, she's nicer than Ethan. But how hard is that? And, though we could try to pin Ethan's own harshness on the reality of his upbringing, truth is (yes, take a seat), you could have a verbally abusive parent and turn out an advocate of nice. Ethan's inner dialogue has just been unmuzzled and on an inordinately long leash for too long.

And how about **Katie**? What do you think her head had to say about all of those food and exercise promises and consequences?

- What the hell was I thinking? I hate celery. This food sucks. I want some f*cking pizza. Bummer.
- Chicken is boring. I hate dieting. I'm never going to be thin. I was crazy to think this would work.
- Nonfat dressing tastes like shit.
- What the f*ck do you do with cottage cheese? Do you eat it or put something on it? I don't understand what you do with it.
- Shit, I don't want to work out. My legs are sore from yesterday. And I'm too busy. I'm never going to get everything done. This sucks! I'm such a procrastinator.
- Divorce sucks. This day sucked. My ex sucks. I need a drink.
- Should I tell the waitress no butter on the asparagus? She's busy. I don't want to bother her. I hate when people are picky about ordering food. Forget it. It's just a little butter. It's not really cheating. I'll wipe it with my napkin. Yeah, that should work.
- I'm starving. There's nothing to eat. I want those damn Girl Scout cookies. Why in the hell did my sister buy them? She knows I'm dieting.
- My sister was supposed to bring me home some sashimi for dinner. They didn't have any.
- She brought me a roasted chicken. F*CK. If I have chicken one more night I'm going to f*cking scream.

If you have a teen (or are avoiding having one), you're probably thinking that thirty-eight-year-old Katie sounds a lot like 'em: lazy, persnickety, with a side order of resistance.

Once you incriminate your head in writing and fully see what it's so busy trying to get you doing and out of doing, you can deal with it head-on. You can put the right promises in place to hush it and, even, redirect it, so that you, *all* of you—your mind, body, and heart—are fighting for the same end goal: your dreams realized.

A PEN FOR YOUR THOUGHTS

It's that time again. Your turn to do the assignment.

ASSIGNMENT FOR CHAPTER FOUR

1. Three times per day, stop and write down the thoughts you were having over the past hour or two. It's a good idea to set a timer, such as on your cell phone, to remind you when it's time to record your thoughts. Give yourself a time limit, such as five minutes, and challenge yourself to write as many thoughts in that time as possible. Don't edit your thoughts, just dump whatever is in your brain on the page. Do this for two weeks.

2. Once you have a large amount of thought data, read through it and see the thought themes that emerge. Make a list of your thoughts' themes, such as:
  * Worrying about what others think
  * Decision anxiety
  * Judging/criticizing other people
  * Self-judging/criticizing or doubting
  * Competitive with others/comparing yourself—feeling better or worse because of that comparison

3. In the three areas you've selected to work on in this book, follow the five steps outlined in this chapter to get your mind under new management: yours.

Moving a Head

Armed with all of this information, you can start to conduct where you spend your mental energy. You can decide where you want to focus your energy and make promises accordingly. Some of your thoughts are embarrassing and you won't want to put them down on paper. But know that the things you hide own you, and worse, they become truth. The key is to have a sense of humor about it all. There isn't one of us who isn't a tad twisted. There is just no chance for change if you hide it or give it that much power over you by thinking it *is* you.

It's not.

Look (probably another sentence starter you should brace yourself for), coming after the very narrative you have held on to your whole life is no small feat. The willingness to dive into the deep end of the pool with me comes with a whole new world of vulnerability, triumphs, and mess. I do not promise you your life is going to get simpler. The fast lane is coming. Thank God. You and I are building courage and inner grit over cowardice and resignation. Please check your seat belt.

Okay, time for your **POP QUIZ**. Ready?

Today's the day! You are going to finally ask out that cute friend of a friend whom you have been flirting with for months on Facebook. You listen to the following advice from your trusted advisor, coach, consultant, guru, intuit, and social planner—your mind:

A. are you an idiot?! Your "one" asks *you* out. This one can't possibly be it. Don't do it. It was a dumb promise to begin with.

B. play it cool. Instead of asking them out *today*, how about you post that cute new photo of you on FB and see how they respond this time.

C. in fact, while you're *not* at it, forward his or her response to your friends who know about your crush and see what they think you should *really* do.

D. tell your head to simmer down. Even though you understand it's scared, your dream is to find the love of your life. Your actions (and thoughts!) need to match the results you want. Set up the coffee date! Be as brave as you want your soul's mate to be.

Yep. **D** for dare yourself to deal with your head and duke it out with your ass-covering double agent, whose sabotaging scheme is to keep you sad, safe, and—yep, at the rate you're going—single.

CHAPTER FIVE

Emotional DNA

Dealing with the Hand You Were Dealt

ARE YOU ~~MY~~ YOUR MOTHER?

No matter how much we love our parents or even how far we've run from them, they provided our basic building blocks. And, though we all at some point in our lives giggle (or choke) at how we're inevitably turning into or sounding like our parents, do we *really* understand the magnitude of it?

Answer: way less than even the most self-aware of us are aware.

I promise you, most of us have never *fully* dealt with how deep the emotional, not just physical, DNA goes. Sure, we all know we have our mother's complexion and our father's nose. But do we ever really deal head-on with the extent to which we not only have our dad's pretty blue eyes, but we may also have his wandering eyes? Or the inclination to marry someone with his wandering eyes?

Sure, some of you really do know this about yourself and may even think this whole concept unnecessary. Either because 1) it's so obvious to you, or 2) because you've spent years working through this and are now, truly and completely, different from them.

Still, isn't that the point?

In some way, shape, or form, who you are today, even if it's the polar opposite of who your parents are or were, is *still* a reaction to them. Is still not wholly and freely designed by you. If we are subconsciously, or even consciously, busy being better than our parents, sticking it to them in some way, and/or improving upon our unresolved childhood experiences, is that even a self-creation?

Or is it simply a reaction?

The child of an alcoholic is sober, never drinks, is staunch, and feels strongly about sending his kids to religious school. The person whose father was a gambler is utterly conservative. They can't spend a dime.

Whether our parents are or were kind and generous, stingy or condescending. Whether they were alcoholics or cheaters, happily married or miserably complacent. Whether they stayed for the kids or ran away without looking back. How could their character traits and issues not leave a permanent imprint on us?

They have to.

GOOD AND PLENTY

When you were born, you were handed a goody bag of sorts, similar to the kind you received as a kid at the end of a birthday party. Except this particular goody bag didn't have any Pop Rocks, Fun Dip, or dollar-store toys in it. It included your physical DNA (molecules, genes, etc.) and your emotional DNA (personality traits, inner dialogue, issues, beliefs, theories). In it was everything you witnessed, learned, mimicked, made up, and endured growing up—from your parents' marriage to society at large. It's influenced by everything from your race to your sex to your pecking order to the schools you attended to the towns in which you were raised. And we all, without meaning to, built our personality from that very bag we got handed.

Had any of us known we were making our own personality, let alone our marriages (or avoidance of them), from that very bag, we would have tried to consciously design it a bit differently, right?

But what can you expect; you were ten at the time!

In some areas, you know *exactly* what you did with your goody bag. You did great things with it. In reaction to your father never having a great career, you worked toward one you love. You grew up with an addicted parent and chose to stay sober. You saw what didn't work in your parents and, without an ounce of venom in it, you upgraded yourself.

You, without question, did better.

However, most of us have *not* built our personality as a source of pride and pleasure, with zero resentment, with zero reaction, and from a place of pure design, forgiveness, and in honor of our parents. And it is that very reason that you and I are doubling back and getting you conscious of how unconsciously you were built.

Because it's only when you can *fully* see yourself, the great and the less than great, that you can take over your narrative—your traits, your theories, and your beliefs—and consciously evolve what you've been given.

In my twenty-plus years coaching, I've seen some truly hellish goody bags. But I swear, no one—and I mean, no one—no matter what it looks like on the outside, has had it easy. Even the most successful, the best looking, the richest, the smartest, come with their own crap "toys" in their loot bag. Regardless, this is your opportunity to pour out your goody bag and get radically honest about what's in it.

You can either deny it or dig in and deal with it.

As before, I think it's only fair that if I'm showing you how much you are a reaction to your parents, I shine a light on the Marsha Marsha Marsha [my mom] in me.

THE BIG C

Sure, by now, we're all pretty darn clear that I come with a side of shallow, but what you might not know, if you don't know me personally, is how much I also differ from my mother.

You see, my mom has a trait that my sisters and I have come to call "the Big C." Thankfully, it's got nothing whatsoever to do with cancer.

What my mom does have, however, is "couch." She likes her things. And, not just any things. The best of things.

We call this trait, her love of things (particularly, fine furnishings), *couch*.

From Park Avenue to the East River to Beekman Place, the label matters to Mom. Even during a period of time when my folks' finances plummeted and they had to downsize, I secretly wondered whether my mom would dump my dad for the daybed* if she couldn't fit the two into the smaller space.

And here we are. Four kids. Three girls. One boy. With that very trait in all of our respective goody bags. My reaction to it, you wonder? Sure. I love a good couch. But guess what? I married a man that couldn't give two shits about material things.

My house is an adorable 1700s a-bit-worse-for-the-wear antique farmhouse. My closet, miniscule. Do I care? I have spurts. But, for the most part, not really. I've grown enamored of my love of not caring and unexpected non-my-mom-ness.

Sure, the Big C was in all four of our goody bags. But it wasn't until I could see my version of it or, better yet, my aversion to it, that I could laugh at it, name it, and design it differently. Of course I want a nice home. So does my husband, David. It's coming. He's building it. But, not because I need it or because any of our possessions could replace what I love most. They can't.

One time, David and I even tried to buy twelve antique chairs that he found online. Did we buy them? Nope. We left without the chairs, but came home with the phone number of two new friends, the chair owners.

Seems, in response to my mother's *couch*, her preference for things above all, I don't collect things. I collect people.

UPGRADING YOUR MODEL

The more open-eyed you get about the goody bag you've been given, the more you can create who you actually want to be. If you can figure out

---

* Nineteenth-century French Empire.

your parents' blueprint first, you can connect the dots and have a say in the design of yours. It is revolutionary to not only know that you have your parents' issues, but that you can intervene on your own behalf and change them. You can have more fun with, and a sense of humor about, your goody bag. You can have a romantic accountability toward what you were given and heal it.

On purpose.

I am arming you here with the ability to truly design your life. To make sure your dreams are exactly that—yours! So that when it comes to your dream about your marriage or your dream about your relationship to yourself, it doesn't have to be a mere reaction to your parents. You can, instead, be able to dial in and dial out of the traits you want to cultivate.

None of us has any idea how pervasive our parents' traits and issues are. How riddled we are with them. It's as if some of us are building a house and we're trying to skip over dealing with the plumbing. Pipe up and deal.

OTHER PEOPLE'S PARENTS

Let's see how a couple of my clients did in the assignment for this chapter, where they had to list their parents' traits and describe how each of their parents' traits play out in them, as well as how their marriage dynamics affected them.

For the sake of having this book not end up the length of *War and Peace*, I have culled through their traits and picked the top few. These samples are not my clients' first take at the assignment. As you can imagine, it takes a bit to fully nail yourself. The ability and desire to cop to things that don't necessarily work about you, *coptuitiveness,** is, after all, not our species' favorite pastime.

Let's see what **Donna** had to say about each of her folks and how

---

* A favorite term that my husband, David, coined.

some of their traits play out in her, particularly the ones that act as kryptonite to her dreams.

Remember *barking direction #1*: Find yourself in these great people.

DONNA'S DAD'S TRAITS

- **A Victim/Complainer**

  Everything is a problem. He can't get a job because he's too old or too qualified or people don't know how to run businesses these days, etc. No one gives him a chance.

  How it lives in me

  I complain about nothing (at least, out loud). People don't even know I have IBS. I suffer to myself and stoically hide it. I am the quiet victim of my illness, husband, time, etc. I married someone that complains enough out loud for the two of us.

- **Passive-Aggressive**

  My dad will mutter and grumble to himself until someone gets the hint. For example, he will complain about taking out the garbage until someone else takes it out.

  How it lives in me

  I do everything myself and resent others for not helping, even though I don't ask for it. Maybe I ask the kids. But we know how that goes. I married someone who has no problem asking for a ton. I ask for nothing, but watch you take and take. You have no idea I'm upset or need anything.

- **Addictive**

  After he went to rehab for drinking, he took up sugar.

  How it lives in me

  I was definitely a sugar addict in my twenties. After I was diagnosed with IBS, I weaned myself off processed sugar. But I have other addictive behaviors. I just realized now that my shopping and hiding my shopping is exactly my dad's drinking. He hid how much he drank. I hide how much I shop.

DONNA'S MOM'S TRAITS

- **Spiritual**

  My mom is very Catholic and is very devout with her praying and listening to spiritual music or having the Catholic channel on. She reads spiritual books.

  How it lives in me

  It lives in me much in the same way. I picked up on this when I was very little, not just from my mother, but my grandmother. Our three kids go to Catholic schools. We go to church on Sundays. There is no maybe (or choice) about any of it.

- **A Shopper**

  She will use any excuse to go buy something. She used shopping as punishment for my dad when he drank.

  How it lives in me

  I can do this too. I can see how, just like my mother, I deserve to shop. Like my mother, I can even walk out of a gas station with things I didn't go in to get. Telling myself I deserved it.

DONNA'S PARENTS' MARRIAGE TRAITS & DYNAMICS

My parents truly love each other. My father was my mother's first love and lover. They did not fight much in front of us. If we ever heard them fighting, it was because they thought we were out of the house or room. They joked around a lot and were always good at hanging out together whether they were strolling through Costco or watching TV on the sofa. I see them as good mates. When my dad goes on one of his complaining, negative victim rants, I can tell my mom is tuning him out, which I think is how she tolerates it. Every once in a while, she would say, "Would you just stop now?" "Enough!" or "Oh yeah, so what's the good news?" I love that! The main conflict I always saw was around my father's drinking and smoking. And the less frequent, but regular fights about spending. That is when my mother would be angry or sad or both.

You might be thinking that you are not as wildly obvious a clone as Donna is to her folks. Sorry. It's not so. Look. I swear, none of this is bad news. If you're willing to get the karmic joke of it all, it's kind of funny. It's up to us to bemoan it or change it.

Okay, back to Donna's list. If I had listed all of her parents' negative and positive traits, what you would have found is that Donna doesn't have a bad thing to say about her mom. Not one. The closest to a negative trait she had was about her mom's shopping. And do you think Donna really thought her mom's shopping habit was truly criminal? You can see how in Donna's description of it, she justifies it for her mom. I mean, after all, it was in response to her dad's drinking.

Here's the thing (*barking direction #4*: Follow me): If Donna positions her mother, the wife of a passive-aggressive pessimist with a dry sense of humor, as the hero of her story...what does that allow Donna to be in her own tale? If love looks like one villain (the husband) and one hero/martyr/victim (the wife), isn't that exactly what Donna is repeating in her marriage? If Donna views speaking up as "confrontation," does she have to ever open her mouth? Did her mom? Do you think that it's a coincidence that Donna is perpetuating her family's lineage, issues, and traits?

It is only through this process of investigating how much we are subconsciously influenced by our parents' marriage, our lineage, and heritage that we can drag our subconscious into our conscious and get to change any of it.

Sure, Donna's husband, John, doesn't drink, but do you think he complains? Do you think he's a happy-go-lucky fellow? Do you think happy-go-lucky is Donna's "type"? Doesn't John's overt griping (like her dad's) allow Donna to not deal with her own inner gripes?

What we can all (and I mean all) count on if we don't do the work necessary on ourselves is this: an upgrade of our parents, from their personality traits to their marriage. If your mom was a hitter, you more than likely won't hit your kids, but you might take yourself away, shut down a bit, be remarkably polite, need a cocktail, and harbor a little resentment. If your dad was a drinker, you might not touch alcohol, but maybe you're addicted to shopping or overeating. If your parents' marriage was loud and uncomfortable for you to be around as a kid, you're more than likely going to swallow your own "loud" feelings.

An improvement? Yes. Enough of one for this lifetime? What do *you* think?

Sure, we are all better, newer models than our folks. We are the new iPhone. But is that enough? Can Donna use the list she wrote to help her get the ultimate karmic joke, the "I = she"? The "we = a version of (or aversion to) our parents"? We're here to not simply point at our parents' foibles (however fun), but to evolve them.

Hell, we're even here to teach *them* how to download the new upgrade.

Okay, how about **Ethan**'s parents? Let's see from where Ethan got his Mopey Dick trait. Remember, Ethan's also got a bonus dad, in this case, his biological.

ETHAN'S MOM'S TRAITS

- **Judgmental**

  She is always talking smack about everyone.

  How it lives in me

  I am a harsh, harsh judge. Of her, of me, of even the type of book she reads, what my mother-in-law paints, what my family posts on FB, you name it, I judge it. Even right now, I'm judging my judging.

- **Martyr**

  My mom is constantly looking for the opportunity to catch someone not appreciating her. She often would have fits, either angry or tearful, about how no one appreciated how much she did for the family.

How it lives in me

I find myself often (full-time) frustrated that no one is: a) helping me, or b) appreciating how hard I work to make things wonderful for everyone. Now, do I ask people for help? Never. Do I "yes" people to death? Always. Or at least until I blow and blame them for over-asking. Did I marry someone that thinks herself entitled, who thinks everything is owed her and should be done for her? Yes. Did I even woo her and other people with my generosity and overdoing things for them? Yes. So, it's a Catch-22, I used my selflessness to lure you to like me, and then resent you for it.

- **Moody**

  Because of my mom's bipolar tendencies, her moods were intense and ever changing. She would rage, cry, act aloof, give the silent treatment, all with a very harsh edge.

  How it lives in me

  I am a slightly softer version of this. I am pouty, whiny, and sad. My wife is a bit unforgiving and cold in response to my mood swings. Which, as I think about it, actually works for my brooder. If she were instantly forgiving and loving, continuing to mope would be harder for me.

- **Creative**

  My mom is always making things. She is a talented artist, but, no surprise here, does not use those skills much.

  How it lives in me

  I have always loved to draw and work with clay, in particular. I do not use the skills I have for much—no longer active in music, never write, and only doodle or draw with the kids. I have lots of excuses for this, but I think it is closer to lack of confidence and doubt regarding my abilities. Maybe I'm too busy judging myself to stop long enough to make art I could then cruelly judge.

ETHAN'S STEPDAD'S TRAITS

- **Instigator**

  He often made fun of my mom's emotional state. He would tease us kids and make fun of his friends' and relatives' peculiarities. He would play dumb or act like the straight man in a comedy routine when my mom was really upset.

  How it lives in me

  I am constantly joking and ribbing everyone (kids, wife, friends, etc.). This often makes a bad situation worse. I can't seem to resist a good joke even (or especially?) at a bad time. My wife, though she can be cold, is also highly sensitive when it comes to being made fun of. She doesn't find my dark sense of humor funny. Mind you, it doesn't stop me.

- **Victim**

  My dad has a fatalistic outlook on life. He feels like other people are less deserving of success and that, based on how hard he has worked in his life, he should have more. He sees life as rigged so that simple working people like himself can't ever get ahead.

  How it lives in me

  I too have played the victim role most of my life. Shitty things have happened and I chose to let that define me. It also made me angry at the world and resentful of others. I developed a quitter's attitude, but reserve the right to be angry about the rules, even after I quit the game.

ETHAN'S BIOLOGICAL DAD'S TRAITS

- **Absent**

  I have never met my biological father, but the one trait that I can definitely speak to of his is his absence.

How it lives in me

I keep emotional distance in my relationships. I have a hard time letting people in and try to push them out once they do get there. I used to feel like running away a lot (from my wife), but not so much anymore. I have not tried to find my dad. I assume he does not want to be found, which I guess makes me actively absent for him as well.

ETHAN'S PARENTS' MARRIAGE TRAITS & DYNAMICS

My parents' marriage was full of conflict. They would fight mostly because my mom was being wacky or they disagreed on how to address a kid's bad behavior. There were a couple of separations, lots of yelling, threats, occasionally violence. My parents had both been in previous failed marriages and came into this one determined to make it work. There were tons of conflicts and fights and bad shit, but they stayed in it and, at the very least, modeled putting the marriage first for me. My parents were always involved in some family drama—lots of gossiping and speculating about what everyone else was up to. I have attempted to bring drama into my marriage by being moody and angry. I perceive conflict when it's not there; I jump quickly to getting mad.

Of course, none of us are that surprised by any of Ethan's parent traits or at how critical he is of his folks, given how hard he is on himself. Right? But then, isn't that the point? If we are harsh on ourselves, doesn't that allow us to be harsh on others too? I can judge you, because I equally judge myself?

But is that really okay?

By seeing which traits Ethan has of his parents, he can start to connect the dots and make promises about doing things differently himself. He can connect the fact that his moodiness, just like his mom's, is directly connected to his not asking for anything. He can see that if his mother had just asked for what she needed, or even for acknowledgment, she would have felt appreciated and, more than likely, less edgy. And Ethan can now really start to question how he does those very things.

It all starts to beg you to do things differently.

To stop pointing only at *them*, to stop being moody about *their* moodiness, and get the joke on *yourself*. If you only point at your parents, you don't have to actually change yourself. Once you've connected the dots and see your personality and the current state you are stuck in, you can also see the gap between your current state and your desired (dream) state.

Ethan can start to see how to get himself from the 5 he rated himself in his SELF dream to a 9/10. He can see that his Mopey Dick trait never allows him to ask for what he needs. It watches people not appreciate him instead of asking for help.

Once he can see it, he can change it.

Barking direction #6: Read that above line again. It's important.

Are you starting to see how deeply spiritual, significant, and non-coincidental all of our lives are? If we spend our lives thinking we have no say over any of this, we get to continue on autopilot, on default about it all. And our lives become only a predictable upgrade of our parents'. And, even if that's great, and it is, is that great enough?

Can you see from Donna and Ethan's assignments how little freedom they (and we) have to design who and how they want to be if they don't first fully understand where they come from? There is no freedom of choice, no design, no authorship when we are simply driven subconsciously (or even consciously) to "not become our folks."

I am arming you here with the ability to truly design your life. Because until you really know what you are up against or reacting to, how can you evolve it?

CH-CH-CH-CH-CHANGES

Okay, so now that you've possibly stopped talking to me, because not only have I called you a chicken, a brat, a weather reporter, and a head case, and I am *now* calling you a reaction to your parents—I'm going to make it up to you.

I'm going to teach you how to put a leash on those negative traits of yours/theirs. But first, no shit, make sure you really want to. Because, as much as you might argue, I promise you, you love to hate, use, and hold on to your lousy traits. Otherwise, you'd have changed them yourself.

I swear, at some point we all figured out how to change a habit that didn't work for us. Think about how you learned not to drink till you puke. Right? Fourth drink, lo and behold, the bed spins. Stick to three. Voila. You changed. It's a miracle.

Here are the six steps you'll need to follow in order to **leash a negative trait**:

1. **Pinpoint it.** Pick the negative trait you want to eliminate that is getting in the way of your dream. For example, if you're looking for love, you will have to deal with some of the traits that are in your LOVE dream's way, e.g., *shy, shallow, cold,* and/or *pessimistic.*

2. **Observe it.** As you did with your thoughts in Chapter Four, you're going to start observing your trait in action. So let's say you are an angry, easily annoyed grumbler. For about a week or two, see how the trait shows up all day long. Remember, it's an operating system. It collects data, processes concepts, and outputs your thoughts, feelings, and actions. Watch it. Catch it. See what triggers it. See how often it shows up. See how you talk to yourself about it. Notice the inner dialogue that goes with the trait. See how it's examining everything from its perspective and finding reasons to grumble.

3. **Name it.** Give it a name. And, make it something funny. So catching it becomes not only wise of you, but also entertaining to you. Catching your nicknamed trait on purpose with a sense of humor is key to developing your higher self. Since we know traits are hardwired and are going nowhere, you might as well turn your lower self into a pet. One that, without a doubt, needs a bath, a bow, a tight leash, grooming, and, on more occasions than not (at least in the beginning), a muzzle, a wee-wee pad, and a cage.

4. **Leash it.** You are now going to leash your trait, which means that

you're going to put in rules and regulations about the trait to stop it in its tracks. Once you understand what you're doing and how it deeply affects others, the impetus to change the crappy behavior, to find the right promise and consequence to stop it, is there. So, if you owe your kids or your spouse or your coworkers ten dollars each time you do your "Busiest, Most Important Asshole in the Room" trait, so be it. Let's see how long it takes you to either straighten up or buy some strong duct tape for your mouth during homework or bath time.

5. **Replace it.** Design the trait that you want to replace the negative one with. So, for example, if you're a relative of mine and wanted to deal with, let's say, your shallowness, you'd replace that trait with depth, with caring to your core.

6. **Implement it.** No surprise here, in order to change something, you have to put promises in place to cause that very change. You have to, uh, keep those promises (or pay up). So, for example, if you wanted to take down "shallow" and evoke "depth," you'd make new promises around slowing down, caring, listening, paying it forward daily, and—oh no, anything but *that* again—tell others about this new you that you're evoking.

HISTORY REPEATS

The more I study people's history, the more wide-eyed and blown away I am with how uncannily I find it repeating. And, not only repeating, leaking into our lives.

I have watched brilliant children of addicts stay proudly sober, but get into business partnerships with addicts, still having to work through the very same issues as their parents and their grandparents, without realizing their plight. Not realizing not only how special it is to intervene on its behalf and on our own behalf, but also how vital it is. Not just to study our history in order to avoid our family's foreseen pitfalls, but so we can fully understand it and truly honor it.

I mean, if we could all get brazenly curious as to our role in our family's evolution, from pawns to participants in it, what would be possible?

Sure, we care deeply if cancer runs in our family, and we should. But do we care that in our same history, there are siblings that no longer speak, failed marriages, and cycles of abuse?

Shouldn't we?

Hell, science has even backed me on this one. According to a new field, *behavioral epigenetics*, our experiences and those of our forebears are never gone, even if they have been forgotten. They become part of us, a molecular residue. The DNA remains the same, but the psychological and behavioral tendencies—good and bad—can be inherited. Neuroscientists at Emory University taught male mice to fear the smell of cherry blossoms by associating the scent of acetophenone, a chemical that smells like cherries and almonds, with mild foot shocks. Two weeks later, they bred with females. The resulting pups were raised to adulthood having never been exposed to the smell. However, when the critters caught a whiff of it for the first time, they became anxious and fearful. They were even born with more cherry-blossom-detecting neurons in their noses and more brain space devoted to cherry-blossom smelling. The memory transmission extended out another generation when these male mice bred.

The more we recognize that what is happening with us is *directly* linked to our lineage and family history, the more we can change those very patterns that are repeating, whether we want them to or not.

Once again, figuring it only fair if I'm coming after your inheritance and repetitive history, I air some reruns of my own.

ET TU, BRUTE(S)?

Turns out betrayal runs in my family. And not just your regular, run-of-the-mill disloyalty, but dramatic, heart-wrenching, Brutus-like best friend betrayal.

Who knew? Clearly, I didn't. My dad? Yeah, he knew.

Ironically, the only reason I happened to discover this family story of mine is because I was stuck on repeat myself. Otherwise, like many a dark, sad, and potentially embarrassing family myth, this one would have stayed buried too.

I'd say it was about the fourth heartbreak of mine with a best friend that had me *finally* get suspicious enough about my own lineage to investigate it. I sat down with my dad (yes, he shut the TV off) and learned the story of my grandmother's younger brother, Sam. At least, from my dad's perspective.

Here's how the story goes.

Sam was a bit of a deadbeat. A baseball player who dropped out of college. My grandfather took Sam under his wing, sent him to night school, moved him in with his family, and eventually made him a one-third partner in his accounting firm.

Yes, hit play on the sad, yet ominous, music score.

One day, when no one was around, Sam and another employee from the firm came into the office, cleaned out their files, and started their own practice, taking 30 to 40 percent of my grandfather's clients with them. The story goes that perhaps Sam justified his actions by believing that as long as my grandfather's actual sons (my dad and uncle) were working for the firm, he would never be a true owner.

But we'll never know, because no one ever spoke to Sam again.

Needless to say, my grandmother was heartbroken. Her brother's actions were not only unfathomable, they were unforgivable. A few months later, on a flight home from Puerto Rico, my grandmother had a heart attack. She died the next day in a hospital in Bermuda. But not before she said, "Sammy did this to me."

And even though my grandmother smoked a pack a day and her own father died at the age of fifty of a heart attack, it doesn't matter to the story. This sad, dark, heartbreaking tale was going down this way. A loving sister deeply betrayed by her brother, who sold out his family to have his own firm. And, though my grandfather and uncle rebuilt their accounting practice, no one, obviously, was ever the same.

And, voila. Here I am. A seemingly smart, hardworking, hyper-trusting person repeatedly stepping in the same pile of poop over and over again. Shocked and heartbroken each and every time a best friend betrays me. I love them. I coach them. I help forward their dreams. I hire them. I even give some of them a piece of my company. And yes, my sister Beth is cofounder of the company; my brother-in-law, CEO; and my dad, our attorney. So, similarly, my friends too might have felt that they'd never be true owners, so long as my family was imbedded in the business.

You can't make this stuff up!

Smart me, duh-mb and on autopilot about it all. Clueless that my affinity for these four friends, my hiring of them, getting hurt, betrayed and stolen from by them, *was* lineage, *was* my family's history on repeat.

It wasn't until I, just like Phil, the weatherman (Bill Murray), in the film *Groundhog Day** finally got the subtle note—four best friends and a couple of employees later—that I could catch a glimpse of my part in the pattern.

You see, *I* wasn't innocent here either.

I turned a blind eye to the people I hired. Each one of these friends whom I loved and took under my wing were not just hardworking, gifted, and dynamic, they were takers and emulators. They were always going to want to own more and never want to give credit where credit was due. Just like Sam, they were hit-and-runners. And, because deep down I knew who they were, stepped over it, loved their love, and used their gifts anyway, I got dinged for it. And, until I finally saw this repeating pattern of mine, and learned the right lesson from it, I was going to keep getting dinged for it.

I bet you anything that my grandfather *also* knew exactly who Sam was and kept him anyway.

It's only when you can fully see your own family's history on repeat that you can have a say over it. Instead of perpetuating a pattern that has been handed down from generation to generation, you (and I) get to change it.

---

* If you've never seen the film, see it. Hell, see it over and over until you too see the you in it.

BRIGHT LIGHTS, BIG PITHY

Ready? Here are the steps for **how to investigate your lineage and family history**. Remember, your family is not in trouble. Quite the opposite. They are helping you crack your own code.

No defense attorney necessary. Bright investigative lights, sure.

1. **Write out your version.** First, you are going to write out your version of your family's history. Particularly, in any of the areas you are working on in the book and in any area where you are, what I'd call, cavity prone, whether it's career, money, love, etc. If, for example, one of the areas you are particularly struggling with is money, you want to investigate what's up with your family and money. All of them. Your mom, your dad, your grandparents. What happened with them and money? Did they sell out? Give up? Embezzle? Borrow? Or, you're having hardships when it comes to love, and, let's say, you just found out your husband has been having an affair and wants a divorce. Even though your parents are still married, do you really know your family's history with regard to cheating, to keeping secrets, to women ending up alone at fifty? Trust me. You want to know. Get asking questions.

2. **Interview your family.**
   - Interview your parents. Find out about their childhood, life, and marriage. Include questions about your grandparents and great-grandparents. Look at aunts and uncles. Search for patterns. Uncover all of the secrets and lies in the families. Leave no stone unturned. Find out the truth about marriages, cheating, disease, personality traits, money, and tragedy. Tackle all of the twelve areas of your life listed in Chapter One.
   - Even if you are not tackling your love or sex life in this book, interview your parents about it anyway. Why? Many of us are tweens when it comes to talking about sex. Certainly about discussing it with our parents. Even if your parents are older,

I promise you they didn't want to discuss it when they were younger, either. This part of the assignment is to get you to grow up about sex. To want to know your parents well. To want to understand their plight fully. Their love life. Their first love. Their first heartbreak. Their virginity stories. Not only because you are like them or reacting to them, but because, if you deeply love them like many of you do, shouldn't you know them better? And, if you don't deeply dig them, shouldn't you, in order to accept and forgive them, know them better?

- Interview your siblings. Talk with them about your childhood and family stories. I promise you, no one is telling the exact same story. Find out what they remember. Get all the facts about your life and growing up in your home.

3. **Interpret the data.** What do you want to change? What dark family secrets could you possibly repeat? Be honest about where you fall in the family lineage. Are you like Aunt Joan who drinks too much and can't keep a man? Or are you like Grandpa Jack, who resents the world and never finishes anything he starts? Who are you in the lineage? You are in there somewhere.

4. **Upgrade your operating system.** Once you've identified the possible pitfalls that come from your traits, lineage, and history, you can start making promises to stop a pattern or change an outcome. Make personal laws for yourself that honor the emotional and physical DNA that comes from your family's history. For example, if there is breast cancer in your family, make a promise to have a mammogram every year. If you see a pattern of quitters in your family lineage and you happen to quit every activity you've ever tried (yes, your brief stint with pole dancing* counts), make a promise to not quit the next activity. If your mom has anger issues that you possess as well, make a promise to "leash" that trait.

---

* Okay, mine. What? I got motion sickness from it!

When I ask people to study their parents and how their parents' narratives have impacted them in their own life, they don't think much of it. Until, that is, they get the deep, profound, and historical joke.

It *is* ours to evolve.

DOWNLOADING THE NEW UPGRADE

Yep. It's that time again. Time for you to dive on in.

Though you could certainly opt to suffer through doing this assignment, I recommend that instead you, once again, locate your sense of humor, your compassion for humanity's plight, and find the privilege in uncovering what you are here to evolve. The only way for Phil the weatherman to stop Groundhog Day from repeating and repeating and repeating was to giddily get busy learning what he was here to learn.

ASSIGNMENT FOR CHAPTER FIVE

1. Make a list of your parents' positive and negative character traits.
   - For each characteristic, give one word that describes the trait, e.g., mean, cold, adventurous, meticulous, etc.
   - For each trait, write a few sentences describing the nuances of the trait.
   - Underneath that trait and its description, write how that trait plays out in you. In other words, your version of it.
2. Make the same list for your parents' marriage traits and dynamics.
3. Pick one of your negative traits and replace it with a new positive trait that is aligned with your dreams; then, create promises (and consequences) to not only birth that new personality trait...but also prove it so.
4. Follow the directions in this chapter and investigate your family history.

The Whole Megillah

Conscious living is about waking up to your traits and your lineage and understanding fully everything that makes you *you*—your family's detailed history from the beginning of time, handed down to you, in all its glory and its gook.

The way to make your life sacred and your parents' lives sacred and your children's lives sacred is to honor the story of your family, study it, and connect the dots in your family's line. Even if it is a sad and sick accounting, which it often is. The correction of it is the only way to make it a proud and great tale.

The more you understand your whole self, the more you can actually direct the future of whom you and your children become.

Ready for a **POP QUIZ**?

Let's say you're an introvert. Always have been. But now, after having done the assignment for Chapter One, you have a dream of being part of a loving, supportive, and social community. You're now gonna need to:

A. buy new dead bolt locks; what were you thinking!
B. design a new "outgoing" trait that matches your dream in the area of COMMUNITY and promise to 1) speak at least two sentences to one to three new people a day; and 2) make fun social plans three times a month.
C. blame your mom for your trait.
D. not only blame your mom, might as well call her too. But make sure it's after two p.m., when she is done broadcasting her live religious radio talk show.

Yep, **B** for badass and the brave new you.

CHAPTER SIX

The Truth about Lying

Becoming Honest about Your Dishonesty

Most of us think that we are kind and loving, generous and tolerant, forgiving and noble; but an uncritical observation of our
reactions to life will reveal a self that is not at all kind and loving,
generous and tolerant, forgiving and noble. And it is this self that
we must first accept and then set about to change . . .

—*Neville Goddard*

LIARS ANONYMOUS

Just like everybody poops, everybody lies. But, where's *that* kids' book?
The problem is that most of us aren't even conscious of our lying or the
negative impact it has on our self-esteem, confidence, health, career, and
each and every one of our relationships. I mean, if we can't be trusted
ourselves to tell the whole truth and nothing but, how can we believe
what anyone else is telling us?

Uh, we can't.

Ever wonder why you sometimes question the sincerity of what others
say to you? Like, if they compliment you on what you're wearing, what

you've written, what you (obviously, not me) baked, etc., you thank them but, simultaneously, you think they're just saying it to be nice?

Why is that?

What if you don't fully believe what others are saying to you because you too can be overly nice, edit before you speak, say yes when you mean no, and exaggerate? What if the very reason you find it difficult to believe others is because you shouldn't be believed either?

In other words, you lie too.

Hell, we're practically born liars. The minute we figured out how to talk, didn't we figure out how to lie? Whether it was to get out of trouble, or get another cookie from Dad when Mom already said no.

Look. The world is full of liars, and it's time someone admitted it, shed a light on it, and lightened up about it. At the moment, no one really talks about lying. It's practically taboo. There is no section in the library about it. Yet it's pervasive. But no worries. We all know how well it goes when we ignore issues at hand. Right?

Obviously, lying isn't something any of us are particularly proud of. It's why we hide it in the first place. And, not only do we hide it, we spend an inordinate amount of time trying to justify it, defend it, and/or blame it on anything else but our own sneaky and cowardly selves.

Lord knows we certainly don't want to be known as a liar, let alone date one, befriend one, marry one, elect one, work for one, or raise one.

And, yet, here we are.

Barking direction #10: As you read this next section, see if you can quiet your inner dialogue, which has no doubt already gathered its legal defense team, as we go digging for all the different ways we lie. Mind you, it's not so you can go beat yourself up about it, but so you can stop it and tell the truth about yourself (like you never have before). So you can connect the dots about the real reason you don't and can't believe in yourself and your dreams. The real reason you can't fully trust yourself. Because, out in the real world, you are not fully being you.

In fact, you have gotten the real you into a bit of a bind.

You have wrapped yourself pretty darn tight in the pretense of who you want people to *think* you are. And, ironically, the only way to discover who you *really* are is by getting honest about who you've been.

The only way out is by outing your liar.

What if what I'm offering you here is akin to *The Matrix*'s "red pill"? What if telling the truth about every which way you don't tell the truth *is* the key to personal freedom? What if the very reason you don't sleep so soundly, you toss and turn at night, grind your teeth, and need that cookie, drink, or pill is from the anxiety that comes with managing everything you need to lie about and hide? (Psst, not to mention the fact that all of your hiding and lying keeps your very vices intact. You know, in order to keep dating that guy or gal, you need to keep smoking. The two go hand in hand.)

Here's the key: Telling the whole truth and nothing but is the ultimate in taking care of yourself. I can't tell you how many clients of mine, once they clean up their lie list and resolve the big ones, cure themselves of their own depression.

Yes. This is when I usually break into my own remake of the song "Fifty Ways to Leave Your ~~Lover~~ Liar."

But, never fear, it's not fifty.

Okay. That's possibly a lie. Truth be told (ha), it depends how long you've been wearing that particular cover-up.

PERSONAL POLLUTION

If I were going to radically change the world, I'd eradicate lying.

Everyone, and I mean everyone, has a list of lies. We are constantly maintaining that list, doing damage control or preemptive strikes to protect it. Twenty years, 22,000 clients later, I've seen your lists. Few of us ever fully understand how much each and every one of those lies impact us. That is until we begin to deal with each one, one at a time, and see that our lies have, in fact, created our reality.

Huh?

If we can smell it, taste it, touch it, hear it, and see it—voila, we know it to be real. But we also know that some things are real without the senses test. Right? What few of us ever realize is that when we think something, believe something, and then hide what we think and believe, it also becomes real.

So, let's just say, I don't like your dress. But I don't tell you that. I decide it'll hurt your feelings because you love it, you are so proud of it, you overpaid for it, yada yada. So nice me hides my not-so-nice thought and spares you my opinion.

To my own self, that becomes true.

Your dress is now frumpy, period. After all, if I had to hide it, it has to be true. And so it goes. The list of all the things we think and feel but decide we can't say gets larger, spreading like mold in a dark environment. Now you're filled to the brim with everything you think but don't say. If you want to truly change you, you are going to have to strap on your sense of humor and, yes, meet your ~~maker~~ faker.

You must face every which way you lie. Not *if* you lie but *how* you lie.

I've listed below seven different categories of lying. See which ones are your particular favorites.

Helpful (albeit, slightly obnoxious) hint: If you want a shortcut to figuring out your own brand of lying, just take a look at your parents' brand. Ouch. I know.

1. **Outright lying.** This is when you lie by completely making something up. Either in an attempt to cover your own ass or get yourself off the hook from something. From the ever-handy, "there was a ton of traffic" to the "I never got that e-mail" to the "I stayed home and did laundry" (when, for example, you were really out with someone you're not ready to tell people about yet), to the timeless classic, "I had food poisoning."

2. **Lying by Omission.** This is when you lie because you don't want someone to know the entire story. Either they didn't ask, so you didn't tell, or you don't think the entire story is actually their business anyway. Even though, if the tables were turned, you'd want to know the whole truth

from them. Maybe you tell people the reason you got divorced was that you fell out of love. Sure, that's part of it. But you leave out the part of the story where you got caught cheating. Another type of omission is when you sell out on something that's actually really important to you and you've been negotiating silently with yourself, trying to get over it. Maybe you even brought it up once and tell yourself you addressed it, but you never brought it up again. For example, your fiancé is not Jewish and, even though you wish it didn't matter to you, it does.

3. **Lying by exaggeration.** This is when you tell a story not in the exact way it happened. You tell it with a touch more pizazz. Good or bad. For example, you say, "My boss came into the office and told me how great I did. He said this and this and this." The truth is your boss *did* come in the office and *did* tell you he liked your presentation, *but* that was it. In your retelling of the event, you embellish so your listener will be more impressed or compassionate.

4. **Lying by under-exaggeration.** This is when you lie by underselling a story. You don't want to boast or actually deal with (or let anyone else know) how good or bad things really are, so unconsciously you make light of it. You deny it. For example, your partner drinks. They may have a few (or more than a few) every night, but you don't face it or let yourself even think there's a problem. Honestly, it's not that bad.

5. **Lying by misrepresenting a story.** This is when you lie by misleading others. When someone asks you if you read this very book, you say "I'm in the middle of it," when the truth is you are four pages in, haven't touched it in a month and, even if you remembered where you last put it, you're still not going to pick it up again.

6. **Lying by avoiding confrontation.** This is when you lie to avoid causing waves, starting a fight, possibly hurting someone's feelings, etc. Maybe a friend asks you what you think of her boyfriend, and even though you know for a fact that he just hit on your other friend last week, you don't say that. Instead, you do your best deer-in-headlights look, and go with the, "I just met him, I can't tell yet" line, and hope she didn't notice how your voice went up an octave.

7. Lying by keeping secrets you are taking to the grave with you.
These are deep-rooted lies that you will never talk about so long as you live. It's something no one can know about you, your family, or your past. They are so hidden, goofy, upsetting, embarrassing, and offensive to you that you've sworn to yourself that you'll never tell anyone. From abortion to abuse to addiction to sex secrets. You're going to the grave with these.

Now that you've caught a whiff of all of our favorite lie variations, you can at least cross off your first lie from your list. The lie that you don't lie! Yay. That's a start.

I mean, come on, aren't we all odd when it comes to full-on honesty? Just look at us on an elevator. How many of us are *really* fascinated by what floor comes after three? And, yet there we all are, staring up.

Isn't that a goofy form of lying?

As before, figuring it only fair if I'm coming after your brand of lying, I out one of my own specialty brands.

PITCHER THIS

Turns out there's not only betrayal in my lineage, there's cheating.

According to my dad (mind you, an attorney), he cheated on my mother one time only. And, for the record, it was barely his fault. You see, as the story goes (and is going to the grave with him *exactly* this way), one time in Texas, a client's wife knocked on his hotel room door. And that was it . . .

At some point, my dad confessed his onetime cheat to my mom and, after some fighting (loud), he was, eventually, forgiven. Much later, my mom copped to at least two makeout scenes with different men over the years. Apparently, in my family, we not only lie and cheat, we also, in dribs and drabs, dole out the truth.

Somewhat ironically and perfectly, not that long ago, at one of our dinner parties where we curate the conversation with a great question, the topic of the evening was outing a lie (big or small) that no one knows about you. Whereupon, my mom decided *not* to take to the grave the fact that during her fifty-eight-year marriage to my Orthodox Jewish father, the reason some of her dinners were particularly more delicious than others was because, instead of using margarine like she was supposed to to keep the meat meal kosher, she used butter.

A confession to which my dad could truly, at this point, only shake his head and fully get the "it takes one to know one" concept.

And, though my mom's version of lying and cheating was not nearly as criminal as my dad's, you can start to possibly see how we all (and I mean *all*) marry similar creatures (or criminals) to ourselves. But we'll get to that more in Chapter Nine.

Okay, so back to *my* version of cheating. The regular kind. Okay. Maybe not the *regular*, regular kind.

Ready?

Not only did I sleep with two brothers, I did so on the very same day. Think brunch, then late dinner.

I know.

Here's how it went down:

Late one morning at the train station, I bumped into the older brother, whom I dated years before. *Nice* me offers him a ride (wink, wink) home. Yes, in both senses of the word.

Off the older brother goes and, on that very same night, I go out with the younger brother, whom I had just started dating. And, yes, what the heck, I sleep with him too. And, for the next two years proceeded to date the younger brother, without ever telling him what (or whom) I did.

Some of you, no doubt, might think that I didn't "technically" do anything wrong. Right? I mean I wasn't really "dating" the younger brother yet when I slept with the older one. Right?

First, you can thank your liar's lawyer for sharing. And, second, you should note how much we liars love qualifying words like, "technically," "mostly," "for the most part," and a good air quote or two.

Needless to say, my relationship with the younger brother was a tumultuous one. Hard to imagine, given the start of it. And, even when we broke up, I was still having a hard time living with myself and could barely look him in the eye. You see, gross me was still letting him like me, even if just as a friend, without ever telling him who the "me" he was still talking to really was.

So I decided to finally tell him the whole truth about me—not only to make myself feel better, but also to set *him* free as well.

The whole truth?

Well, I wish I could tell you that the only crime I committed with this guy was with his brother. But it wasn't. *Technically*, there was the ex from camp, a graveyard* blow job, and a kiss or two over the years...

You know what he did when I told him the whole story?

He poured an entire pitcher of beer over my head. And how do you think I felt? Embarrassed? Shamed? Guilt-ridden?

Nope.

I never felt better in my entire life. It was like my own cheating, using, finagling "Baby Lauren" trait was finally walking the plank. That cheating chick was going down, coming clean, and getting her comeuppance and the hate she earned.

Finally, I got to pull the veil off of the me I never showed him, and he got to look at me like the asshole I truly was. And I got to start dealing with the asshole I truly was. No smokescreen. No excuses. No sarong.

Years upon years later, when I was working on my patterns of love, lineage, and lying, I called him to apologize fully (as I was fairly certain he hadn't heard or accepted my apology as he was pouring the beer over my head). I got to tell him how, in the name of him, and in the name of the grossest thing I've ever done, I have done a lot of good work in the world.

In my book, that's correction here on earth.

Since then, the two of us have hung out. I could call him anytime. In

---

* Mind you, not a late-night-shift one. One in an actual cemetery in Manhattan! Anyone know the statute of limitations in New York for indecent exposure?

fact, I just did to make sure there were no lies in my story about my lying and to not only get his perspective, but to see who forgot more of it.

He won.

YOUR IN-HOUSE PUBLICIST

If, on the inside, the real you is managing all the *mishegas** (inner dialogue, traits, beliefs, theories, and now lies), what's the outside world get to see?

There really is a real you, and then there's the persona you let the rest of the world see. When you are lying, managing your appearance and what other people think of you, and telling only partial truths, you're acting as your own PR agent. It's the persona you let out in the world to maintain your relationships and save face.

But is it really saving face, or is it saving false?

After all, the real you is not allowed out. The real you is being managed by the fake you. The one that is selling and justifying half-truths, always smiling, bringing coffee to people you don't like, saying many more yeses than you mean, and pretending you're really happy when you're not.

But how could you be really happy?

You're in the middle of manipulating everything everyone can see about you, and the real you gets stuck in the back, running the puppet show. The more you let your PR agent speak for you, the smaller and more lost you get.

For example, let's say you're out on a third date with someone, and you really like him or her and you have a list of questions you wish you could ask them. Your inner dialogue, scripted by your PR agent, is saying to you, "Don't you dare. They are going to think you are looking for a commitment," uh, even though you are. And guess what? You're not going to ask all of the questions that matter to you because your trusted advisors—in this case, your PR agent and chicken—have sold you that

---

* Yiddish for "craziness."

it'll ruin the date. I mean, if your date turns out to like you, was it really *you* who was on that date?

Learning to tell the truth is an art.

If you can start to see and feel the difference between who you are being when you are honest and who you are being when you are not, you can bridge the gap. You can fire your PR agent who sells you that they are only protecting you. Sure, they are. They are just also suppressing you.

If there are people in your life with whom you can't be truly yourself, those relationships are already damaged. They are fake. And if they are with important people in your life and you want them coming with you on this new ride with the new and real you, rock on. And if it turns out, sadly, that your previous lies have indeed caused too much damage for them to forgive, it really is okay to *make a new plan, Stan. You don't need to be coy, Roy. Just get yourself free.*

Truth is, I really did lose a lot of people in my life when I opted for an honest one. It wasn't their fault. It was mine.

WARNING

This process of setting yourself free, of shedding some old friends that knew and loved you when you were not you, is part of growing up and becoming true to yourself. It is neither a short process nor for the fainthearted.

It truly took me *years* to figure out how to do this and find out who wanted to stay for the ride. But trust me. The friends that really love *you*, warts and all, are your very favorites for good reason. They love you for who you really are. You gave them VIP backstage passes to your puppet show and not only did they show up, they stayed.

SECRET SOCIETY

If we can't tell the truth in a relationship, what's the point of being with that person? If the real you is hidden from the people you love, manipulating what they are allowed to know, is that real love?

Are you really okay with that particular definition of love?

Transparency, what we all aim for, is sharing the real you. Unfiltered and unrehearsed. When you are being fully transparent, everyone in your life gets the real, unedited you. You feel totally alive, honest, current, and are dealing in your life fully.

Some people claim the right to hold on to their secrets under the guise of privacy. You know, "it's their life, their thoughts, their feelings, they should be able to choose with whom they want to share them," right?

Uh, wrong. And, here's why:

- **Secrets create reality.** The act of keeping and hiding a secret is what gives it weight and credence. We hide it because we want it to go away, but that is exactly what causes the *opposite* result. Our secret becomes an underlying cause of discord in the very relationship we are trying to protect. It gnaws away at our happiness and keeps us stuck in a form of purgatory that we don't even know we're in, but we feel.

- **Secrets hide the real you.** Somewhere along the way, it became okay for people to be good secret keepers, admirable even and an act of love and loyalty. People who hold on to their secrets sometimes treat them like protective armor. However, if they do this long enough and keep insulating themselves with secrets, they inevitably lose touch with the self they have so deeply hidden away. In essence, they become their secrets. They are bound by the very lies they told, which spiraled until they're stuck with them.

- **Secrets manifest problems elsewhere.** There are big secrets and little secrets. Many people can grasp how keeping a big secret, like cheating on a spouse, is significant and would impact a person. But what about the little ones that pile up when we don't speak our mind or when we lie to make someone feel better? For example, I had a client once who couldn't bring himself to tell his girlfriend that she had gained weight. And, even though she repeatedly asked him how she looked and was clearly bummed about it herself, he said nothing. He justified not telling her because he felt shallow and knew she was already upset about it and why add to her upset. Right? Sound familiar? But the more he didn't say, the more *he* himself obsessed about it. So much so, it got to the point where he was no longer physically attracted to her. He thought he had erectile issues. But, I'm thinking, it was way more vocal than penile.

- **Secrets isolate you.** Building a relationship on a foundation of secrecy and lies is like building a house directly on sand. You cannot sustain deep connections with people who only get to see the carefully edited "you." When you don't say what you really think, people don't know you. You never feel fully loved for who you really are.

KARMIC RELIEF

Yes, it's that time again. Someone else's!

But, before we go over Donna, Ethan, and Katie's assignment for this chapter, do you wanna hear one of the biggest hypocrisies about lying?

Our number one reason for lying—to protect another's feelings—is itself a lie.

Sure, we care about other people's feelings. But it's not the first and foremost reason we lie. What matters most to us (even to the nicest of us) is self-preservation, protecting our comfort level, and our desire to be liked by others and not *ever* be known as the shallow, judgmental, petty, mean grudge holder we may be in our minds.

However, here's what's even more ironic.

Do you actually hate any of my clients thus far in the book? Sure, you may have judged a line or twelve of theirs, but didn't you, more so, just relate to them? Even like them? And even admire and appreciate them for their unabashed (albeit anonymous) honesty?

Our foibles, issues, lies, and idiosyncrasies are not the problem, I swear. Our hiding of them is. It's what leaves us not trusting each other and not developing ourselves to become trustworthy.

Truly, people don't hate me more when I tell them the two-brother story. Of course, many are glad they didn't date me back then, but I swear they find the ease with which I tell on my dark side a breath of fresh air. They find it enviable that I don't have an ounce of shame about ratting out Baby Lauren to everyone in my life (you included) and using my bad stories to do good in the world.

What would your life be like if you could be *that* honest about your dishonesty?

Yes, the fessing up assignment is coming soon to a theater near you. No priest necessary. Just courage, compassion, and a sense of humor.

Okay. So, let's see how **Donna** did on the assignment for this chapter, where she had to list out all of her lies.

PS: Just so you know, I SO know that you have many, many, many more lies than you are first going to list when doing this assignment yourself. I often have a client go back and add the ones they purposely "forgot," before we even begin. Remember, I speak liar fluently. I am one.

In the name of brevity, I've kept my clients' lie lists to about ten each.

DONNA'S LIE LIST

- I faked sick to stay home from school.
- I stole money from my dad out of his wallet.
- I have lied to my husband, John, about loads of things. How much I spend, whether or not those shoes or those trousers are new, or where I bought them from. I lied to him about why I couldn't go to Spain with him this year. I told him my mom couldn't come. I really just wanted a break from him. I have lied to him about my whereabouts. My secret office that I've been renting behind his back (and where I ship my purchases to). I have lied or not told him things so that the kids don't get into trouble with him. I didn't tell him I have been having Juvederm.
- I have lied to my kids about why I was late picking them up. I told them I was at an appointment, when I was really shopping. I kept

things from them, like when I was hurt or angry at their dad or when I felt like he was in the wrong. I lied to my kids about calling friends for play-overs when I didn't find it convenient.

- When people ask me how I met John, I often leave out the part about my having been married.
- I lied to my doctor that I was still taking a drug she prescribed for me. I didn't feel good about taking the medication and didn't believe it was helping, so I took myself off. My hair started to fall out and it freaked me out.
- I deceived my neighbor. When her oldest daughter started being really mean to my daughter, I would tell the mom that she was at a playdate when she was just playing at our neighbor's house two doors down. Technically not lying, but deceptive just the same.
- I have lied to myself about being ill. I tell myself I am fine and that it will go away. I also tell myself that what I am doing (lying) is okay.
- I have lied to John and my mom about being ill. I didn't want to worry my mom and I didn't want to hear John say, "It never ends with you!"
- John and I eloped. When we did I told my family, but John was too chicken, because he thought his mom would be angry with him. So for two years we pretended not to be married when we visited them. Even though I was not happy about it, I went along with it.

Everyone's lie list has its own flavor. Donna's variety of lies sounds like many of ours: secrets kept to perpetuate Donna looking like the good wife, mother, and friend. But on closer examination, you will see in order to manage all of her lies, Donna needs her PR agent full-time.

Clearly, there's a Donna in each of us. Many of us could go through that list of Donna's withholds, misrepresentations, and outright lies as if we're at a closing on a house, initialing right next to our similar ones. Sign here, here, here, and here again.

Right?

But, question for you: Do you think that Donna's husband, John, really doesn't know that Donna has been overspending? Do you think any of our parents *really* didn't have an inkling that we were disobeying and manipulating them? And even if our folks didn't know all the diabolical details, it was not because we were such good liars. It was much more likely that many of our parents or our spouses either 1) preferred not to know, and/or 2) were lost in their own shenanigans.

Another question for you: Do you know why most people won't confront you about whether or not you're lying?

Because they don't want to be questioned themselves.

I can't tell you how many people I coach who, for example, lie in their online dating profile and then walk around appalled, flabbergasted, and shocked by how many people they've gone out with who lied about their age, their weight, and what they're really looking for (sex).

But when I go probing as to why my client didn't vet the other person better about their real age or real intent, I swear it's because my client is too busy being mortified by everyone else's crimes than taking a look at their own.

Okay, so maybe you didn't verify their age, but you still can't believe the audacity that they turned out five years older than they had posted. Except, *technically*, you haven't yet mentioned that you have a kid. You know, you were waiting to see if they were worth telling that private info to...

Trust me, we're way more manipulative than naive about a thing. Our PR agent would never want to publicize our own lies. Wisely, they will have you point only at the other persons.

Okay. Back to Donna.

What do you think happens when Donna fesses up the truth to her husband, to her mom, to her kids, and yes, even to that neighbor? Did she get a sake poured over her head? Did she have to move? Do you really think Donna's neighbor didn't know her tween daughter could be mean? Do you think that any of our dads didn't notice money went missing from their wallets or our moms didn't know we faked sick?

Barking direction #11: Tell your PR agent to pipe down for this question. Guess what happens when you responsibly tell someone the truth you've been hiding? No matter what your PR agent tries to sell you, telling someone your truth is way more magical than malevolent. You, for the first time in what feels like forever, are actually present and fully yourself with that person. True friendship (or the honest end of a fake one) is possible. And the age-old saying "The truth shall set you free" is proven age old, for good reason.

But, Lauren! Isn't it selfish of me to tell someone the truth to make myself feel better? Shouldn't I just live with the guilt?

Though understandable, is it really that honorable? Doesn't the other person in the scenario have the right to react the way they react? It's all about respecting the other person enough to let them deal appropriately and fairly with you.

As petrified as Donna was when she sat down with her husband, it turns out 1) it was wise of her to put in the sex promise (Chapter Three) way *before* the fessing assignment, and 2) she had already put in promises to leash her over-shopping and overspending as well. So both their relationship and their bank account had already improved a bunch before this confession.

Which helps.

In her first round of fessing, Donna told John about all of her needless shopping, and though he had an inkling about it, and had noticed some of the new clothes she was wearing, he had no idea of the extent of it. He was shocked and embarrassed that he didn't know. But at the same time, the guy was relieved that his wife was starting to come back to life. He loved her. She was adorable, bubbly, and fun, but he had chalked up her growing lethargy and Stepford Wife sullenness to the day-to-day wear and tear of raising three kids, combined with her illness. He didn't realize what was really going on—how unhappy and dissatisfied she had truly become. Donna also got to see that in order to keep lying and hiding, she had to keep John—not her own addiction—earmarked as the villain, the bully, and the reason she was lying in the first place.

Donna also got to witness and feel how much John really cared about the marriage. He was not a jerk. Sure, he had his own jerky traits that needed leashing and a muzzle. Just as Donna needed to put in her own promises about being a grown-up with him. But he was willing, even eager, to have these conversations with her. He listened. He cared.

Later, in another sitting, when Donna fully braved up with John about the office rental, this round was a little tougher. John was definitely caught off guard by her renting a secret shipping address he had no clue about. Admittedly, he thought she was a little crazy. She didn't disagree. But, when he calmed down, he could even understand it. After all, this was the same guy who had her lie to his entire family about their elopement and marriage for two years!

John forgave her and even (eventually) managed to find the funny in it. Both of them did. Which they definitely needed to as they, more conscious than ever, raise their three children.

What John and Donna also got to discover when she confessed her lies was that there was lying on *both* sides: the blatant things Donna was actively hiding from John, but also John's hiding how much he felt Donna had gone missing in their relationship.

Both brands of lying were stifling their marriage.

The more Donna cleaned up her lies, the more connected she felt to John. The more honest she got about her dishonesty, the more she felt known and loved. The better, no kidding, the sex got! You see, Donna was *now* being fully loved for her true quirky self—shopping bags, hidden office, irritable bowels, passive-aggression, and all.

The whole process was also a way for Donna to see, even more, how she truly was her father's daughter. She could connect the dots between her father's drinking and hiding of it, and her shopping and lying about it. As well as the dots to her mother, a devout woman who revenge shopped, smiled, and said nothing. Subconsciously, Donna had just upgraded her mom's closet!

I am sure, at the moment, you are panicked about the damage fessing your lies might do. And you think that, although Donna survived the telling of hers, you won't.

Here's how I view it.

This is an opportunity to pay your karmic debt now. You are setting everyone in the story free. Allowing them to have their true and honest reactions. The truth is, the people on your list will either forgive you or not. But either way, the relationship is now a real one.

I have found with ALL my clients that there are so many more success stories that come out of these confessions than anything remotely close to their PR agent's or chicken's predictions. Though I do understand how scary this whole process must seem to your inner dialogue—to your chicken, weather reporter, double agent, and now your PR agent (whose very job your *entire* life has been to keep your liar under wraps and the true you in a suit of armor, protected forever). Unfortunately for your tight security team, there's no easy way to become the real you without getting real about all of it. And, um, is it really such a surprise that self-love requires loving your real self?

Not by hiding it, by being it.

Just know that all that really happens when you out your truth to someone is this: Either the big-deal-ness of the lie dissipates and you discover it was only a big deal because it was hidden and grew exponentially bigger (as lies do when they stay in your head), OR, the lie gets dealt with. Period.

The minute you actually tell someone the truth about what happened, the "what happened" finds its final resting place. Where it belongs. Learned from and no longer in your current reality.

How about **Ethan**'s LIE list?

ETHAN'S LIE LIST

- Regularly faked illness or injury for attention. Would walk with a limp or fake symptoms by warming up a thermometer or putting soap in my eyes to make them look red.
- I am embarrassed by my mom's behavior when she is acting loud or trying to be funny, get attention, etc. I am embarrassed by my mom's racist comments.
- Stole a banjo from my dad and left it at a friend's house.

- Told my ex that I did not sleep with her roommate when I had.
- Never told my parents that I got my girlfriend pregnant in high school and she had an abortion.
- Forged a check from my friend Tod's bank account.
- Used to make fun of a friend behind his back for wetting the bed.
- Told an ex that I wanted to break up because I wasn't sure I wanted to be in a relationship but it was really because I heard another girl wanted to go out with me whose friends told me she was a nympho.
- Got high on my wedding night and didn't tell my wife.
- Went out with some friends one night and drove around shooting cats with a BB gun.
- I was caught slashing tires along with some friends and convinced one of them (who already had a record) to take the blame for the rest of us so we could stay clean.

Okay, for all of you cat lovers out there, please note, Ethan, while cleaning up all of his lies (yes, all of them), sent a check to the ASPCA with an explanation and an apology.

Lauren, do you really make a client go clean up all of his or her lies, big or small, even from childhood?! I understand the big lies that may still haunt us, but why deal with the silly and irrelevant ones? Why not live in the present by leaving the past where it belongs—in the past?

Here's the thing (uh-oh is right), from everything that you've read thus far from Ethan, do you think he's free from his past? Do you think he thinks highly of himself? Remember, the minute you start to sell out on yourself, start to hide things, to lie, the smaller you stay, the less YOU you are.

Ethan opted to go on this karmic set-yourself-free ride. It's not that each actual lie on its own was so particularly big, but to clean up his whole life, and to set himself wholly free, he had to come to the realization that the only reason he wasn't telling the truth about every last thing (little and big) was because he was protecting people from knowing who he had really been or was or still was. And, he wanted to end the right, once and for all, to be *that* guy. Just like I wanted to grow up and time-out Baby Lauren.

And when faced with having to tell it all, for Ethan, it was worth the telling.

Because, guess what? Once you tell everyone who you've been, let's say, oh, I don't know, that you've been sneaking food for years, they are *now* always going to look for the crumbs on your face.

It changes you.

The gap between who you are (current state) and the dream of who you want to be and all that you want to accomplish (desired state) is wide. Its width depends on how willing you are to get conscious about what you are currently not conscious. The minute Ethan got to see how much of his past still infiltrates his present, he could do something about it. He could upgrade his current operating system. He could shift his emotional integrity (how he feels), his physical integrity (what he does), and his spiritual integrity (what he thinks).

The minute Ethan started copping to every "out integrity," every promise to himself he didn't even know he had, he started to lighten up and actually like himself.

Turns out, of course, that Ethan's parents already knew he drank, smoked, and was promiscuous back in high school. It's so funny, and truly never ceases to amaze me, the amount of people I coach who think they invented sex, drugs, and rock and roll.

I mean, what do you think Ethan's parents were like back in high school?

And, when he confessed to his mom about what bothered him about her, do you know what she did? Take a seat. She apologized to *him*. It bothered her too. And, you know what Ethan got to see in that very moment? He got to see for the first time ever that *maybe* she was not the sole problem. Sure, she was a bit crazy. But she had a legitimate doctor's note.

What was his excuse?

When Ethan fessed to his wife, Regina, that he was high on their wedding night, you know what she said? She knew. The same people that got him high asked her if she wanted a hit. Do you think she didn't know whom she was marrying?

Unless you open your mouth and out yourself and all you hold against yourself, whether you are aware of it or not, you will never know how truly heavy those lies weigh on you. Yes, even the seemingly inconsequential ones.

If you don't have to spend your life managing your lies, managing who knows what about you, you'd have so much more time to just be you.

Speaking about being yourself, let's see what **Katie's** got in her own closet:

KATIE'S LIE LIST

- I was eight years old and my older brother caught me in bed naked with one of the boys in the neighborhood. I swore I'd never do it again. I did. As a matter of fact, there were at least four more boys I did that with from my school by the age of eleven. No one knew.

- My best friend and I stole a bottle of wine from my dad's wine cellar and drank it on my street corner in the middle of the night. I was fourteen. It was a Château Lafite, a crazy-expensive, special bottle of wine. My siblings got blamed. I played innocent. I didn't say a word. I would steal beer, wine, and liquor from the basement and my parents' liquor cabinet. I have no idea how my dad didn't notice. He supplied me with drinks throughout my high school and college years.

- Once I was old enough to drive, almost every Sunday I would get dressed for twelve thirty p.m. Catholic Mass at Saint Patrick's Church and leave the house and go three blocks away to my friend Jeanne's house and have breakfast with her family. I would stay forty-five minutes, drive to church, grab a bulletin, and then go home. My parents, who almost always went to the earlier Mass, would ask me about the service. I'd lie. Even saying I spoke to the priest on my way out of the church. I did this my entire high school years.

- I lost my virginity in my parents' bed while my mom was in the hospital having gallbladder surgery and my dad was in Asia on business. Didn't wash the sheets either.
- I had a fling with one of the assistant soccer coaches at college. No one knew about us. When a friend suspected something and asked me about him, I lied.
- I got into a fight with my college boyfriend one night at a bar when we were living together. He left me there. I stayed and had another drink. I met another guy at the bar, cheated on my boyfriend that night, came home around three a.m. and lied about where I was.
- I cheated on every guy I've been with. I cheated on my husband before we got married.
- I got pregnant by a boyfriend I loved when I was twenty-four and living in LA. He cheated on me and we broke up before I knew I was pregnant. I had an abortion and never told him.
- I worked as a bartender in Santa Monica while I was going to film school. One day I walked into my boss's office and told her my dad had a heart attack so I could get off work for four days.
- My boyfriend during film school flew into town from London (we had a long-distance relationship) and surprised me and asked me to marry him at a party with fifty of our friends. I said yes. I lied. I didn't want to marry him. He's now my ex-husband.
- I lied to Lauren, my life coach. I said I was 192 pounds on our first coaching call. I was really 207 pounds. I also lied to Lauren about how much I was drinking. I didn't want her to fire me.

Nothing terribly shocking in here, right? Except, I guess, how much Katie played nice on the outside, when she's not nearly so innocent at all. Right?

She drinks. She cheats. She even lied about her churchgoing.

But let me ask you something. If you lie to keep other people happy, do you ever have to confront the fact that you must think that other people are more important than you? More important than your own truth? That by lying in the name of others, you are, in essence, locking yourself into being second fiddle, forever.

When someone cares more about pleasing others, they erode their own self-confidence and self-respect. They diminish their relationship to themselves.

So, whenever I have a client who is lacking in self-confidence in an area of their life, I ask them to look at where they are lying in that area. Where are they acting like number two and making everyone else in their life number one?

Though we can obviously all understand, at some point in our life, lying to authority, whether it was to our parents, to our teachers, to our bosses, to a traffic cop, etc., how do we explain all of our lying to our boyfriends, friends, and fiancés?

What you will find is that you have just gotten used to lying as a method of dealing with reality. It's as if it's become an addiction and you've lost sight of your own values. And, until now, you've never connected the dots that you are the source of your own problems.

People pleasers and martyrs like Katie don't believe in their own dreams. If Katie sells out her dreams for everyone else's, does she ever have to be accountable for her own? Does she have to speak up? Or, can she look like the victim of her parents, of her ex-boyfriend that "got her pregnant" (where was she in the bed?), and even a victim of a marriage proposal?

The minute Katie came clean with her ex-husband about all of her own lies, including the one that she didn't want to marry him, but did anyway, you know what happened? The two could not only find genuine compassion for each other, but even forgiveness.

SPIRITUAL ACCOUNTING

Yes, it's that time again: your turn.

I imagine at this moment, possibly worse than ever before in this book, worse than dreaming in more areas than you ever cared to care, worse than listing out how much more you are your parents than you knew, you are for sure thinking that I should, once and for real, bugger off. That you are not going here.

That you're not *that* bad and, even if you were, why would you *ever* go back ten years and forty friends later? And while you are at it, you're thinking that lacking in self-confidence, self-respect, and intimacy—if it means you don't have to tell you-know-who about you-know-what—is a fate you chose.

I get it. And, in truth, even that admission is already an upgrade to where most of us started! However, what you should *also* know is that every time I coach a client, even the most successful, we will hit an area in their life where they are stuck. And even if we think there is not one stone we haven't turned over, when we go digging for the lie that lives in that very area, we inevitably find one. The time they didn't buy that house. The child they wanted, but didn't have. Something that's still rankling, even after all this time.

I swear there is not a more fascinating, mind-blowing process to set yourself free than to own your own lies. Than to see that, in any area where you are stuck, you piled a lie there, there, there, and there—and all of a sudden, you can't get out of that door.

Decades after I discovered that one of the keys to personal freedom is to stop lying, I was still cleaning up my own lies. For the big liars out there—myself obviously included—yes, we're an Exxon spill. It's gonna take some time to clean up all of our personal pollution.

But for what else are we here?

ASSIGNMENT FOR CHAPTER SIX

1. Make a list of every lie you've ever told in your life that you can remember. I recommend you take your time as you do the assignment, as you have a whole lifetime's worth of lies to uncover. Remember, have a sense of humor when doing your list. Use the following categories to help you:

- Outright lying—saying something that isn't true.
- All the things you've hidden or hide on purpose or don't want people to know.
- Exaggerations.
- Partial truths: You shared only partially what happened.
- Misrepresentations.
- Withholding information that you should have said.
- Thinking, but not saying, things that would hurt someone else.
- Faking something, like injuries, or being someone's friend. These are where you think one way, but act another.
- Avoiding confrontations.
- Keeping secrets that are "no one's business."
- Hiding opinions or judgments that you think are too detrimental and mean to say.
- Adding drama to what you say.
- Secrets that you are taking to the grave.

2. Make a list of everything you were lied to about.
3. Select five lies from your list that you are willing to clean up. Start with the easy ones.
4. Write down the situations that your PR agent shows up in your life.
5. Read the warning label below. Then, read it again.
6. Follow all of the steps laid out below and clean up the five lies you picked in number three.

WARNING

There really are conditions for cleaning up your life. Obviously, the more on your list you can and are willing to clear up, the freer you will be. Personally, I cleaned up every last lie I ever told. Every one of my coaches and coaches-in-training have cleaned up every last one of their lies, too—and have lived to tell about it. (And yes, their partners have lived too.)

However, I do **NOT** recommend you pick up the phone and blow up your life.

As with any and all of this coaching, you need to do what feels right for you, on a gradient that works for you. Some of the bigger conversations (e.g., the affairs, the thievery, drug use, the sexual deviation, etc.) are going to be harder to craft and to responsibly deliver. I do not have every client blow up their marriages and destroy their divorce proceedings. But what I do have them do is draft a *spiritual contract* of sorts with themselves.

For example, I had one client that had cheated on her husband for ten years who wanted to come clean with him, but who also didn't want to create a shit storm with her divorce, with her kids, etc. So she designed an exit plan that worked for her. Sure, a plan that scared the crap out of her, but one that also rang true and responsible for her. She asked for a divorce. She promised herself (and me) that five years after the divorce, she would tell her ex-husband about the affair. She promised that she too would tell her children about the affair when they were old enough.

Her deal truly had integrity for her.

There is a level of misery and integrity that we are each willing to live with. There's an amount of Prozac we're willing to pop in honesty's stead. It is not for me to assign you guilt or to have you blow things up sooner than sits right with you. To each his or her own.

Find yours.

What I know to be true, no matter what, is that love, happiness, self-confidence, and personal pride are on the other side of the truth, and always will be—when you are ready.

For Immediate Release

Now that you've done the assignment (or at least contemplated doing the assignment) for this chapter and safely written down your lies (in hieroglyphics, Vulcan, Dothraki, pig Latin, some sort of code, and/or your best indecipherable script), I'm thinking it might prove easier for me to show you how to clean up your lies rather than solely write the steps out for you.

Below is an actual accounting of a forty-seven-year-old woman's confession to her dad. For the sake of anonymity and, as it's a great nickname for all of us hiders, we'll call her "Heidi." Heidi's eighty-year-old dad was a teacher, social worker, guidance counselor, and an active layperson in the church.

I had Heidi write out, in her own words, what transpired with her dad when she fessed to him that she had an abortion. You can tell by how intricately she remembers it, how important it was to her. And, for you out there whose arm hair just stood up and want, once again, to ship me back to Long Island, believe you me, I understand.

However, I promise you, this lie landed on *her* list. Out of the gazillion lies that you've told over your lifetime, the ones that need to end up on your list, will. They will almost natter in your head to get put on your list, even though, without a doubt, your PR agent (and all of their affiliates) will want to talk you out of counting certain ones.

Scribble those down too, however indecipherably.

I promise you, your higher self that you have done so much yoga to find knows which lies belong on your list.

Here's Heidi's recounting:

Heidi: Hi, Dad. I want to have a conversation with you. Could you meet me at Dunkin' Donuts so I can talk to you? It is important that I tell you something, but want to make sure that we can talk and not be distracted or interrupted by things going on at home.
Dad: Yes, of course. I am always ready to listen. Is everything okay?
Heidi: Yes, it's all good. I want to share something with you that I never told you and I really want to. It is time to get closer to you.
Dad: Let's meet. And, remember, you can tell me anything.

Here's Heidi's thought process:

Meanwhile, I have this nagging whisper in my mind: yes, except *this* thing, which is not just "anything," but something that is going to have you judge and hate me.

At Dunkin' Donuts:

Heidi: I brought you here because there is something that I have been hiding and therefore lying about to you for the last twenty-seven years. I am scared to tell you, but I know that I want to get closer to you and this lie is going to keep you from knowing the real me. I am worried about what you are going to think of me, but I have to tell you anyway, because I love you and want you to love me and not the me that I have been pretending to be. God, I am scared…

Dad: Just tell me. It's okay.

Heidi: When I was in college, I got pregnant and had an abortion. I have kept it a secret, because I know how strong your faith is and I thought you would judge me and never speak to me again. I hid it and never told you, but it has been killing me on the inside.

By now, I am looking right into his eyes and totally unaware of anything else—it was like the world stopped and it was only my soul talking to his, everything else around me was silent.

That is when he took my hands in his and said:

Dad: Did you think that I wouldn't love you anymore?

I could only shake my head yes, because no words would come out.

Dad: I love you. There is nothing that you can do that would ever change that. Remember that. There is nothing that you could ever do to make me stop loving you. I am sorry you didn't tell me, so I could have loved you through that hard time. I am sorry you had to hide and suffer in the hiding. I am sorry I missed all these years of the real you. But I see you now. And I love you as much—no…even more.

I never felt more loved and free in my life than in that minute. We stayed there in that Dunkin' Donuts, just sitting and just being together for a while. I got home that afternoon to my phone ringing. It was my dad.

Dad: Can you meet me at the Dunkin' Donuts tomorrow? I have a secret that I haven't told anyone in fifty years.

So, back to Dunkin' Donuts I went the next afternoon. There, my dad told me about how when he was studying to be a priest, he was approached sexually by one of the other men who was much further along in the program. My dad stopped him and then went to the head of the program to tell what happened. The head of the program shooed my dad away, saying that it wasn't a big deal and that nothing happened, so my dad should let it go. But my dad couldn't because he knew it was wrong. Soon after that happened, my dad left his religious studies there.

My dad said he never told me because he was afraid that it would affect my faith and give me a bad taste about my religion. He was afraid that it would make me quit growing my own spirituality. He said he was sorry he hid it. He apologized for lying and pretending. He was so inspired by my courage and honesty the day before, that it prompted him to do the same. To match me. He saw the opportunity to speak about something he never was going to, and not only bring closure for himself about it, but allow for an intimacy with his daughter, an intimacy he had no idea, until now, was thwarted by his own hiding. In his pride of me, he got to find his own freedom from the past and I got to see my dad for the human he was, not up on a pedestal, not below me, eye to eye, and love him even more for it.

Our relationship grew much stronger after those two days of honesty. I am grateful for facing my fears and telling my dad the truth. He was grateful that my courage inspired his own.

It changed our relationship forever.

For those of you that still want, besides a tissue, the basic **steps on how to fess,** I've included them below.

Remember, these are just the basics. Tweak them to make sense for you and what you are fessing. See how, in the example, Heidi took care of her dad, setting up a time to speak, a context for the conversation, and for why she was bringing this up with him now, after all of this time. And though your answer may very well be because Lauren Zander made you, come up with a better one. I mean, after all, no biggie, it's *only* the whole, real, and true you that has been heidi-ing, all this time. No urgency (cough, cough)...

1. **Confess** what you need to confess. Yes, in detail. Admit your role and feelings. Apologize for your part in it all or for hiding it for this long.
2. If applicable, **ask** them their experience, their memory of the incident, and now their experience of hearing what you confessed.
3. **Listen fully** to their response. If they have one. Then say back to them what you heard, so they really know you heard them.
4. Once they have heard your confession and accepted your apology, **forgive yourself** and close the book on this incident so that you never have to revisit it.
5. If appropriate, **make a promise** about future behavior. And, while you're at it, attach a consequence!

Here's what I am promising you out of doing the work above: a pride in yourself that maybe, if you're lucky, you've allowed yourself to briefly experience before. Maybe it was when you were finally honest with your boss and quit, or asked for the divorce you've been wanting to for years, or really told your mom (and mine) that when they tell you your hair looks "fine," you truly know what that means. Except now, you can have direct access to that feeling anytime you want.

How, you wonder?

Tell the truth with grace and wisdom all of the time, particularly when you don't want to. Better than any cookie, smoke, or drink. It's got no calories; in fact, it probably burns some and has you be who you've always wanted to be: you, only better.

Okay, time for your **POP QUIZ**.

You've been dating someone for a few months now and it's really going great. You haven't liked someone this much since, you can't remember when. There's just one thing that's bothering you: they have bad breath. You have no choice but to:

A. regift this book. You know, out of sight, ~~out of~~ back into mind.

B. research online what you can slip into their food and drink that might help. Then, make sure you delete all history on your computer.

C. sit them down, look them in the eye, and tell the truth—you dig them a ton, but have something a little embarrassing to fess, and last thing you'd ever want to do is hurt their feelings, but you also always want to be honest with them, so, here goes. And, then, together, come up with a plan, e.g., regular dental cleanings and/or a fun Costco run for mouthwash.

D. lie through your teeth. You are sure halitosis gets better with time and age…

Answer: **C** for care to be gracefully honest. By all means, if you want to fully trust someone, be trustworthy. And, heads up. Be prepared for more honesty on their part too, e.g., check your own toe fungus.

CHAPTER SEVEN

Hauntings

Unraveling Your Past

GHOSTED STORIES

Ever notice that no matter how many kind and appreciative e-mails/ texts/calls you receive, you only really care about the one lousy one you got? Hell, you talk about it for days, forward it to friends, and though you don't bring it to an art store to frame, you might as well.

Why is that?

The reason is more peculiar than you think. The reason we love to hate an e-mail, a crappy call, a snide remark, or interpreted eye roll is not just because it hurts, but because—drum roll, please—we agree with it. Consciously or subconsciously, it gives us evidence for our own beliefs and theories.

And how about those particular childhood memories that we are still haunted by and can't seem to shake? Sure, the reasons some of those particular *hauntings* stick around are obvious, right? Like the time our parents announced their divorce or the time we broke our leg right before soccer camp. But what about those other less obvious memories that still haunt us?

What if we haven't put those memories to rest, similar to the framed e-mail, because they are connected to our greatest fears?

You see, unless the memory is somehow still serving a purpose for us, I promise we'd have already filed it away with the many other not so great ones.

Understanding why those particular memories still haunt us is very important to fully understanding ourselves. Many of the decisions we've made about our life or about what to do next with our life come from those haunting moments.

The reason you need to study your hauntings is not just because you and I are out to leave no stone unturned (that too), but because each of them contains important information, you, their owner, are not aware of.

You don't have all the facts.

In fact, you don't even know what really occurred. You have a deep and significant memory that happened with, let's say, your father or your mother or your brother or your best friend, but you haven't spoken about it in twenty-five years. They said or did something that deeply hurt you. It changed how you viewed yourself, how you speak up or don't. But you have never even asked anyone involved what happened. Sure, you think you know what transpired, and you keep running the same narrative over in your head, but you actually have never interviewed anyone else about it.

Five years, ten years, twenty-five years later and you still don't know all the facts.

In those haunting memories of yours are also crimes that were done to you or that you did to someone else. And even though they are buried, like any lie, like any unspoken family myth, they fester. They grow. They spread. They become even more significant over time. And, though you may never have spoken to whomever again, it lingers.

Worse, it shapes you.

It shapes what you think about people, what you think about yourself, and what you think about life in general. For some of you, you don't even know how much what happened *actually* upsets you or should upset you.

You think you got over it.

Whether it was an abortion you secretly had, or even something more overt, like your dad got hit by a bus. These events influence you. They haunt you, even if you don't explicitly think about them every day. But instead of realizing the root cause of your issues, you walk around a bit mystified as to why you are anxious and can't get on an airplane...

In fact, you might even *prefer* your version of reality, devastating, destructive, depressing as it may be. It is, after all, what has fueled your inner dialogue forever. It has been in charge of the narrative in your head for decades. When you look in the mirror, it has scripted all of your not so nice Snow White evil-queen-like lines: "I'm fat," "I'm ugly," "I'm not that great and never will be." All of your weather reports, your "I've never been good at money," "I'll never find love," or "I'm terrible at getting up in the morning."

It has backed your storyline for as far back as you and your narrative care to remember.

How do I know?

After twenty years of doing this, I've watched the stories unfold and unravel. I've watched your narrative's "defense attorney" not weigh evidence fairly and care only about proving your hauntings true. It doesn't matter, for example, that your father hugged and congratulated you when you got engaged, what matters is the one line he said after your announcement, about how expensive the year was going to be (which it will, by the way). The one line that evidenced your narrative, permanently branding your dad as "stingy" and "uncaring," and that you are "less important than his bank account." Your hauntings' attorney has no interest in including your dad's hug, his teary eyes, or his brag to his friends about you in the evidence file.

And, truth is, if at any point you had wanted the haunting to go on record another way, smart you would have investigated it better.

Right?

Or, smart you, who prides yourself on how up-front and honest you are in relationships, isn't even *remotely* curious as to why you are suddenly too "shy" to share your true feelings with your father.

Truly, smart you could have and would have found holes in your own narrative, or at least have been curious about poking around for them. But you weren't.

We aren't.

Remember, we're way too smart a species to ever claim ignorance.

We are way more perceptive about how this plays out in others than in ourselves. And we are way too attached to being twenty-five years accurate about something than twenty-five years inaccurate about anything. Especially if that very thing not only hurts, but it also proves our theories and beliefs about ourselves, and about the world, to be true.

Once again, I figure if I'm coming after what haunts you, far be it from me not to out one of my own skeletons.

CAMP FIRED

Around the same time in my life as I was reeling about being betrayed by some of my closest friends, there was another person from my past about whom, when I'd catch a glimpse of her on Facebook or I'd hear her name mentioned by mutual friends, I grumbled.

And, well, given that I was in the middle of investigating my own issue with backstabbing friends in the present, I figured I couldn't very well step over another potential one from my past.

Even after what she did to me, dot dot dot.

Cue dark, melodramatic music.

What had she done to me, you wonder? A long, long time ago at sleep-away camp,* she and I were friends. And, during the particular summer in question, the love of my life, my boyfriend from the previous summer, told me he was moving on. In turn, I did what most teens would do, I told my three closest girlfriends to stay away from him.

This one didn't.

And, well, we've all seen the movie. On a camping trip, shortly thereafter, I walked in on the two of them messing around.† Clearly, marking the end of her for me.

---

* If you were my folks, wouldn't you get rid of me for eight weeks, if you could?

† I am pretty sure that had I told this particular story *before* I told you the story about the two brothers, you might feel a little more compassion for me.

But there I was. Years later. In the middle of being hurt by yet another best friend of mine, and I found myself *still* mumbling about this camp one. I mean, something had to be fishy, right? Figuring, once again, just maybe, I ought to try my own method on, uh, me.

So I called her.

And guess what? She called me back, not only quickly, but enthusiastically. She was actually happy to hear from me. Which already messed with my narrative about her. I mean, according to me (see: uh-oh), she hated me too. But, no shit, there she was, happy to hear from me.

Note to self: Don't believe yourself.

Turns out, this person was tickled to talk to me. I told her that I was calling to talk something through with her and asked her if she'd be willing, in the name of clearing up an old haunting, to take turns listening to each other's version of the same story.

She was game.

So, I proceeded to tell her how I "remembered" (accurately or not) what happened. How I told all three of my closest girlfriends to stay away from my ex that summer and she didn't. And how I couldn't believe she would do that to me.

She listened to my version of what happened and, though she didn't remember *any* of it, she apologized for all of it, saying it certainly sounded like something she'd do back then. But, what happened next was even more fascinating. She told me *her* version of what transpired that very same summer. A way different part of it that *I* didn't remember at all.

I mean like, *zero* of it.

Turns out, later that very summer, when I was sitting on her bed in her bunk (apparently I must have forgiven her), there was a letter on her bed from her friend, which I asked if I could read, and she said, "Sure," forgetting what was actually in the letter.

What was in that letter, you wonder?

In that very letter, her friend revealed a secret my camp friend was hiding. Turns out, she had been lying the entire summer about her age. She was actually two years younger than what she had told *everyone*.

And what did "Poor Lauren" do with that information?

Not only did I confront her, I ratted her out. I told *everyone*. And, deeply embarrassed by what she had done, she left camp four days later. And the kicker (besides me)? She never, for a moment, hated me for what I did. She had been suffering over her lie the entire summer. She thought my turning her in was, you know, very like me, honest and up-front. Robin Hood–like, if you will.

Robin Hoodwink is more like it, no?!

Ironically, I swear, I did not remember that part of the story, at all. I forgot the very same part that we all *magically* forget when it comes to what we're haunted by—our part in it.

In fact, the very reason I was still haunted by her was *not* because what happened to me was so crazy devastating, or even undeserved. I mean, sure, it sucked. But the very reason I was still mumbling about her and haunted by the story was that there was a lie in the story—not hers, *mine*.

Can you see, if I only tell a tale as the victim of it, I never have to fully deal with my part in it? I can keep picking Brutuses as my besties, screaming perpetrated, but never having to see or deal with my *own* perp.

The only reason I was still haunted by this particular campfire story is that I was not remembering the story accurately at all. I was remembering it to suit my sad story of Poor Lauren, betrayed by best friends, and *not* where I can be an interesting picker of friends and an interesting friend myself.

I was not learning the *right* lesson.

The lesson I had always taken away from that camp story had been to "watch my back" and "pick my friends wisely." What I learned after my conversation with my old friend was that I should also watch my *own* self-righteousness and two-facedness.

In the face of cleaning up old haunts, I got to free myself of any evidence of Poor Lauren and actually got to help and coach this old friend (turned *actual* friend twenty years later) to rid herself of a bad boyfriend, figure out her financial situation, and design a career that made her much happier than the one I found her in.

And now we get to love each other, genuinely.

SPIRITUAL DENTISTRY

What if the longer we don't deal with the memories we are haunted by, the more these memories, like long-ignored cavities, become not only painfully sensitive, but require a root canal?

Our haunting memories stick with us, not because we are being punished for them, but because there is unfinished business, something festering within them. There is a lesson in each of them that, I promise you, like me, you haven't learned yet or it wouldn't keep repeating or weigh so heavily on you. The minute you learn the right lesson and own up to it, I swear, you are freed from it. There's a release, a revelation, and a profound experience of having grown up about something that has haunted you for a long time and has shaped you.

Typically, I have clients go digging for what haunts them in the following cavity-prone areas:

- When you think of a person and you don't want to see them.
- Anyone from your past whom you once loved and don't anymore.
- Anything you haven't told your parents: for example, you used drugs, stole something, had an abortion, etc.
- People who have betrayed you or you betrayed.
- Anytime you ever cheated on someone or have been cheated on or won't even consider that cheating possibly occurred.
- Lies you're taking to the grave.
- Embarrassing events that happened in your past.
- Deep moments of making decisions with yourself that you still remember.
- Dreams you have sold out on.
- Anything you have quit or failed.

As easy as it is for me to type up that list, I promise you, I know that none of this digging is easy. In fact, the fact-finding that's involved in unraveling a person's hauntings is not a natural inclination for any of us.

Especially given how attached we are to our theories, our beliefs, and our weather reports about who we are and from where we came. To go digging, only to possibly discover yourself umpteen years inaccurate about something, let alone uncomfortable and vulnerable in the quest itself, who of us is quickly heading to that dentist's chair?

None of us.

But, once again, the only way out of our hell in any area where we are flailing is with a flashlight and a drill. Right? I mean, if we could get out of it by avoiding it or by numbing it, we'd all be blissfully ignorant as I type. But, boy, are we ever not blissful.

Without realizing it, we are repeating the same mistakes over and over again in our lives. It's critical to see our patterns and figure out the lessons we are supposed to learn.

Investigating and unraveling what haunts us brings truth to our current and possibly inaccurate translations of important life events, allowing us to grow up, move on, and even rescript our own narrative.

OTHER PEOPLE'S HAUNTED HOUSES

Yes, it's that time again: theirs!

Let's take a look at a few of my clients' hauntings. The first part of their assignment (and yours too) is to list out the memories that still haunt them. Once we have listed them all, we go through them one by one. Together, we see what sounds odd, illogical, and in need of investigating. Together, we seek out what is possibly haunting you from your past that is connected to what's not working in your current reality. So, for example, if you have issues with love and intimacy, like Katie, we are particularly searching out hauntings that are related to sex, intimacy, and love. If you have financial troubles, we are actively seeking out hauntings in your past related to money.

What you'll find, as each of my clients did, is when our hauntings are written out and told on paper the very way we remember them, from our own young perspective, holes appear. In the light of day, out of your head and onto paper, you can start to sniff some funk in them. I promise if there weren't something funky in them, they'd have been filed away and not stinking up the back of your fridge, like the long-forgotten leftovers they are.

As I list out some of my clients' hauntings, see if you can smell what's odd or inconsistent in them. Given how you know each of these clients pretty intimately—you've read their traits, their thought logs, lie lists, heard their chickens cluck and their brats tantrum—see if you can spot where their theories are getting fueled by their narratives and their current reality. See if you can figure out why they'd keep these particular hauntings in their back pockets on purpose. Because, I promise you, if these memories didn't somehow serve a purpose, my clients would have resolved them or gotten over them long ago.

We are haunted by a memory because, in the remembering of it, there are some distortions, misunderstandings, missing information, one-sidedness, and lies. Otherwise, it wouldn't make the list. But, remember, what's important to us is how invested we are in keeping our haunting intact. If we unravel the haunting and call it out for what it is (a memory filed incorrectly), your narrative is in trouble. It has, after all, been held in place by your lies, your memories, and your fears. If we were to unravel your haunting, finding out that there is no boogeyman in the closet except the one you invented to stay scared and safe, the ground you've been standing on for all of this time is indeed changeable.

If, for example, you had to give up the memory with your judgmental father or unwell mother that locks in place your "I'll never lose weight" belief, what's possible now for you? Yes, losing weight. But, first, you'd have to be willing to face what you never wanted to face before—all that *you* didn't say to your father or mother. Everything that *you* made something they said mean, which they might not have meant at all. You'd have to be willing to be thirty years completely disproven. And what human wants that?

Answer: few, if any.

But, until you break these very chains you bound yourself with, there is no designing, there is no dreaming. The only way out of your current operating system is to shed a light on the outdated operating system's faulty old and archaic design.

Let's take a look at one of **Ethan**'s hauntings and see how he, with my help, untangled it:

I have never met my biological father despite having lived in the same small town as he for eighteen years. I always denied wanting to contact him, feeling that it should be his responsibility at best and "f*ck him if he doesn't want to have me in his life," at worst. As I get older, I am really feeling the need to at least know about that part of who I am. It also bothers me that I have at least two half sisters whom I have never met. I don't want to screw up his life or be a complicating incident, but I feel like I have the right to know a little bit (if only to complete my medical history when I go to the doctor).

Ethan's haunting is completely understandable, right? But let's see how he did when I had him go back into this haunting and flesh it out some more. To tell more of his truth about it, his worries, and seek out any cavities in it. You know, hire himself a really good dentist and/or a prosecuting attorney to cross-examine his own memory.

Here's Ethan's fairer take at it:

The reason that I never contacted my father (or at least what I tell myself) is that I don't want to upset his life. When I was younger, I would say that I didn't care about having a relationship with him and that he had an opportunity to take responsibility and contact me, but he refused. Therefore, f*ck him. What's more honest, is that I'm afraid that I'll get rejected again. Everything in my life, as it relates to him, has felt like rejection of my very being. I don't want to risk him ignoring me and I don't want to hear him say, "I don't have a son, I don't know who the crazy woman is who keeps telling you that I'm your father, but it's not true."

At least, in this accounting, Ethan is more honest about his fear. About why his chicken has kept him cooped up this long from ever seeking out his father. Right? But, remember, you and I are coming after every which way we evidence our theories and beliefs. Every which way we speak about ourselves like the weather. Like we have no say over any of it. No say over how, in this case, our biological father will react. Do you think our inner chickens and PR agents would ever, and I mean ever, think it a good idea for us to risk being that vulnerable and call our biological father?

Not a chance.

So instead, your PR agent, backed loudly by your inner dialogue, would draft up a press release stating that your very own father would deny even knowing you.

You know why?

So you wouldn't have to pick up the phone and risk being hurt by someone other than yourself. So, in its stead, you will say all those mean things to you, uh, on his behalf, pretending they are true. Pretending it's what you are sure he'd say. Even though you have never even met him.

Unfortunately, for your psychic inner chicken, the only way you will truly know how someone is going to respond or not is by being brave and grown-up enough to ask the other person.

And that's just what Ethan did.

I contacted my father by telephone and had a short, awkward, but positive conversation with him, where he stated that he would be open to discussing our relationship. We exchanged e-mails for a few weeks and eventually set up a time to talk. I called my father and explained that I have only heard my mom's version of his story (and the one I have made up in my head) and that I would appreciate it if he could just give me his side. He started with their relationship and told me that they dated for a few weeks and then my mom disappeared. She came back a year or so later and said she had his child, but did not want anything from him. He went in the army and did not hear from her for a few more years. He said there was a court hearing where he admitted to possibly being my father, but then nothing came of that. He heard nothing until seven or so years later when my mom confronted his wife at her work and then nothing after that until I called him. He was very apologetic and accepted responsibility for not acting on this. He admitted to feeling guilty and for screwing up by not trying to contact me all these years. We made a commitment to stay in touch and work on our relationship. The next day I got an e-mail from his wife, thanking me for being nice to my dad and saying that their family would be interested in getting to know me better and that there is "room in their life" for me.

Holy shit, right?!

Now, now. Of course, sometimes these first calls don't go as poetically as this one did. Although most really do go beautifully, it's true that a few don't. I'll show you one of those too. But, either way, even when these conversations don't go as we want them to or worse, they go south, they are still valuable. The person we had to be to make the call or send the e-mail is *already* a different human.

That said, I truly believe Ethan's call went down as beautifully as it did because he did not come at his dad as if his dad wronged him, as Ethan easily could have and many of us would have. And because Ethan was willing to be this brave and genuinely wanted to know his biological dad's version of what happened, his dad did not need to defend himself. His dad was not in trouble. He could freely just tell his truth, and even apologize. And, Ethan, poor thing, could, in turn, be *years* inaccurate about how unloved he was.

Just look for yourself.

I visited my dad and his family over my birthday in March. It was amazing. We talked about our lives and the assumptions we had made and a plan to move forward. He and his wife had a mini family reunion for me with my sisters, grandma, and nieces and nephews. They are my family now and it has changed everything in my life.

What your PR agent and narrative's legal team will never and I mean, never, want to concede, is that losing this case and being years upon years inaccurate is exactly where freedom, happiness, love, self-esteem, and the real grown-up you resides.

Obviously, Ethan's flavor of haunting is not necessarily yours or mine. What's important to note, however, is how, no matter what, whether your parents were absent or abusive, your childhood uneventful or tumultuous, each of us holds tightly to our hauntings. No matter how deep, dark, or shallow our hauntings are, we slip them in our back pockets, in our clutch and clutches, and we keep them intact as they are what has helped to design our long-lived narratives.

Having an honest conversation with our parents about the very things we spent years upon years hiding is a big deal. It's also an opportunity to grow up about the very things that we are actively, albeit subconsciously, avoiding. It gets us to also wake up to the fact that our parents have secrets they are busy hiding from us too.

Imagine that. Our parents are human, as well.

Heading out and actually asking our parents, our partners, our ex-wives, ex-husbands, our friends (Facebook and real ones), our neighbors, or our classmates means we have to deal head-on with exactly the issue at hand.

Come on, Lauren, what if we really have gotten over these events? Why bring them to the forefront again? They are only relevant if we make them relevant.

You know what's always so interesting to me?

How resistant we are to dealing with what matters the very most to us—proving that our lives mattered. Proving that who we are and what we did is remembered. And to our core, it kills us that, quite possibly, our imprint, our impact here, might not matter. But, instead of dealing with that deep, honest, and even profound fear, we protect our narrative and our hole-ridden memories and refuse to face our very own fear about our actual history. We are reluctant to go back to people whom we loved, who deeply mattered to us, or who had the power to hurt us and to not *only* clean up what may or may not have happened, *but also* to forgive them. And even believe that our forgiveness is not only wanted, that it matters.

Until you make that phone call and get whatever apology you think you're owed and restore a love you left for dead, you have no idea how blocked your emotional arteries have been. You have no idea that if you are even *minutely* haunted by it, so are they. I swear, everyone you love or loved, everyone you remember, also remembers you.

It's a *spiritual quid pro quo*.

Yet, in the name of comfort, of potential embarrassment or of possibly being forgotten, most of us opt to avoid resolving it. I mean, come on. Would you really be upset if someone called you from your past to apologize for something? Or if they called you to ask you to apologize for something? Wouldn't you do it? Even if it was, for a moment, uncomfortable. From my perspective, I'm always a bit shocked at how *few* of us are getting these calls.

Wouldn't the world be a more beautiful place if we actually believed that what people have done to us or what we have done to others matters enough to acknowledge it, fix it, forgive it, *and* change how it shaped us?

Note to the cynic (and/or my brother, Matt): Even if, ultimately, you think none of this karmically matters, then simply buy its placebo effect. Because it turns out, even just the act itself—of courageously confronting our ghosts, of believing ourselves to be the very source of change in our own life, of stepping up and caring enough to change ourselves—changes us.

And, anyway, do you really have a better idea?

Let's see how **Stephanie** did in digging up her hauntings and then unraveling some of them:

In my earliest memory I am at Bloomingdale's with my mother and I am playing under the clothing racks. I can only see her feet. I hear a stranger approach my mother and say "Oh my, what a beautiful daughter you have." My mother immediately grabbed my hands out from under the rack and pulled me to my feet, putting my hands out for the woman to see. "Look at how ugly her hands are. She has very ugly hands."

Retell:

I asked my mom about this incident that I remember like it was yester-day. In fact, I had a long list of incidents, just like this one, where my mom was mean to me. My mom was diagnosed as clinically depressed and a narcissist. She doesn't remember any of them. Regardless, she apologized for not being well and whatever she did back then.

I was thirteen and my sister came home very drunk. I was home alone. She went to leave the house again in the car and I knew she should not be driving. I stood in front of the car in the driveway to keep her from leaving. She drove toward me and I jumped out of the way as to not be hit.

Retell:

My sister is an addict. She doesn't remember this incident. We were not close back then and still aren't. I sat and judged her and judged my parents for how they treated and coddled her. So, even though I might have been doing the heroic thing back then, the memory certainly comes with my favorite flair to it. Poor Stephanie, in a sea of losers, tries to save "them," but to no avail "they" always suck.

I have had more than one abortion in my lifetime.

Retell:

The truth is, I've had two abortions. And, up until now, I have not for-given myself. But, instead of just dealing with the plain truth that I was reckless about a variety of things, I beat myself up about it. I also know that because my relationship with my mom has never been great, my upgrade to her crappy parenting has been subconsciously avoiding parenting. So, perhaps my abortions that I have quietly suffered over have been a silent f*ck-you to her as well and I hadn't seen them as such until now. I also didn't tell one of the men involved. So I think this also goes on my lies-to-clean-up list.

I haven't met a client yet that didn't opt, at first, for their sad, single-focused narrative over the more honest telling, which happens to integrate, um, the other person's version of reality. Right? As if Stephanie's mother wanted to be sick, mean, and vindictive.

Stephanie got to see that if she could keep evidencing her theories that she was indeed screwed, the victim of a mean mother, a sick sister, a boys' club at work, the dating scene (or lack thereof), etc., then she never had to stop pointing. She could always find a "they."

But when is there not a "they"?

Last thing a child of a clinically depressed narcissist ever wants to deal with is how similarly sad and self-centered they are.

Did you ever wonder why so many of us believe that we'd never get an apology from our parents for all of their wrongdoings, *but* also never ask for one? I mean, if we asked for an apology and, in turn, they apologized—wouldn't it prove our longtime narrative fallible *and* malleable? And, if our narratives were truly that malleable, wouldn't that put all the power back entirely in our hands?

Yup. And uh-oh.

The minute we are willing to find the holes in our own narratives is the minute we can rewrite our entire autobiography. It is the minute that who we have always thought ourselves to be can change and get rewired.

Stephanie had to be brave enough, just like Ethan, to go to the source—in this case, her parents—and question her favorite sad and long-standing theories about herself, about love, and about vulnerability.

No longer to prove them but, to disprove them.

Now, let's see what haunted **Katie**. Brace yourself, this one is particularly dark.

One day, when I was six years old, I was sitting on my front porch when an older boy from my school walked into my front yard. I went off to play with him. I was missing for hours. The whole neighborhood searched for me. He did sexual stuff to me. I escaped from him. My neighbor found me crying in the street. I never told anyone what happened that day. At some point, I blocked the memory from my mind. All I remembered was walking off the porch with him and then being found by my neighbor. Earlier this year, I was working on a video promo for the AmberWatch Foundation and the memory came flooding back to me like an old 8mm movie.

After I started coaching with Lauren, she had me investigate what happened that day with my family. My mom said it was the worst day of her life. My dad didn't remember that day. My sister thought she was never going to see me again. My brother (who was in class with him at school) remembered how he just wanted to kick the boy's ass for taking me home with him. And thought it was weird.

Can you see how Katie's first telling of her haunting is obscurely obscure? And, even though she doesn't remember a ton of it, even the part that she is willing to tell seems, for such an impactful event, vague.

Let's see how Katie did in her expanded version of her haunting.

Retelling:

I'm six years old. My older brothers, older sister, and several of the neighborhood kids were playing high jump (track and field event) in the backyard on an old mattress that my parents had just thrown out. I wanted to play with them, but they told me I was too little. I got pissed, stomped away, and sat on the front porch alone.

I'm not sure how long I was sitting there before I saw him walk into my yard. He was eight or nine years old and in my older brother's class. He was the weirdo kid at school, whom no one played with at recess. I told him I had no one to play with. He said he would play with me. I ran upstairs to my mom's room and told her I was going to Kenny's house (he had the same name as the boy next door). I knew she thought I was going to play with the neighbor. I remember thinking when I was leaving with him, that my siblings should have let me play with them.

We walked to his house, which was in the next neighborhood. I met his mom. She seemed nice. She offered me a snack. I said no. I was allergic to peanuts and wasn't allowed to eat at other people's houses. We went to his bedroom to play. We played a game he had made up. He had me take off my clothes and then he did weird, sexual things to me. I started crying and told him I wanted to go home. He hit me, which scared me. I didn't say another word after that. I remember he was on top of me. I think I blacked out. Then it was like I was outside my body and looking down watching us. I don't know how long we were in his room. I remember putting my clothes back on at some point. Before we left his room, he said that if I told anyone about our game, he would hurt my family. I told him I wouldn't tell anyone. We went outside. I said I wanted to go home. He said I was never going home, that I belonged to him now.

At some point, he turned his back on me and I took off running; he ran after me and tackled me to the ground. This happened a few times before I literally outran him, sprinting through different backyards until I ended up on a street I recognized. I had been missing for hours. One of our neighbors was driving their car, looking for me, and found me wandering in the middle of the street crying. He told me to run home through the backyards as fast as I can, my family was worried about me. I ran home.

I remember walking into my house and hearing my mom and sister crying. They were sitting at the kitchen table. When my mom saw me, she yelled through her tears, "Where have you been?! We thought you were dead!" I told my mom that I had been at Kenny's house who was in my brother's class. My brother said that he was a weirdo and had no friends. My mom asked if he hurt me. I told them he hit me. But didn't say anything else.

The next day at school, my brother beat him up. A few days later, I remember walking down the hallway at school and he was walking toward me. I was afraid to look at him but I did. I wanted to scream that I didn't tell anyone. That was the last time I was alone with him. Sometime after that day, I blocked out the memory from my mind. All I remembered from that day was walking off the porch with him and then being found by my neighbor. Earlier this year, I was working on a video promo for the AmberWatch Foundation and the memory came flooding back to me like an old 8mm movie.

Obviously and understandably, Katie did not head back into investigating this haunt happily. Thirty-plus years later, Katie not only didn't want to deal with it, she was blaming her reluctance to resolve it on what the boy, who made the threat back when he was eight or nine, might do.

Ready for my "why bother to brave up now" case?

If you are *truly* claiming, like Katie was, that the reason you shouldn't head back into a haunting of yours is that 1) it happened so long ago; and 2) *for the most part*, you got over it; and 3) you even understand that the perpetrator was unwell him/herself; then why is it such a big deal to call him/her and clear it up this many years later?

I mean, if you truly don't care, then why do you care so much about what they will be like on the other end of the phone? How come your comfort matters more to you than letting justice truly happen? What's it really going to hurt by going back into your autobiography and manually correcting it? Wouldn't going back and redoing that moment in your life give *you* back the very power you relinquished?

Katie truly understood that the more hidden she kept this incident, the more real it became and the more she allowed it to define her. After some deliberation, some cheerleading from me, and some scripting of what she was going to say when/if she reached him, she called him.

Update:

I found him and contacted him via e-mail giving him my phone number, saying I wanted to talk to him. He called me immediately, which surprised me. He wanted to know why I was contacting him. I asked him if he remembered the day I went over to his house to play. He said he did. I told him I had nightmares about that day and had blocked it from my memory. And after I split up with my husband, the memories came back to me. I told him my recollection of what happened. We were in his bedroom. I was naked and he was touching me and doing things to me. I didn't want to play with him anymore. He hit me and wouldn't let me go home. He said he didn't remember anything from that day. Then he said he may have tried to kiss me. Then he apologized for anything he may have done that hurt me. We got off the phone with him saying he was going to think about what happened and let me know if he remembered anything else.

Our conversation didn't help me find out any more information about that day, but it did allow me to let go of that day and stop being scared of this boy. I had nightmares about that day since I was a kid. I don't anymore. But, in reality, I saw by contacting him that he was just a kid too. Who knows what happened. I think I do, but I don't know for sure. It was through the eyes of a scared six-year-old. What I do know is that I blocked that day from my memory for thirty years and used it to stay disconnected from myself, from people in general, and, certainly, from men.

Some hauntings, like Katie's, obviously stay ingrained in our minds because in them there is a deep hurt and a true crime that was committed. Some get resolved like Ethan's, and some don't. Some of us hold on to our haunts, like Katie, to keep ourselves, consciously or not, disconnected from people. Except, truly, how could our most important life lessons have anything to do with hiding, lying, distrusting, and not being ourselves?!

They can't.

What was ever so important for Katie (and us) to see was that her ability to hide throughout her life stems back to this very first haunting of hers. And not just what happened with the boy, *but* what happened after. Katie came home and *kept* hiding. In the name of protecting herself, her family, and what people might think of her, Katie justified lying about and hiding certain things from then on with the people in her life.

And, though I absolutely can understand how going into your narrative and correcting the inciting event might make you huff at me and question whether it will work or if it's too contrived, you, like Katie, would have to be willing to see that by courageously heading back and placing yourself as the hero in your own life, you can set the record straight. You can develop yourself into a person you are proud of, one who is brave enough to seek out and slay your own ghosts. To, once and for all, bring justice to yourself and release your own victim. Not because you weren't one, but because in the very way you carried the crime for your entire life, you didn't bring justice to the crime at all. In fact, whether you even remember the crime fully or not, in the very way you think about yourself, call yourself *shy*, an *introvert*, or a *hider*—you shaped yourself.

From the crime forward.

And, by connecting all of her dots, Katie could set herself free. She could start to understand how everything in her life, from her traits to her lineage to her heritage to her hauntings, created her *default mission* in life. And, until you, like Katie, can set the *whole* record straight in your life and figure out how you are at the source of it *all*, you will continue to default on your life's true mission.

The moment you start to unravel your own hauntings and discover that your personality is *indeed* malleable, you can rewire yourself. You can go from your default mission to your *true* mission. And wouldn't taking over the design of your life make it all that much more meaningful? Wouldn't solving your own riddle—what you are riddled by—be part of your mission? Wouldn't making ourselves a society responsible for our own personal pollution turn us into a humanity we could all respect?

Now, now. Give me some slack. This is the first time I've even come close to singing "Kumbaya." But, you see, I can't help it. The theory is that everything in your life matters. And by extension, you can fix anything in your life that hasn't made you wholly proud and call it "healed." This is, in my view, the very point of being alive. It's the way to set up the next generation to become the humanity we'd all want to meet.

You know, my version of conversion.

Look. Many of you have had real moments of profound hell, like Katie's, or even worse. There is no doubt in my mind that these events cause deep and lasting damage. Except, what if the reason we suffer most about the insufferable is that we are not connecting the dots and correcting what happened in a way that truly sets us free?

LIFE STORY COLONOSCOPY

Heading back into your life to dust off and decipher old memories allows you to fully grasp how much power you have *always* held in your life. It helps you start to see that the way *you* have stored your memories and the role *you* played in them can be altered by you at any moment. Truly. At any moment in time.

Hell, with *one* phone call.

I remember gasping at how right they got the premise in the film *Back to the Future* as I rewatched it with my kids. If you could truly go back and relive one moment in your past differently, how would it change everything about your current reality? And, really, the power of that *is* the very power of us.

To not only wish it were different, but to cause it to go differently.

Somewhat graphically (and certainly less than coyly), I have been known to call this process of clearing up old haunts a *life story colonoscopy*.

As unattractive a metaphor as that may be, it's kind of apropos, no?

I mean, here I am, in order to unclog you of all that haunts you, asking you to swallow a ton of information (akin to the ungodly amounts of liquid you must imbibe before the procedure), so you can be freed up, rewire yourself, and fully reconnect to your dreams. And, though this might not be the most appealing way to set you up for the assignment for this chapter, it's honest. And, just like the actual medical procedure, it's also, at some point in your life, for your life's sake, mandatory.

The very same warning that I issued for the "outing of your lies" assignment also applies here. For those of you who are contemplating blowing up your life, interrogating friends, bullying old nemeses, please don't. Please take care of the people in your world. They are in your world for good reason, even if they are stuck in your minds for bad reasons. Proceed with care, and dare yourself to be many years inaccurate about a whole slew of things.

I promise you, you are.

ASSIGNMENT FOR CHAPTER SEVEN

1. Please write out the incidents from your life that haunt you. Dig deep—there should be at least ten incidents on your list. Each haunting should have at least a three-sentence description.
2. Go through your list of hauntings and write down any patterns or themes that you see about yourself and your life.
3. Choose three hauntings to unravel and follow the steps below to unravel them.
4. Read and heed the warning below.

Okay. Here are the **steps to unravel a haunt:**

1. **Have a huge amount of compassion for yourself.** This whole process (hell, the whole book) takes an inspiring amount of courage.
2. As with the guidelines for how to fess a lie, you will need to **frame the conversation,** letting the interviewee know why you are interviewing them. Letting them know that this is for you to learn more about yourself, and to help you figure out what is real versus made up, as you want and need to know the truth. Reread both Heidi's fessing conversation with her dad (Chapter Six) and my Camp Fired conversation in this chapter for examples of how best to set up a fessing conversation.
3. **Show compassion and gratitude for the interviewee.** Do not put him/her on the defensive. Ask questions that are thought provoking and engaging, and not ones that might result in one-word answers. You are out to have an appreciation for what it must have been like for him or her to be on the other side of your reality, not put them on the spot. You can even tell them just that.
4. **Prep them, and get their permission** to talk about what might not be such pretty stuff. You can tell them that you understand it might not be comfortable for them. But you can also explain how

you've discovered that the things you've kept hidden are much worse in the dark of your mind than when spoken about out loud.

5. **Explain to them that you need the truth** from their viewpoint.

6. While you're at it, **explain to them that you are simply gathering the facts** from each person's perspective, and that this is not about being right or wrong. They are not going to get in trouble, no matter how they respond. Obviously, don't promise it and not mean it. Figure out how to mean it first, or you'll end up adding it to your list of lies from Chapter Six!

7. **Make sure, once again, that the interviewee understands** that you need honest answers only, as this is not about you judging them or their responses at all, this is about you ending your right to ever make stuff up about your own life.

8. Lastly, please **understand that I know there are other important issues** that you need to resolve before diving headfirst into these. For example, it was hugely important for Katie, before she faced her hauntings, to lose the weight, stop drinking, and figure out what she needed to deal with about her career. Katie also resolved many other hauntings before she dealt with the incident with the boy. Not everyone wants to speed through this, nor should they. Find your gradient. See what has integrity for you. And don't do it alone. Find someone whom you allow to deeply know you, who has got your hand and back as you do this.

Come on.

This is a call to arms. To claim your right to rewrite it all. To care about what matters most to you: mattering.

Okay. It's that time again, time for a **POP QUIZ**.

Over dinner, your wonderful, albeit conservative, parents express how proud they are of you that you are not turning out like your cousin who has thrown her life away by moving in with a man before she's married. You have no choice but to:

A. nod in agreement. Even though just the other day you were at your favorite cousin's new apartment, told her how genuinely happy you were for her (and meant it), and asked her to see if there were any other apartments available in the building for you and your significant other.

B. add this incident to your hauntings list.

C. while you're at it, add it to your lie list too, because you ain't never telling them.

D. call a coach or a friend that has successfully outed herself or himself to parents who were as "understanding" as yours.

E. with your friend or coach's help, and after having practiced a ton, sit your parents down, one at a time, and carefully, gracefully, lovingly, tell them both what you haven't been telling them.

Yes. When ready, **D** and *then* **E** for dare and evolve.

It takes something to be brave enough to evolve your lineage in honor of it. Lying for your parents' sake keeps you from growing up. Worse, it blames your parents for why *you* still can't speak up. It oddly has lying and hiding as an act of love.

No matter how old-school your parents may be, you are not. There is an inherent risk involved for all parents that their kids might, oh, I don't know, turn out to be who they were meant to be! No matter what, proceed with care and compassion. Remember, you are not a rotary phone, but the new iPhone. Here to teach *them*.

CHAPTER EIGHT

Unstuck

Finding Your Way out of Purge-atory

PURGE-ATORY

Whenever a client is upset, stuck in an uncomfortable situation that they swear they want to change but seemingly can't, I have them do a *purge*. A purge is when you write down everything that is upsetting and frustrating you in a stream of consciousness. And I mean *everything*. From what pisses you off about a coworker, online dating sites, your commute, your career, your tween, the economy, the gluten-free frenzy—even the latest nor'easter that is headed for, oh, I don't know, let's say Westchester County (mine) *again*.

A purge is about letting out every last part of the narrative you have in your head. In all its detailed detritus. Because *until* you get that very last thing that is running rampant in your head out of your head and onto paper,* the entire saga feels real.

Worse, all those contradictions in our mind *are* what shape and inform our reality.

You will be amazed at how what you are upset about sounds legit in

---

* Or your i-Whatever.

your head, but when it is written down on paper, it's nothing but your inner dialogue's lousiest and most convoluted hits on a subject.

It's the very reason why I have you put your purge to paper.

To incriminate your inner dialogue, which is doing a damn good job at keeping you from finding a solution. And to shine a spotlight on the narrative in your head that is shaping your reality, your attitude, and your opinions into a false reality.

In those very purges are the thoughts that directly influence your actions—that directly affect what you, for example, put in your mouth. And many of us truly believe that we've always just "been this way" as opposed to understanding the truth: that it's a narrative in our head that we keep repeating, so much so that it actually becomes our reality.

There is a huge, life-altering difference between thinking "we are just that way" versus understanding that "we just keep acting that way." *Barking direction #6:* Reread that last sentence. Though seemingly innocuous, it's crucial for you to fully understand the difference.

Once I get someone to put everything they are thinking down on paper, I can tell what's really going on with them. What gets unearthed in a purge is the very thing you need to step back to see, figure out, and change. It's the very thing that's stopping you, haunting you, and keeping you stuck. But, until you unearth it, you can't change it.

It remains your life's weather.

Most of the time, we just stay locked in our minds, replaying all of those negative thoughts—and instead of discerning what's what, we go get a cocktail or a cookie. We turn on the TV. We put in our teeth-grinding bite plate. We do *anything* to avoid having to spend more time with our cockamamie mind. The more purges you do, the more you can understand the undercurrent that you've been busy proving your whole life. The business your head's been managing. The different companies it compartmentalizes and runs—your body's company, your relationship company, your family company, etc.

You see, whatever you believe and keep in that head of yours, you're proving.

A purge allows you to set your narrative free, off leash, so you can see it fully and use it to learn from it. In all its mess and mayhem.

Speaking of mess.

Thinking it's only fair if I hold your bucket as you purge, I'll show you what's in mine.

PIG (WITH A) PEN

As much as I'm always working on you, you should know I am also working on myself too. And just in time. Three things happened concurrently that had me think it a good time to put my own Baby Lauren trait in a time-out: 1) my older sister, Beth, moved into a fabulous new and immaculately clean home; 2) my kids hit the age where they're old enough to cook, leave dishes in the sink, change their wardrobe an impressive amount of times, and use beauty products in (and all over) the bathroom; and 3) all of a sudden, my house reminded me of a squirrel house. For the first time ever, I was jealous of my siblings' houses. They all seemed to have a better deal than me. You see, theirs were clean.

Suddenly Baby Lauren had an internal tantrum.

As brats do, she started to plot how she was going to soothe herself. She even contemplated having her once-a-week cleaning lady come thrice. However, Baby Lauren also knew, no matter how much she pouted, there was no way her money-saving MacGyver of a man would ever concede to it. So, eventually and wisely, I decided to instead see my tantrum for what it truly was—a purgatory of sorts. One it was definitely time for me to come out of and one that, undoubtedly, was ~~my mother's fault~~ in response to one of my mother's traits.

Which one?

My mom's the maniacally neat one. The one that, when I was growing up, had us take our shoes off as we entered the house. The one that had us not use the brass sink, um, as a sink, etc. Just as I collect people, my mother collects dust. There is no quicker picker upper than my mom.

In fact, it's why a decade or so ago we gave this trait of hers the nickname "Walks with Sponge."* Because, for as long as I've known her, my mom has been cleaning.

Except, besides being accurate about my theory that my mom is a cleanaholic, let's tell Baby Lauren what other prizes she wins during her stint in purgatory:

Well, Baby Lauren, behind unkempt curtain number one, you win: 1) three piglets (kids) whose closets make your own look pretty darn good; 2) no fighting chance to find what you're looking for in your own closets and drawers; and, the kicker, 3) no deeper relationship with your mom, to whom you are obviously still reacting (and not honoring by evolving).

So the best way for me to decipher what was really going on in the mess that was my mind was to purge.

And here's an excerpt of what came out:

After all the work I've done on myself you'd think I'd get the joke and stop blaming you for being the way I am. But I don't. And the funniest part is that I know I'm lazy. I don't want to care about cleaning or being organized. I don't want to care about things like you do. Even though I know why I hate this trait, it still doesn't change anything. Sure, I wish I cared more than I do and would stop bitching about it or whining about having to do it or being jealous of others who do it and stop feeling like a baby about it all. I mean, I need to not just force my kids to care, I gotta force myself? What a purgatory! Obviously, I can't be upset about forcing my kids to care, but that seems like a bad joke, because that means I'm being her. Ha. I hated Marsha for caring so much about cleaning above being connected to people and how everything had to

---

* I imagine, by now, that you more than likely think me ridiculously ruthless with regards to my mom. But, in my defense, you should know: 1) I have an equal amount of nicknames for myself, and 2) this nickname, in particular, is one of *her* favorites. The only issue she has with it is that she'd prefer if I updated it to, "Walks with Bounty," as sponges are so bacteria infested, she wouldn't be caught dead today (for fear of the death it would cause) walking with one.

be just right. For me, it seems simple, pleasurable, and right to abolish a trait of mine that is a reaction and the opposite of an upgrade. The real upgrade would be to do it, care, be intimate, and enjoy it.

And then it really hit me.

Not only that I don't necessarily speak grammatically correct English when I mind dump, or that I can be spoiled, entitled, and bratty, *but* the fact that the biggest crime I held against Marsha was that she'd rather clean than be intimate.

An association *I* made.

Not her truth. Not the truth. My made-up truth. One I watched, judged, and penned. One that ever conveniently justified my reluctant cleaner.

A truth, however, that was purely based on a *syllogism*. A great word for bad logic. A word whose definition, I joke, just may have been the best thing I left college with. My syllogism went something like this:

Marsha is a cleaner; Marsha has three friends; therefore all cleaners need only three friends.

And, given that:

Baby Lauren wants intimacy; cleanliness precludes intimacy; therefore Baby Lauren can't clean.

And, voila. For Baby Lauren, the affiliation made perfect sense. It allowed Baby Lauren to do what was predictable for her—be intimate, not clean, blame her mommy, *and* make it a matter of principle.

In that moment of oy, I realized that the *real* and *honorable* evolution of my mom's trait would be to love to clean *and* to be intimate. To stop blaming my mom for a connection I made. To apologize to her for wiping my own dirt on her. And do the very thing I'd make you do.

Make promises.

Put in the right actions to take down my brat and forward my dream of having not just a cleaner house, but a deeper relationship with my mother. I made a date with my mom to read her the purge I wrote. I also made a promise to clean my house, three hours a week for three weeks in a row, before meeting with my mom. And, brilliantly, I hired my husband's fabulously talented aunt Maggie to help me organize and spruce up the look and systems in the house.

And you'll never believe what happened when I cleaned.

Turns out, if I put music on, I truly had nothing bad to say about the act of cleaning. I even (sorta) enjoyed it. Shit, I may even have my mom's gene. I even got the therapeutic part to it. The peace and satisfaction that came from it. Something, clearly, Baby Lauren had no intent to *ever* discover.

Guess what else looked better, post-cleaning? My mom.

After reading my mother my purge and apologizing, she said something so cute that I never would have guessed could come out of "that woman's" mouth. My mom paused and said, "You're right. You know, I learned that from my own mom after my sister, Barbara, died and all my mother could do was clean, instead of being with her feelings about her daughter's death, and still have to deal with raising me. I really should be more intimate."

And in that moment, sitting across from my mom, I could finally see my whole narrative about my mother for what it truly was, a *spiritual purgatory*. How I kept my stuff straight but not spotless, decent but not great, always at a 6.5/7 at best, with days of an 8 (the day the cleaning lady came). And, once I saw the purgatory for what it was, it changed the level of love I had for my mom forever. The love I had always wanted from her *was* there to be had. I just did nothing about it, except ultimately, lazily, becoming a little bit of a pig.

By the time my mom was done holding *my* purge bucket, we were scheduled to meet and connect intimately every other week. Far from a baby step for Baby Lauren, a leap. One that wasn't going to happen on its own without a purge and a willingness on my part to examine what was in my own slop.

SPRUNG CLEANING

Truth is, any place that you're really below a 6 in an area of your life, you probably (I'm being nice) owe a purge. What I mean by "owe a purge" is letting the whole drama out of you. To, once and forever, break up with a long-standing relationship of yours—your narrative.

There really is a specific way you tell the story. The way you're mad. The way you see things and your side of everything. And, it is that very way of thinking that is wholly yours that you need to fully catch, fully be able to hear, pinpoint, speak clearly about, even (eventually) giggle about, in order to change it.

But, Lauren, what if it's not just me? What if everyone else around me agrees with my purge and agrees that my father is a [fill in the blank]?

By now, you should have more than an inkling that your closest of friends are your very closest of friends, not only because their narrative and yours are of similar minds, *but also* because you have potentially bizarre and seemingly coincidental overlapping themes (divorced or alcoholic parents, similar sibling dynamics, etc.). So, even though your nearest and dearest happen to agree, it still doesn't make your purge *the* truth, just a shared one.

Below are **steps on how to purge**.

Not to worry; as before, I will give you enough samples of my clients' purges that the alternative—not doing a purge and keep talking to yourself about the issue at hand—will no longer sound like your sanest idea.

- Write out everything that's in your head on the subject (area of life or a person) and get it on a piece of paper/computer/what have you. Get it out of you. It could be something you are afraid of, angry about, sad about, etc. Include your feelings, frustrations, blame, guilt, excuses, justifications, and doubts.
- Write your purge in the first person, e.g., "I hate weddings. I don't want to go. I can't believe I have to wear that bridesmaid dress, let alone pay for it. And sit at the singles table. She's always had it out for me, etc."

- Be brutally honest. Dump it ALL out. Don't worry if you con-
  tradict yourself. Just say everything in your head. Allow yourself to be wildly honest, illogical, evil, crazy, and make no sense
  whatsoever—it doesn't matter, this is a safe space to just say it
  all however it sounds in your head. You know, let the real reeling
  you out.

OTHER PEOPLE'S PURGES

Time to hold a couple of my clients' "buckets." See if you can decipher
what Stephanie and Katie have been chewing on and swallowing.

Here's what you are looking for within each of their purges:

- Bad Logic (BL)
- Theories (T)
- Excuses (E)
- Traits (TR)
- Chicken (C)
- Brat (B)
- Weather Reporter (WR)
- Missing Actions or Promises (MA)
- Hauntings (H)
- Missing Information (MI)
- Lies (L)

First up, an excerpt from **Stephanie**'s purge on dating.

Heads up. Many of our narratives, since they rarely see the light of
day, let loose lengthily when unleashed.

Can I give up?! I mean, really, who has time for this anyway!!?? No one
is on these dating sites. It's a meat market. A numbers game. And if
they are here, they're losers or predators or both. I can't go out with

fifty-year-olds. In two minutes they're gonna need a pill, if they don't already. I've worked too hard, too long, to settle now. If he's successful, he's traveling too and we can have what, Skype sex?! I don't even look great on Skype. And, shit, any of the great ones by now are going to look at me as dried up or ticking-clock crazy. I should have just married Jason. I could have made it work with him. Nobody is perfect, right? F*ck love. It's overrated. You're independent, successful, and own a two-bedroom apartment in Tribeca. Quit complaining. You don't need anyone. You'll be fine alone. Better off, even. Just accept it.

If you're single (or once was), more than likely, you can relate to Stephanie's purge. You may even have said some of these lines or certainly toasted to a few of them with friends at a bar.

Right?

But, if you and I are on the hunt for all the hidden (or not so hidden) elements in this purge, let's see what we unearth.

In Stephanie's purge, like in all our purges, are a plethora of our favorite excuses, theories, traits, bad logic, and long lingering, unresolved hauntings, etc. The combination of which keeps our favorite narratives, our all-time favorite jukebox songs, locked in place.

On repeat.

So even though we may have a deep desire, in this case, like Stephanie, to find true love, we also can't get ourselves out of our own theories' way to find it. And, truth is, as much as we say we want to change our minds, it's not necessarily so.

The minute you can sit back and look at your purge as the road map it is to your narrative on a subject, is the minute you can have a say over it. You can get the venom out of your system, lessen the power your inner dialogue holds over you, and help yourself see the issue at hand from a different, more constructive position.

You get to decide what *you* want to think.

You get to have a say over what your mind says. You get to see what you have, for a long time, made up about a subject that has purposely kept you in the exact same spot and sport in your life. You get to see how what you are thinking creates your reality. You get to see how your inner dialogue, your *pigeon,** is often the one driving the bus. You get to see what information you've culled that is not based on logic or reality or even what happened, but on what happened according to, uh, you.

Whom you should not necessarily trust.

The truth that you should not necessarily trust yourself, however insulting, turns out to be the best news *ever*. It allows you the ability to fire your lower self from your advisory board. It allows you to say no to that persistent and pesky pigeon!

Let's see what **theories** Stephanie's got in her clutch and clutches:

- No one is on these sites.
- It's a meat market.
- It's a numbers game.
- In two minutes, they're going to need a pill [Viagra], if they don't already.
- I look like crap on Skype.
- I'm dried up.

How about Stephanie's favorite brand of **excuses**? When in doubt (or fear), blame:

- Time
- Work
- Work
- Work (ha)
- Men in general
- Skype

---

* If you don't know Mo Willems's Caldecott Medal–winning children's book *Don't Let the Pigeon Drive the Bus!*, check it out. It was introduced to me by a dear friend, Professor Jim Phills, then at the Stanford Graduate School of Business, who quipped, "the pigeon is your bratty inner dialogue."

- Erectile dysfunction (a low blow)
- Age

Can you tell from Stephanie's purge whom she possibly has some unresolved hauntings with?

- Men (Jason, in particular)
- Herself with regards to her age

Until Stephanie was willing to purge, she could not see the losing game she was playing when it came to finding love. Do you think her advisory board (her narrative) was really out to prove love—magical, easy, and for her?

No way.

Once you fully get who or what is actually running the show, you have the chance to fire your current board, evict your inner squatters (chicken, brat, WR, double agent, PR agent, etc.), who are pretending to act as your wedding planners. And, once and for real, get into the right dream-pursuing actions like, writing new theories and proving *them*, or having—oh no, anything but *that*—fun dating.

Suffering is not only optional, it needs to become suspect.

TAKING THE STAND

After I have someone spew every last thing they have on a subject and go through their own purge to cull and decode the detritus, I have them do what I call a *talkback*, where they get to talk back to each line of their purge in **bold** and in **ALL CAPS**, playing their own defense attorney, their own sleuth, on behalf of their higher self. Forcing you to step up and be brave enough to spit logic back at all that was illogical in your own tirade. Forcing you to debunk your own favorite theories. Your own—yep—lies. Poking holes in your self-declared seemingly impenetrable issue.

Let's see how **Stephanie** did in her talkback (in all caps) to her dating purge:

Can I give up?! I mean, really, who has time for this anyway!!??

GIVE ME A BREAK, I CAN DO MY JOB IN MY SLEEP. I HAVE PLENTY OF TIME IF I REALLY CARED.

No one is on these dating sites.

UGH, NOT TRUE. TWO OF MY CLOSEST FRIENDS MET GREAT MEN ONLINE, EXPLAIN THAT.

It's a meat market.

SURE, BUT I'M PRIME BEEF.

A numbers game.

POSSIBLY, BUT THEN GET PLAYING AND HAVE FUN.

And if they are here, they're losers or predators or both.

I'M SUCH A BITCH. WHAT? REALLY! I DON'T KNOW HOW TO WEED OUT AND EVEN HAVE FUN DOING IT.

I can't go out with fifty-year-olds.

SO DON'T.

In two minutes they're gonna need a pill, if they don't already.

UGH. JUST PLAIN MY-MOTHER-LIKE AND MEAN OF ME.

I've worked too hard, too long, to settle now.

SO DON'T.

If he's successful, he's traveling too and we can have what, Skype sex?! I don't even look great on Skype.

HA. IF I CARED AND TOOK MY HAIR OUT OF THE SCRUNCHIE I PUT IN WHEN I GOT HOME, I'D LOOK GOOD.

And, shit, any of the great ones by now are going to look at me as dried up or ticking-clock crazy.

MY MAN WON'T.

I should have just married Jason. I could have made it work with him.

NOT TRUE. IT WAS GOOD, IT WAS A LOT OF FUN, IT WORKED, BUT IT WAS NOT DEEP ENOUGH. IT DIDN'T FEEL

LIKE WHAT I WANTED TO FEEL LIKE FOR THE REST OF MY LIFE. IF THIS WAS IT, I WAS IN TROUBLE.

Nobody is perfect, right? F*ck love. It's overrated. You're independent, successful, and own a two-bedroom apartment in Tribeca. Quit complaining. You don't need anyone. You'll be fine alone. Better off, even. Just accept it.

WHOA. I'M A BABY/BITCH WHO IS STILL SO PISSED AT EVERYTHING THAT DIDN'T TURN OUT AND HIDING FROM DEALING EVER AGAIN. AND REALLY ABLE TO POINT THE FINGER AT EVERYONE BUT ME. AND SINCE I LOVE WORK AND MAKING MONEY AND BEING ABLE TO BE INDEPENDENT AND IMPORTANT, I CAN HIDE THERE, AND NEVER HAVE TO DEAL WITH WHAT I TRULY WANT, WHICH IS LOVE AND FAMILY, AND THINGS WORTH LIVING FOR OTHER THAN MYSELF AND MY CAREER.

Can you see how much fun Stephanie actually had doing her talkback, getting her chicken back in its coop, putting her higher self on the stand against her lower self, and magically, perfectly, knowing how to win the case?

A much better case to win—her LOVE dream's.

Now let's check out an excerpt of **Katie**'s purge. This happens to be Katie's first sober Saint Patrick's Day, since she was probably sixteen. Clearly, Katie's drinking buddy, her brat, which she's nicknamed "Lucy," was less than tickled. In this purge, I also had Katie mark up what elements (Weather Reporter, Brat, Chicken, Traits, Theories, Bad Logic, and Lies) she could see whining within it.

If you're willing to see what your head truly does for a living, you can fully hear and fire your advisory board, which, for your dreams' sake, you need to.

I am not happy. All I do is work. I work and work and get no rewards. (**WR**) None. Everyone else in the world has escapes. I don't. I'm trying to make shit happen. (**WR**) That isn't going to get me to New York. I never should have been a writer. (**BL/C**) No one knows what it's like being on this journey alone. (**C/TH/TR**) AND I have all these promises and promises and lists of promises that I have to follow and try to keep them in order, which I do with a sheet, but I still forget stuff sometimes by mistake or say I'm going to call someone and forget. Saint Patrick's Day is my day. It always has been my day. I'm 100 percent Irish. (**WR**) And I just wanna go out and drink. (**B**) 'Cause I don't want to be Katie today. I just want to disappear. (**C/B**)

Now, let's see how Katie did in her talkback.

I am not happy.

THAT'S A LIE. I AM SO MUCH HAPPIER THAN I'VE BEEN IN YEARS. I LOST SIXTY POUNDS. I AM PROUD OF MYSELF. I LOVE WHAT I'M DOING NOW. THIS IS JUST ME SOO WANTING TO DRINK. LUCY (MY BRAT), YOU'LL SAY ANYTHING TO GET A DRINK.

All I do is work. I work and work and get no rewards. Everyone in the world has escapes. I don't.

ANOTHER LIE. I PLAY PLENTY. AND WHAT EXACTLY DO YOU WANT ESCAPING FROM, KATIE—FEELING?

That isn't going to get me to New York. I never should have been a writer.

I LOVE WRITING. AND TO TELL THE TRUTH, I'M JUST SCARED TO TAKE THE LEAP AND GO TO NEW YORK.

No one knows what it's like being on this journey alone.

WHO AM I KIDDING. I PREFER BEING ALONE, NEVER MIND, I HAVE LOTS OF PEOPLE WHO LOVE ME AND ARE THERE FOR ME. ALL A LIE. AND GOING THROUGH A DIVORCE IS A COMMON EVENT. WOW, LAUREN WAS RIGHT. I DO SOUND LIKE THAT PIGEON.

And I have all these promises and promises and lists of promises that I have to follow and try to keep them in order, which I do with a sheet but I still forget stuff sometimes by mistake or say I'm going to call someone and forget.

QUIT COMPLAINING, LUCY. MY PROMISES HAVE GOTTEN ME TO LOSE WEIGHT. MY CHECKLIST HAS SAVED MY LIFE. I AM HAPPIER THAN I'VE BEEN IN YEARS. I LOOK AWESOME. STOP EXCUSING BEING SLOPPY AND BREAKING PROMISES.

Saint Patrick's Day is my day. I'm 100 percent Irish.

YES, IT HAS BEEN MY DAY TO PARTY AND GET DRUNK AND ESCAPE. I DON'T NEED TO ESCAPE. I ACTUALLY LIKE MY LIFE NOW. AND THE AMOUNT MY DRINKER LOVES BEING IRISH IS SHOCKING.

'Cause I don't want to be Katie today. I just want to disappear.

WOW, NO WONDER I KEPT LOSING THE FOOD AND ALCO-HOL BATTLE. THIS FEELING IS BRUTAL. LUCY IS MAKING AN ADDICT'S CASE TO NOT DEAL WITH LIFE AND EAT OR DRINK INSTEAD. F*CK OFF, LUCY. I'M HAPPY. CHECKING OUT NEVER MADE ME HAPPY. NOT ONCE.

Can you see how Katie's traits—martyr, lone ranger, and victim—are in full form? In order to drink, her narrative had to work up a good tailspin to see if it can talk her out of her promise to stay sober and somehow make it everyone else's fault—from the divorce, to her career choice, to no one fully understanding her plight.

What Katie failed to mention in her purge was the reason she was pissed (angry, not drunk) and not allowed to drink at all was not that her promises around drinking (that, FYI, *she* designed) were so ruthless or that I was going after deprivation. I wasn't. Katie had simple drinking rules. But, because Katie not only kept breaking her promises around the amount of drinks she could have but also was lying about and hiding it for *months*, even I got to the end of my rope. I was concerned if she couldn't keep her promises re: drinking, then I had no choice but to think her an addict. So, you see, at the time of this purge, Katie was in the middle of paying her own self-imposed consequence for going on a bender and lying about it: no booze for a year.

If only our inner dialogue were as supportive of our dreams as it is of our vices.

Our inner dialogue is way more interested in hosting a *pity party* than fighting the right fight against our brat and chicken. I mean, after all, most pity parties are not only catered affairs, in Katie's case, they even have an open bar!

THE REEL YOU

Ready? It's your turn to let your narrative loose.

This is your opportunity to find out what your feral and deeply opinionated head *really* thinks about a subject, and get wise to your narrative's ingenious ploy to have you think *you* have little say over what *your* mind says.

ASSIGNMENT FOR CHAPTER EIGHT

This assignment is meant to help you discern some of your deep, negative theories about why you can't have something in your life.

1. Follow the steps in this chapter and do a purge about a person, a situation, an area of life, etc., that you are stuck or struggling with. Write down everything in your head about the subject. It could be something you are afraid about, angry about, sad about, etc. Include feelings, frustrations, blame, guilt, excuses, justifications, and doubts. Literally dump your thoughts on the page in their rawest and most unedited form. Your purge is a rant. Write it in the first person. This is a safe space to just say it all, however it sounds in your head.

2. Located in the purge is a bevy of insights and information about yourself or the situation. Go through your purge and label the elements below:

- Excuses
- Chicken, Brat, and Weather Reporter
- Traits
- Lies
- Hauntings
- Bad Logic
- Theories
- Missing Actions/Promises/Practices
- Missing Information

3. After labeling all the elements in your purge, make a separate list for each element. That way you can see all your traits at play and hear every way you clucked, tantrumed, pontificated, lied, and used bad logic throughout your purge.

4. Once you have dissected your purge, do a talkback for each line in the purge, pointing out why the line isn't true, or how you could author that line differently instead of being a victim of it.

5. Write out a list of action items to work on from these insights— e.g., confess to the right person, find out the truth about a past incident, interview a family member, make a promise. Anything that will help you get to the truth.

In Your Defense

There really is a voice inside you that knows what to say in response to your purge. It's more than likely what you'd say to your friends if they were down and reeling. But, when it comes to yourself, you've somehow misplaced that ability.

Find it.

If you can catch your inner dialogue, you can deal with it. You can drag your deepest, darkest theories out of your subconscious and see how they're influencing your current reality. Like Katie, you can see your muck for what it is and decipher it. You can put yourself in the right actions to get you out of the hole in which you are seemingly stuck. You can build a case against your narrative's case. You can find your favorite sad songs, your favorite themes, your longtime count-on-able deep hurts that, I swear, you have equal evidence to poke holes in.

Counter your purge with your truth, and let your truth triumph.

Okay, time for your **POP QUIZ**. Yes, even though this entire chapter was a bit of a midterm exam.

Your husband/wife/partner is getting on your nerves today. Worse than ever. And even though, after Chapter Three (The Promise Land), you threw caution to the wind and promised to have sex with him/her once a week, somehow it's already Sunday. And now, you not only don't feel like having sex with him/her, you also don't want to keep your self-imposed consequence (that you happened to giggle and brag about last week) and forfeit *Game of Thrones* tonight. So you:

A. fake nice, claim migraine, turn on HBO, and add the fake illness to your lie list. After all, what's a lie list for?

B. who needs paper? Purge all over your person. Hell, they deserve it.

C. say nothing, stay passively pissed, and skip *Game of Thrones*. This season isn't that great anyway, and there's a good chance that Khaleesi won't even appear in tonight's episode.

D. figure out you're just being lazy, take a shower, get your game on, and jump him/her in time for the show.

E. sit down at your computer, light a pity party candle, and go for it. Purge. Rant. Curse. Let it rip. Much better on paper than on your partner. See what's really going on and deal. Ideally, get this all done in time for a quickie, before your TV show begins.

Answer: **D** and/or **E** for detritus. A fancy word for "crap."

Sometimes, what you uncover in your purge really does have something to do with the very thing you thought. Sometimes, somewhat surprisingly, it doesn't. Sometimes, it truly is just your chicken or brat at play, trying to get you out of, in this case, keeping your sex promise and managing to somehow sneakily blame it on your playmate.

CHAPTER NINE

The Mother Load

Cleaning, Unloading, and Putting away
Your Dirty Laundry

THE ALTER

Staying in love with your partner and staying connected with your parents, spawn, siblings, best friends, business partners, etc., takes practice and accountability. The reason many relationships deteriorate over time is that we often don't know how to address and resolve issues as they come up. The result: We wind up with a looooong list of unresolved complaints about each other. And by now you've certainly gotten your PhD in what happens when thoughts fester quietly in the dark over time, right?

They grow. They spread. And, they become more and more true.

I promise that each of you has a list that details all of the things your partner, your parent, your kid, and your boss does "wrong." You can choose to use this list as a weapon, or you can use that very same list as a tool to build a better, more mature, and fulfilling relationship. If there are areas in the relationship where you've been suffering, you might have given up the idea that there is anything you can do about any of it.

You would be wrong.

You, after all, are the CEO of it all. And, as such, you have the choice to find being responsible for everything in your life either taxing or liberating. It puts you (and not that pigeon) in the driver's seat of your bus. It puts you at your life and relationships' helm.

The author of it all.

Most of us are pretty tolerant of our relationships being "fine," right? But, truth is, if we're not deeply happy or inspired by ourselves in the relationship, then odds are we have a laundry list of issues and resentments. So many that we've become two-faced, separating what we think about a person and what we actually say to them. This creates two realities, a fake outer one and a "real" inner one. In order to keep relationships healthy, we must address and resolve all issues *as they come up.*

Truly, there is no simpler formula for staying in love. Until we tell the deep, honest truth to ourselves about what is not working for us, there is no getting intimacy back.

THE LAUNDRY

Now that you've practiced purging on paper in Chapter Eight, compiling your laundry list on someone should be easier (and at the very least, freeing). After all, keeping a shit list on a person, no matter how much you think it doesn't affect you, does.

You know how to tell how "real" your list is for you?

Your inner dialogue has already started wondering how to write that list in some indecipherable language or code, just in case anyone should *ever* come across it. You're looking for ways to hide. Again.

But here's the problem with that. If you're never willing to show someone else your list (or are even devastated at the notion that they might have a list on you), you're left in the land of "The Emperor's New Clothes." Left missing the very joke that if you have a list, they have one too. And the more you keep a tally of a person's faults, the less interested you are in seeing anything else—it becomes your truth about them. Except, do you really think the person you've got a list on doesn't feel it?

Imagine if the world talked about *all* of it. If lying and hiding weren't available options. I mean, wouldn't it be much simpler to not have to manage what you say or don't say, all in the guise of pretending it's about protecting someone else (when really it's about protecting everything you are scared to think, say, and do)? If you had to be transparent, the facade would have come down a long time ago. And that very facade is worth a lot to you. Not only does it safeguard your narrative, it allows for the cookie, the cocktail, the watching TV instead of having sex, etc.

Wouldn't it be freeing to not have a list on anyone, because everything new on that list got cleared up when it happened? Because, in fact, there was nothing you, the CEO of your own life, weren't saying?

The laundry list is a compilation of everything that bothers you about the other person. It is an opportunity for you to clear up old hurts, grievances, and points of anger that cloud your relationship and keep it from being honest, intimate, fun, and flourishing. When writing the laundry list, you are going to open up about your innermost thoughts and feelings. Some are scary to say. Some are mean. Some will disappear over the course of this exercise, because as soon as you type them or say them you realize, once they hit the light of day, you don't actually even believe them. Some of them, obviously, are true and deep for you and really need working out.

Remember, this is not an attack list. In honor of the relationship, it is ending your right to be two-faced with someone who matters enough to you to even *have* a list on them. Everyone has a list. If you are hiding shit, they are hiding shit. The expression "birds of a feather flock together," I promise, holds true in this case too.

Listen. I soooo know that this is scary as hell. I mean, though all this truth telling sounds like a good idea in theory, I know your inner dialogue is no doubt, at this very moment, wildly squawking like, er, like a pigeon?!

Trust me. Give it a try.

Here are the **steps on how to compile a laundry list** on a person.

1. **Spew on paper.** This is your opportunity to first face the truth with yourself. To get up on your soapbox (figurative or literal) and purge every last thing you have on the other person on paper in list format.

Let your subconscious and your conscious inner workings just go for it. It's why we hide it in the first place. It's unruly. It's mean. It's ruthless. It's hypocritical. We'd never let anyone see or hear what we've been saying to ourselves. But here's your chance to unleash it safely on paper. Not to worry, this is NOT the list they will see. This one is for you. Your own come-to-Jesus with yourself. Your chance to clear out every last thing that is going on in your head about the other person and get it out of your head and onto paper. For some, it's actually an exorcism. Make sure you include in this spew everything you are:

- Hurt by
- Angry about
- Hiding
- Unresolved about
- Haunted by
- Holding on to
- Still upset over

Until you get all of this craziness out, you will not be able to decipher what's real and what's ravenous rancor. Purging this list is a chance for you to face the truth.

2. **Step away from the list.** Go for a walk. Brown-bag breathe. Whatever you need to do to step away from your seemingly reality-based list for a bit, so you can come back to it in a day or five to see it with fresh (not in the nasty sense) eyes.

3. **Get real.** Now that you've stepped away from your initial list/spew, go back over the list and modify it to be more truthful. Make it 100 percent more accurate, balanced, and fair of a telling. Be more grown-up about it, and start to see the other person's side. And, from that perspective, tell it more accurately and with their version considered. Rewrite what you need to in order to tell the truth and understand the other person better. So, for example, let's say you're upset and frustrated that it feels like your partner doesn't care about sex anymore and doesn't get how hard taking care of a

baby really is. Except, if you had to tell it in a more balanced way, you might have to cop to the fact that while you are madly in love with being a mom, you haven't lost the last twenty pounds yet. You're exhausted, sure, from mothering, but also from staying up insanely late playing *Candy Crush*; and, by the time your partner comes home late, you don't really give a shit about sex either. Can you see how *that* is a slightly more honest telling than the "you're not physically attracted to me anymore" bullet point that landed on your initial laundry list?

4. **Have compassion.** Sorry. It is true that being two-faced and collecting evidence on someone you care about comes with our species' packaging. This entire list-writing process is not meant to have you feel crappy about yourself. Quite the opposite. It's meant for you to have insights about yourself, your collection process, and to have you hear your own narrative at play. To get you in your current reality. Would your inner dialogue think this a wise exercise? No way. Your inner dialogue wants to pretend that all of your list items have been long-term filed away and justifiable. Don't listen to it. Smile at your inner squatters and hear them for what they are.

5. **Keep it real.** See in the list where you are prone to exaggerating, to using words like "never" and "always." Although it may feel like it's indeed *always*, your exaggeration will give less credence to what you are saying. The other person won't be able to hear it and will feel it an unfair attack. So, for example, your first instinct might be to say "you're so mean when we fight." Even if it feels true, it's a bit general. What works better would be to say something more specific like, "I hate it when you, at the end of two out of three of our fights, say mean things like, 'You're a lousy father,'" or, "if you think *this* of me, maybe you should divorce me," storm out of the room, or hang up the phone.

6. **Cover everything.** Make sure you cover everything, even if it's something you two have openly discussed before. If you are still thinking about it, it belongs on the list. Address all areas of the relationship. What complaints, opinions, and issues do you have in

each of the twelve areas of life in the chart (that apply) from Chapter One?

7. **Give examples.** Be specific. Eventually, when you go over the list with the person, you want them to know exactly what you are talking about. Be sure to include what the other person does, doesn't do, says, doesn't say, or implies. Do they give you a certain look that bothers you; do they have a habit that annoys you? You want to make sure that the list really makes sense to them. The person to whom you are reading it should not be left with any questions as to what you mean. They should not be left thinking:

- Huh?
- When was the last time I did that?
- Always?
- Yeah, but I've gotten better.

If you think the other person will react with one of the above responses to one of your bullet points, then go back and ask yourself the truth about the situation. What would they say in their own defense? What does that mean about your version of the story? What would be a truth you could both agree upon?

8. **Keep it current.** If the issue is a complaint you've made many times before and things *have* improved but are still not fully handled, say that. Keep it up-to-date. For example, "Since you've gained weight I haven't been physically attracted to you. And, even though I know you've been on a diet and lost weight, which is great, I'm not there yet." That way, the other person is not left with the need to say, "Yeah, but." They can just understand your experience and what your truth looks like. And, however harsh that example may have just sounded, I promise, if you're the one that gained weight, 1) you are not so happy with yourself about it either, and 2) you were not necessarily thinking or caring about your sexiness when you stopped taking care of yourself. So, though we'd all like to simply gasp a good, "How could they?!" we actually already know how they could.

9. **Keep it on the list anyway.** Even if you think that one of your laundry items sounds hypocritical, juvenile, or mean, even if you can sometimes talk yourself out of feeling that way in an attempt to get it off your list, you should, if you ever entertain it, still include it in the laundry list.

10. **Notice.** As you work on this list you might discover that some issues, once written down and practiced out loud with a trusted friend, may dissolve or disappear. You might not feel the need to say it to them anymore. Mark those items on your list as resolved. Write down what you learned about it. On the other hand, sometimes some unresolved issues might get more apparent, louder, and point to the work that will need to be done. This is all normal and part of the process of fessing what you've been holding against the other person.

I'm not going to lie, learning how to become one voice and end being two-faced in your life ain't easy. It's intense. But it's the best leap you'll ever make. The best gap you'll ever bridge. One that creates a spiritual moment in your life. Where you become one secret-free voice out in the world.

For those of you who are scared to take this leap, at the very least follow the steps and do the list. No matter what, it's a stunning way for you to balance yourself on paper. And, if the best contract you can make right now is that you are willing to go face-to-face with your two-facedness, but not resolve it yet, that is *still* huge from where you were yesterday.

OTHER PEOPLE'S LAUNDRY

In relationships, you really could have whatever you want. But building the relationship you desire requires that you treat the relationship as sacred, that you understand that the very way you perceive the truth puts the word "truth" under the right scrutiny, where your facts and your narrative meet up. It gets you to start to be accountable for how hidden and misused the truth has been, and gets you and your partner on the same page of accuracy or inaccuracy about it all. It has you both balancing out your two narratives to create one truth between the two of you.

After all, the truth is not a one-person sport.

What's "true" has got to live between two people. There are facts, and then there's your narrative about the facts, right? Writing and clearing up a laundry list is about getting both of your narratives on the same page. If you are willing to understand that your perspective is just that—yours—and not, necessarily, true for the other person, it lightens the loathe (so to speak). It gives you the opportunity to get in the other person's shoes, understand their perspective, and have compassion—and realize that, of course, you were meant to have these very conversations. Is it really so shocking that the truth is a deep and important part to take on, head-on?

What if integrity is spirituality? If integrity is knowing deeply who you are, by all the actions you take? If integrity is asking for what you want? And is getting it, duh.

From all you've read thus far about Donna and her husband, John, I imagine by now that you're pretty clear that she's got a decent-size laundry list on him, right? What's ironic about this assignment is we walk around thinking what we actually have on this list is so original and so shocking, when in truth, however incredibly hard our listed items are to communicate, they're actually vulnerable, real, forgivable, and even lovable.

Let's take a look at what **Donna** had on John. This far into the book, none of this is going to be a huge surprise for any of you, or for John either. Do you think John doesn't know what doesn't work about himself? The only thing semi-surprising about this list, *possibly*, for him is how well Donna has kept her anger a secret.

I had Donna write up everything she had on John in letter format. Even though it feels a bit formal, for some, it makes it easier to read to the other person. Yes. I typed, "read," not e-mail, text, or mail. However, if doing this assignment as a list is easier for you, by all means, make a list.

Either way, just be sure to read the warning *and* follow the directions in previous chapters on how to have a hard conversation, fess your lies, or resolve your hauntings, etc. The same steps apply here when clearing a laundry list. This is *not* about blowing up a relationship. It's about getting gracefully honest in it.

Dear John,

I am writing this laundry list in an effort to out and end my quiet complaining martyr. She listens, complains to herself, and suffers in silence. She is very judgmental, victimized, and blaming as she watches people (mainly you) hang themselves. I am working with my coach on creating promises and consequences around suffering, complaining, and staying quiet. I am not allowed to stay quiet when I feel something is off or if I am unhappy about something. Nor am I allowed to sit back and judge, blame, or watch you hang yourself. Being afraid to make you or anyone else angry by telling my truth is not an excuse to keep quiet or a measure of how well a conversation has gone.

I am ending my right to swallow my opinion or thoughts and be more open and loving with you. I am sorry for holding this laundry list against you like a file I keep adding to. I am very clear that I haven't let you be the love of my life. And, the more fake I am with you, the more I never give you a chance to love the real me.

Please hear out this laundry list, but please also know that I am well aware that I have been walking around meanly watching you flail and doing nothing to help you. Believing that I wish things were different, but doing nothing differently on my end.

Many of these items on this list we've started to talk about. I know you must have a list on me as well and I deeply want to hear it. This list is ending my right to point and pout and not be the best friend, partner, lover, and teammate I've been claiming I want you to be.

Here goes:

It feels like you think there is one rule for you and one for everyone else:

For example, while it is impossible to walk into your office without tripping, because it is so messy, no one else is allowed to have a messy room, desk, or area. *They* are the lazy slobs that don't care, whereas you are not.

Our family's sloppy trait:

The kids eating bacon with their hands is no different from you eating salad with your hands. In fact, yours is worse, because technically, bacon is finger food. Salad is not.

Your closet is only kept tidy because our cleaning lady keeps it that way. Even she gets pissed off when you wad up your just-ironed T-shirts. Even she says (in a whisper), your closet space is like the kids'.

Yes, I do get the joke that we have a housekeeper that grumbles under her breath with me about you.

Our weird rules around swearing:

You can swear all day and even tell the kids they "f*ck everything up," but it is not okay for any of them to speak that way? How is that fair?

Your complaining:

You complain about the kids "moaning" and "complaining," which I find ironic because you complain a ton yourself. Whether it's about the kids, the mess, your ex-business partner, or even about our room on vacation in paradise (Fiji). Even if the room *was* noisy, you complained about it even after we switched rooms.

But did I say anything to you about your complaining? No.

Instead, I complain in my head about you as much as you complain, but don't see how I am the same as you. At least yours is in the open.

Where I feel you can be mean/cold:

The energy often shifts when you come home. The kids and I are on red alert. So many times, we end up slumping away from the dinner table. But I also see that my suffering martyr doesn't mind walking away feeling bad and being silent about it. Watching you fail us, just like I watched my dad fail me.

What I feel when I hear you say "WHY????"

When something happens (the dog pees on the floor, there is a mark on the wall, a dent in the floor, a ding in my car) it is suddenly MY car, MY dog, MY floor, and you need to know why this happened. It doesn't feel like you are really asking WHY?? In my mind, you are asking, "Who is to blame?" "Who can I blame?"

Now, do I say any of that? No.

Am I responsible for the dog, the house, the floor? Yes. If I can point at your sensitivity and make it erratic and unjust, do I have to see how I blame you for things that fall under my care that I am careless about? No.

After writing this whole list and stepping back from it, I can really see how I have not been on your team at all. It has been me, the kids, and even the housekeeper against you.

I promise, John, from now on, I will stop complaining about your complaining and do something about it all. I promise to tell you when I hear anything from this list coming up and not silently get hurt and think, if I never say "ouch" and only smile fakely that you should just know something was hurtful. I'm done setting you up and thinking myself and the kids the victims of you and not equal perpetrators.

The silencer on the muzzle doesn't make it any less of a crime.

~~LOATHE~~ LOVE THE ONE YOU'RE WITH

The first part of fixing a relationship that you truly, and I mean *truly*, want to fix is by doubling back and going after what's missing and retrievable, by understanding that there was a level of caring and commitment you had for each other when you first got together. A time when you really wanted to get to know each other. It was juicy becoming best friends and sharing everything. You developed a deep connection and figured out how to make it work. But then, over time, you started caring less about listening to or taking care of each other. The excitement faded or the relationship got a little boring. You became less committed.

There was a point where that switch happened, right?

You might even know when you started to notice it, but you aren't really sure what triggered it. Was it when you had kids? When money got tight? When work got more stressful? When an aging parent moved in?

If you find yourself unhappy in your partnership and have a long laundry list on them, what is more than likely at its root is that the original contract you made with your partner in several areas of your relationship (e.g., kids, money, sex, romance, etc.) has been broken or changed somehow. Most of us aren't even aware of the fact that, all along, there are spoken and unspoken contracts being made. But there are.

There truly is a business side to any great relationship. There are *departments* that need to be managed well, or the relationship won't flourish. Every couple divides up the "labor" in a relationship—from who's in charge of finances, food, vacation, romance, and yep, even the dreaded science fair projects. Sadly, there's rarely an equal distribution of departments. (But, ladies, do you really want your partner in charge of children's wear?)

A marriage is not only an intimate relationship, but also a business partnership, and it's important to run it like that or the business will fail. Determining who should be in charge of which department is very scientific. Ready? It's a little tricky, so pay close attention: First, discern who is actually better at the area in question and voila! that person is manager of that particular department. If it's not easy to figure out who is better in the area, then pick who complains about the area the most, and they win it.

Can you see in Donna's laundry list that most of her issues with John are around his parenting and piggishness? And, even though John may think Donna is in charge of the children and housewares department, he has a huge amount of complaints about how those particular departments are run. However, do you think John *really* wants to manage those departments or should? He sure complains the most about them, but I'm not so sure Donna would vote him manager. Would you?

Can you see that one of the real problems here is that, until now,

Donna hasn't fully stepped into her CEO position in that household? Now, now. As CEO, Donna doesn't have to do *everything*; a good CEO doesn't. But she does have to make sure that all departments under her management are running well. She has to parcel out what she needs John to do. Yet, that would require Donna having to open her mouth, get talking, start delegating, and stop playing victim of the contract she signed. Donna can't continue to play Mother Knows Best, CEO, *and* subjugated employee. Her company (her marriage and kids) will not thrive.

Can you also hear how this, more than likely, is very similar to the companies in which Donna and John were both raised? And, unless Donna deals with her own true feelings and opinions with John and starts speaking them, she's stuck silently suffering in a purgatory, which she could feel in her gut. Literally.

Once Donna read John her laundry list, the two of them made a plan to meet every Sunday for the next six months. During those meetings, they moved through each item on each of their lists, addressing every issue in turn. At first, the meeting went for two hours every week (they had a LOT to figure out). They sat down and got to work on clarifying their contracts, divvying up the departments in their marriage, and getting in the right promises and consequences for all of them—kids included.

When I help a couple renegotiate their original contract, I make sure there's no wiggle room, so that two years or five years or even twenty years down the road, they're not trying to break, change, or get out of the contract. The more you understand the agreements between you and your partner, the more you can understand when something goes haywire and starts to fall apart. I have found in my coaching of couples that any relationship can be fixed, as long as the couple has a strong foundation of deep love, a commitment to stay together, and a willingness to do the work.

Donna and John are doing the work.

Truth is, once you fix the list you've been holding on to, your relationship truly has a chance to get stunning. There are always a finite amount of things that need fixing, most of which, I promise, are fixable. There really *is* a happy ever after. Once you realize that your relationship is more important than your individual point of view. That's where the true definition of a "union" lives.

UNDER THE HOOD

Have a seat and chew on this (*barking direction #12*)!

What if whatever you haven't resolved in your life, you are picking? In other words, you are dating, marrying, or partnering with someone at the very same level of development as you. Neither one of you, as much as you'd like to think, is more ahead than the other.

You are *two peas in a pod.*

In fact, subconsciously, some of us even pick slightly bigger criminals than ourselves, so we can hide behind their criminality and don't have to deal with our own. And, even if we think we managed to veer far from the old apple tree of Chapter Five and picked our own "Golden Delicious," I promise, all of our picker's roads point back to our lineage and heritage.

Yep. To that very apple tree.

You see, it's rarely an accident how or why you picked whom you picked. The only surprise is how little we've investigated our own lineage and patterns.

Speaking of interesting pickers, let's take a look at the list I had **Katie** write up on her ex-husband, Shaun. Instead of doing a laundry list on him, I had Katie do a list of how she and Shaun were similar, and, in fact, two peas in a pod.

Yes. Katie was as tickled about compiling this list as you can imagine.

KATIE AND SHAUN'S SIMILARITIES

- We both grew up Catholic and were the youngest of four children.
- We are both intelligent, creative, and writer/filmmakers.
- We're both arrogant and angry at the world. He's overt and loud about his anger, while I'm covert and silent about mine.

- We both got citizenship out of the marriage—his US and my Irish.
- We both had a secret when we got married. He questioned his sexuality and hid it; I wasn't in love with him and didn't want to get married.
- We both married our fathers. My dad is arrogant and has a loud opinion like Shaun. And Shaun's dad would escape by drinking and then disappear like me.
- We both repeated our parents' marriage. My parents' marriage looked to me more like a business deal, with one or both spouses settling. While his parents' marriage was abusive, full of anger and fighting, just like ours.

Wow, right?

Can you see how Katie and Shaun, without realizing it, were both following in their parents' footsteps? Shaun picked Katie, a sad hider who preferred to swallow her feelings, stay quiet, and numb herself with food and alcohol, just like his father had done. And Katie was emulating her mom's traits and patterns—a woman who, she said, was sad and stuck having settled for a man she didn't passionately love. Around Shaun, Katie could continue being the victim of her own life, just as she had always viewed her mom. The victim of Shaun's narcissism, and of his arrogance. Katie could justify lying and hiding, eating and drinking— and she could blame Shaun for all of it.

I mean, what better pick for a people pleaser than a narcissist?

If Katie only pointed at Shaun's lying, she got to not see her own. If she only pointed at Shaun's anger, she got to bypass dealing with hers. If she only pointed at his hiding, she got to miss the fact that she too picked him to hide behind. Once Katie could see her and Shaun's sameness, she could find true compassion for herself *and* for Shaun. She could tell the truth and apologize from there. She could even understand why she married Shaun in the first place—and as she did the work to have some hard conversations with her ex about this, she managed to slowly heal herself and set them both free.

Below is an e-mail Katie wrote to Shaun after one of the times she tried to open up with him in person, but he got too triggered to hear her out.

Dear Shaun,

There are so many things I want to talk to you about and apologize for. We haven't been able to get together and have a conversation without it going in a bad direction so I decided to send you an e-mail to express what is going on with me, what I am feeling, and what I want to say to you.

I have spent the last six months looking at myself and my life. I am waking up to who I have been the past thirty-five years, and I'm not proud of many things. That includes the way I treated you. My whole life I have never really expressed myself or told people the truth about who I am. I don't want to be that person anymore. I don't want to hide from the world anymore. I want to be honest, real, and truthful.

So I am sharing the real me with everyone I know. I am going through my life and confessing any lies I may have told or kept hidden from people. You have been one of the most important people in my life the past eleven years, and I wanted to confess and apologize for my behavior and who I was when I was with you.

I am truly sorry for the pain I caused you during our marriage and the whole breakup process and divorce. I'm sorry I have been cold and distant to you over the years. So many times you tried to open me up and have me express my feelings and I wasn't willing. I wish I was back then. It would have changed everything. I am sorry if I made you feel unloved. You have a lot of love inside of you and I ignored it.

Since we split, I know the past two years have been difficult for us. I wasn't looking at it from your perspective. I only saw my side. I was selfish. I didn't think about or care what you were going through. It was all about me. I am sorry for anything mean or hurtful I said. You know me better than anyone, and when I get hurt I lash out or shut down. And that's what I did with you. I'm sorry. We've had a roller-coaster ride of a marriage, but no matter what happened between us, we were always buddies. And I never wanted to ruin that.

First of all, I want you to know that I care about you and only wanted the best for you, but if I was truly honest with you ten years ago, we wouldn't have gotten married. I was afraid to tell you the truth. I am afraid to tell most people the truth about anything. I hold back and don't express myself. And I know you know that. I didn't know how to tell you I wasn't truly in love with you. I didn't want to hurt you. There was a love, a friendship, fun, and an aligned purpose, but underneath it all you weren't telling the truth about what you were scared of and I wasn't telling the truth about what I was scared of. And together we created a facade just like both of our parents did. And, instead of seeing all of that, I have been blaming you, because when you started to come out as gay, I could blame you and pin it all on you, and that was dishonest of me. I know you loved me, but we never talked about your sexuality or the fact that you got your green card and I got my Irish citizenship from our marriage, or my lack of honesty about where my heart and mind were most of the time.

When you flew into LA from London and proposed to me that Thanksgiving, I was thrown. You had hinted about wanting us to be together, but I had no idea you were going to propose. And I resented that you surprised me and did it with fifty people in the other room. I felt like you put me on the spot so I couldn't say no. I never looked at it from your point of view. It was romantic to fly in, plan a party, and surprise me like that. But I only coldly saw it as you cornering me into saying yes. And I did say yes. I didn't want to hurt your feelings or embarrass you or be uncomfortable or be honest with you.

Even after I canceled the wedding in Maryland and we were dating again, I was still trying to figure out what I wanted to do. I didn't really want to get married. All I cared about was my career, and I know you knew that. But, again, I agreed to get married in

Vegas. About six months before we got married, I cheated on you. I had a one-night stand with a guy I didn't even care about. You were in London. We had gotten into a fight over the phone a few days beforehand about the wedding and being together. I felt pressured to plan the wedding I agreed to plan. I went out to a bar to have a drink and the guy sat down next to me. I grossly managed to make my cheating on you your fault. And it started our marriage on a lie that would cause irreparable damage. And when two people get married, they should be truly honest and real with each other; we weren't. And I, certainly, wasn't.

I kept several other secrets from you. Including the fact that on our wedding day, I had a mini breakdown. After we got into the fight in the casino (before getting the marriage license), I came back to my suite and lost it. I didn't want to get married. I knew it wasn't going to work. I knew we had trouble communicating. I knew I wasn't in love with you. After a few hours, I calmed down and went through with the wedding day anyway.

None of this was fair to you.

If I had just been honest, maybe the two of us wouldn't have gone through so much pain these past few years. I am so sorry, Shaun, for everything I did. I see myself and who I am and I just want to cry, because I never understood myself or saw all the damage I was the source of in our relationship. I didn't think the truth mattered. I lived in compartments and never respected the truth. And I know much of this (and our backgrounds) led to our abusiveness with each other. I am sorry for how I treated you and for all of the abuse I did to you. I'm sorry for anything I lied about or said, did, pushed, shoved, broke, or for any way I hurt you over the years.

It's up to you whether you want to forgive me or not, but I can finally see my part in all of it and I am deeply sorry that I blamed you for everything. It wasn't fair of me.

Love,
Katie

Once Katie fully got that she was not the victim of her marriage, she could shift how she saw everything. She could get her own power back. She could even admit to having sensed from the very get-go that Shaun was lying about his sexuality. Katie, on their second date, asked him if he was bisexual. When he answered, "No," she believed him. But, see the fine print in the LA (Liar's Anonymous) handbook. Will someone who manages what others can and cannot know about themselves *ever* outwardly question another hider/liar?

Answer: nope.

Katie got to see how *she* used Shaun to stay quiet and that she had the choice to either, once and for real, step up and deal with finding her voice and speak up in her life *or* not. It took Katie a long time after she did this initial assignment to actually get to the ultimate truth about her relationship with Shaun. Even after Katie lost all the weight and did every assignment in this book, and had all the confidence to go with her looks, all she really wanted, when it came to love, was a "Mr. Saturday Night." A man who "performed" Saturday nights only and maybe an occasional Tuesday night here and there, but who required absolutely no cuddling or sleeping over, ever.

Each time Katie thought she found someone to fit the bill, each one of them (three), who swore they had never had an erection issue, had issues.

By now, you know how I feel about coincidences.

Even Katie couldn't help but smirk and think that *maybe* it was she. That *perhaps* she and I missed something, as the path Katie was on was clearly not letting her go anywhere. It's what I call *divine spit*, when something out there, whatever "it" you believe in, was clearly not going to let Katie get away with something.

And, certainly, nothing on a Saturday night!

Three figurative flat tires later, Katie and I had a phone conversation about her love life. It wasn't the first time we've had this very conversation. But, it was the first time she *really* went there. And, when she got there, and connected all of her own dots, she got quiet and her voice cracked an, "Oh my God. I never wanted this to be true. I think it's true.

I think I might be gay." And, for a moment, Katie's terror went to joy. Back to terror. Then, back to joy.

I had dinner with Katie a few days after our conversation. She was a completely different person. Her energy was freer, lighter, and more relaxed. For the first time, Katie looked comfortable in her own skin.

THE PARENT TRAP

Whether you love them, loathe them, live with them, live thousands of miles from them, or even if they have passed away, who you were and are with your parents affects you today. And, until you deal with who you are or were with your parents—great, good enough, or ghoulish—you can't get out of the possible default or reactionary mode you're currently in when it comes to designing your own dream partnership.

We all have things we think about our families that we keep to ourselves and have not said to our parents. In the parent letter exercise, you will get to write your truth about your experience growing up with your parent. You will get to write how the experiences affected you and what you thought they meant. You will get to go back and visit yourself and remember the times you felt unloved, abandoned, or alienated by your parents.

The letter is a critical place to sort out fundamental character lies.

There are events in your memory with your parents that are inconsistent with the facts. This exercise will enable you to realize the truth about those memories. To finally be able to spend enough time with those events to hear your own truth. For some of you, the very thing you may be punishing your parent for could be the purgatory you are currently living inside of. The very connection between your own self-loathing and the loathing of our parents is truer than we know and vital for us to figure out.

If we could suspend whatever we need to in order to believe that our parents are our very entryway to our life's purpose, isn't that a better way to take responsibility for everything that came before us and everything that comes with our being the upgraded model? And wouldn't we (even the cynics of us) rather believe that we didn't come here to be screwed by what we're stuck with anyway—our parents' programming (see Chapters One through Eight!)?

Once again, I am asking you to hire a good defense attorney, but this time, not only for your higher self, but for your parents as well.

I know that some of your parents truly did and said awful things to you. This letter is the beginning of correcting that, rewriting your family's history, and healing. This letter is for you to finally get to say every last thing you need to say to both of your parents. It will be the end of your own two-facedness with them, and theirs with you.

Each client's parent letter is different. Each is profound. Each is an opportunity to rewire what has long been wired, possibly faultily, and grow yourself and your parents up, right before their eyes. There are **four main phases** to the letter. Each phase typically requires many rewrites and revisions and, if you were working with a therapist or coach, there could be many back-and-forths with them.

Phase One of writing the letter is your opportunity to purge everything you have on your mother or father,* to tell the truth about everything you have been afraid to say, ask about, or tell. Everything you are hurt by or mad or sad about, and anything you can't forgive or understand. This is your opportunity to unload every last thought you have ever hidden from them.

Barking directions #3 and #5: Don't worry, and go for it. They will never see Phase One's draft. This draft is for you to get it all out of your head, your heart, your gut (if you're like Donna), and onto paper.

Phase Two is when you are going to sort out all of the discrepancies in the letter. You are going to act like a journalist and fact-check. Because after you purge in Phase One, you will likely be left with some

---

* Though these letters are primarily for parents, they also can be written to siblings, spawn, best friends, etc. Truly, to anyone who matters to you that you've let matters get in the way.

holes in your story. You will end up having to figure out what you don't know. You will have to take into account all that you have learned thus far in this book and see that you have *always* had more of your parents' issues than you ever cared to recognize. This is your opportunity to find your own hidden truths.

Phase Three of the letter is when you actually figure out your real questions and have some investigative conversations. You get to unravel your own version of what happened and connect all the dots. You get to find out your siblings', aunts', and uncles' perspectives, remembering that each is going to have their own point of view. This is where your higher self and your journalist need to team up to find out everything you don't know. Because once you have a clue, you can figure out what you are really upset about—and tell it fairly.

Phase Four of the letter has you get the pigeon out of the bus and get writing the real letter. It has you see that even though your parents did do some shitty things, the adage "it takes one to know one" might once again apply here. You'll see how unforgiving and disconnected you've been without ever knowing all of the facts.

Ultimately, this process is a reckoning for a new future—one where we, the new generation, are in charge of building as healthy a relationship with our parents as possible—as an act of love and honesty.

Until now, many of you have been living in a worst-case scenario—that they won't forgive you or apologize to you. This process is so powerful and deep that it will show you how all-encompassing your narrative has been. And if you're willing to do the work, this process will take you to a new, more mature state—one where you get to grow up and take over your own narrative with your entire family.

The whole process of growing yourself up is so moving that the writing of a father letter was a pivotal part in a Netflix documentary film produced by Ed Norton called *My Own Man*. Written and directed by a friend and client of mine, David Sampliner, he took his film across the country, teaching college students about forgiveness and acceptance.

For those of you who have sadly lost one or both of your parents and think that this entire section does not apply to you, it does. Truth is, if we were set free from our parents when they died, I'd have much shorter sessions with people. From parents that are long deceased to biological parents we've never met, they matter. We feel them.

Our parents are right there with us.

WRITE OF PASSAGE

All right, it's that time again: someone else's.

The last thing any one of my clients wants to do, whether they are twenty-one or sixty-one, is to really speak their hidden truth to anyone, let alone their parents. Maybe things are finally good, or good enough, or better than it has ever been with them. Maybe things have always been great and you're fine with skipping over any long-forgotten and fairly forgiven crap.

Water under the bridge and all.

Some of you have already done a ton of the work and truly, wholeheartedly believe that your parents did the best they could. And you mean it. But let me ask you something. Is believing our parents did "the best they could" really forgiving them *or* is it giving them a handicap parking sign? And not only that, is it writing yourself a "get out of having possibly the most uncomfortable and vulnerable conversation with your aging parents ever" permission slip?

Going back to your parents and growing yourself up is a rite of passage, where you and your parents can get, as best as possible, on one and the same page with the story of your lives. Not as a blame game, but as a means of accounting, accepting, and forgiving.

I do, however, make one exception to the rule of resolving every last thing with a parent. That is when either of your parents is emotionally unwell. Because shouldn't you get that holding an unwell parent up to normal standards is a bit, well, crazy of *you*? And, if the truth is, you *can't* go there with your parents (or you tried to go there with them, but still didn't fully resolve anything), then at the very least know that you went for it. Know that by even venturing there, you are a hero for yourself and for your children, and for your children's children.

Hokey but honest, you got to be the change you wish you see.

This *is* the way out of your life on repeat. This is the remote control that has access to the play button. Truth is, there is no play button if you are still pissed at your folks and never forgiving them.

There are only reruns.

Let's see how Stephanie did with one of her parent letters. This slightly abridged sample was, obviously, many drafts later, perfectly imperfect, and very Stephanie-like. Written by someone who is cold and judgmental, like her mom, who has more to own and apologize for in her relationship with her parents, than someone who has had a sadder childhood. Remember, the entire process itself of writing and rewriting these letters is part of the profundity of the exercise.

Let's take a look at **Stephanie**'s letter to her mom.

Sure, it's long. But it's well worth *several* reads. If you need to muzzle your brat that is now rolling its eyes at reading such a long letter, by all means, do so. We all know it's spent way more quality (cough, cough) time on Facebook.

Dear Mom,

I am writing you this letter in order to heal our history. This letter is a way for me to be accountable for my behavior, for my fear and lack of compassion, and to begin a path of being more caring, more loving, and more acknowledging of you. This is my way of finally becoming an adult and moving on from the baseline tension I've been holding in my body around you for far too long that I know you've felt.

I know you've always wanted to be closer to me and I never really *let* you be. I'm sorry. This is a letter in which I get to be responsible for it, honest about it, and apologize fully for not having created that sooner.

It's time.

The more work I do on myself, the more I understand you and see you and your love—and I'm done holding back my love. There was a moment when you fainted in the hospital, when I was holding you up and you looked me right in the eyes, barely able to hold your body up but fully (I think) aware of yourself, and I swear neither of us knew whether this was it or not, and I saw you.

I saw your love and your vulnerability and I will never forget that moment, and I want you to feel my love the way I loved you that day, every day. I'm convinced that while you were so strong and unbelievably impressive, I made you stay alive so I could write and read you this letter. And feel it.

In order to create the adult relationship I want with you, I need to start by being fully honest and open with you here. In this letter, I will account and apologize for all my judgments of you, and I'll also recognize for what I'm grateful.

Please know that there is nothing in here that is meant to hurt you and none of it is a blaming of you. In fact, this letter puts an end to my right to ever blame you for my very own coldness over the years, and my own avoidance of intimacy.

First, the judgments I've been harboring; most of which you've heard. All of which have been cold and unfair on my part in that I never fully addressed any of them with you to resolve them. Instead I sat back and judged only you. These points lead to the reasons why I'm sorry, and this is me owning my part in everything.

1. Judging Dad.

When I was young, and still to this day, I've often judged you for judging—and what seems to me as belittling—Dad. As an adult, I know now that Dad is not innocent, nor am I an expert in marriages or relationships. But, throughout my life, I've sat back and coldly watched you roll your eyes, make faces, belittle him with words and mumbles, and demean him, both privately and publicly. You've called him stupid, fat, made light of his efforts to lose weight, and given him complaints and tense tones instead of support. I *told myself* it was hard to watch, but I now see that if I could make you the sole villain, I'd never have to deal with my own version of this, because I do it and never saw it clearly until recently!

I can also see that I've picked men throughout my life who would "disappoint" me in the very same way it seems Dad has disappointed you, so I could have the same dialogue in my head about them: how incapable, how blind, how absent. I want to own that in judging you for doing this, and playing the "victim" of it, I've lived this same story, and now that I'm working on that, I can see how I created this in my own life.

2. Staying in the relationship.

I've judged you and Dad for not getting a divorce. I made up that you were both consumed by trying to "look good for the neighbors" and for staying together for money, for appearances, for all the wrong reasons. I can remember certain times we'd be out in public and it felt "super close and connected," then it felt like there was a shit storm of anger brimming over the minute we were in private, in the car as a family, when one of you would start in on how angry you were about something that had happened, stuff you'd never express in public in that way.

To wonder if this was going to happen again just plain sucked. For whatever I contributed to that maelstrom over the years, I'm sorry. I can even see how I added to it and got to play the victim, stay cold and angry and not in my heart.

Now, of course, I've chosen to spend my life looking good in public, being so great in public—and I'm ashamed of certain times I was so shitty in private. This particular part has no place in my life and was making me sick. Over the past years learning so much, I've redesigned my existence so I can be proud of who I am, tell the truth with kindness, stay in my heart, and stop playing the victim with the violins in the background.

3. Not being good or loving enough.

I've judged you for not "earning" Dad's attention. I made you the criminal for not "loving him enough" or "holding the peace in the house." I know now that I had zero compassion for you, and blamed you like crazy whenever you wanted more attention. And then I picked men who often withheld their love from me, the same way you did from Dad. So with this letter and these confessions, I get to stop that pattern.

Most importantly, I made this dynamic of being conditional and taking love away, never being satisfied, all your fault. And now I can see I do the exact same thing. I pick men either I cannot be satisfied with that I judge, or I pick one that does that to me.

4. Wanting more attention.

I've judged you for wanting more attention. This is a big one. I've observed in family settings and public settings alike when I coldly watched you—wrongfully and judgmentally—when you've "interrupted" (my label) meals several times to say where a plate is, or in some way "insinuate yourself" (my label) on the conversation. I'm so sorry for this.

Then I've found myself doing the exact same things, with friends, with men, anywhere. What is funniest is that I've even chosen a profession that makes me super center stage. Instead of having compassion for you, or accepting your need for attention and validation as your heart's deepest desire (like all humans!), I saw it only as you being self-centered, and didn't tell you, or ask you about it. I'm sorry for this. It's infected many of our conversations and moments and it's over. You do you and that's what I'm here to love: you.

5. Wanting more intimacy and closeness with me.

I've meanly judged you for wanting more intimacy with me. Way back when, I've *pretended* I've wanted intimacy, but I really didn't—intimacy with you was impossible because I was blaming you in my mind for being mean to Daddy. So that made my coldness with you a justifiable thing. I didn't want to hug you when you were mad and complaining about him (even though a part of me could sense that your anger and issues were absolutely valid).

And, even though I was an angry, complaining liar myself so many times, I made *your* version worse and judged you for being somehow different from me. Fact is, I didn't *want* intimacy because it was easier for me to keep your love at a distance, and hold on to my own anger at you (and blame you for it), easier than dealing with our sameness, or my penchant for distrusting, nitpicking, and keeping a distance. Plus, I told myself that you failing at being a great mom made me a victim, instead of me just finding my heart.

6. Gossiping.

Another thing I've judged you for, mostly in the past, is gossiping about other people. I remember times when you'd talk about friends in some judgmental way in the house or the car, then they'd call five minutes later and you'd be super nice to them on the phone. This felt fake, and was fodder for my judgment of you all this time. But then I chose it for myself, as my own method.

I've loved having secrets in my life (cigarettes, pot, cheating, gossip), because it felt like I had control, and I see how fake I've been in certain situations. I'm sorry for judging you, because in judging you for it, my own gossip became less noticeable.

Again, I "won" in my victim mind in those moments—but I'd really lost the chance to just be in my heart and talk openly about the fact that it didn't feel right to me.

7. Money.

Another thing I've judged you for is how you handled money. Because of what you said about it, I knew we were just getting by, yet I completely wanted and loved the luxury of our trips, camp, and my Ivy League school. That conflict lived in me, yet it became another reason to judge YOU instead of owning my internal shame—of loving the luxe yet knowing we really couldn't afford it. I called you a fake in my head, and I was being so fake about it. The most f*cked-up part is that I knew it was hard for you, and yet I let you buy me everything I wanted. I could enjoy the indulgence and judge it. Ultimately, it let me get away with being a hypocrite. Let love be a measurement of giving me those things, when I knew the truth that it was causing problems in your marriage.

Now I'll list a few apologies I've owed to you for a long time.

1. For not being more kind.

I apologize for not being more kind and not listening much more carefully and caringly. I know you're getting a version of me that is full of expectation and vitriol even recently, and I am sorry. I have been holding back in some strange way to get back at you for what I was still *wrongly* holding against you. I know you still feel where you don't get the "real" me. You still get a part of me that is holding love back from you, and I promise to grow up and be fully loving with you.

2. For not giving you the "me" I give to others.

I have an experience of you of not truly "getting" me, and I told myself that I really wanted to be understood by you, and I'm sorry. I used to hate how you talked to me when you gave me advice, and I'm sorry for that too. I only wanted to be clapped for and to never need your advice, so when you gave it, I was always rude.

I always sickly thought you were jealous of my life, which gave me a great reason to be distant and superior rather than talk to you about what I was feeling. I'm so sorry for this.

3. For ever thinking that you'd abandoned me.

I always had this feeling that you abandoned me when I was small (you had to be helping your sick daughter, and I get it. I'm just admitting what my *inaccurate,* invented feeling was at the time). Then, later in life, when you tried to get close to me, I invented that you weren't giving me the space I was asking you for, especially in my twenties, when you kept asking me to be in closer contact, to call more, to come visit more. I invented that as "needy" on your part, and "too late to fix what was already broken." I'm sorry for being such a bitch and cold and icky and gone for you.

4. For distrusting you.

I had experiences of you where I (wrongly) felt I couldn't trust you, and out of this distrust I invented more reason to be cold to you. I didn't believe you when you would say that everything was fine with you, because I knew even before you started being honest with me about it that you were unhappy with Daddy and deeply sad inside. I could *feel* it.

Bottom line: *You couldn't win with me*, so even when you said nice things, I stayed cold and distant, and was only nice to you in public, and in front of other people, because I didn't believe you due to your saying you were fine when things were bad. I was always wonderful to you in public because it "looked good" for us to have a nice relationship. I'm owning that I'm *that* vain—that I would be kind in public even though I was so cold in private, and I'm sorry for that. Deeply, deeply sorry. This is a big one. I'm healing this.

I'm seeing that the people I love most in my life are the ones with whom I go cold, and the ones from whom I withhold my love—I point to their neediness, weakness, and meanness, instead of dealing with my own fear of getting closer, being truly needed, and being vulnerable myself. Intimacy depends on the truth alone, and it's time to keep things clean by addressing them instead of "being polite."

I've done this with you; I did it with all of my boyfriends prior. By keeping secrets from them, from everyone, I shunned creating powerful, real intimacy. I'm talking about this with you now, because I want intimacy with you, and I want it for my life, in all areas. I no longer have the right to withhold and blame others for *anything* I experience.

5. For not being real and vulnerable with you.

I'm sorry for never leaning on you for support. I was determined to be tougher than you. When you were sick in the hospital, I secretly felt a weird power in helping you, in being stronger, finally, and in having the upper hand when you needed me there. This is hard to admit, but true. And please know that I ultimately came from my heart and was subconsciously healing this entire story in all those moments when I *was* helping, touching, aiding your healing—and I apologize for the moments when I had to work or distract myself those times in the hospital—those were a true combination of both being overwhelmed with work, and trying to avoid the fear of losing you.

For all this, I'm truly sorry. I know now that I'm here to learn about sharing my heart, and letting go of judgment, and embracing my (and others') strengths, talents, experiences, and behaviors.

I'm sad and sorry that all of this resulted in me being distant from you and resisting knowing you. I'm sorry that I haven't been more kind to you as an adult. I'm sorry that I haven't expressed all the gratitude I owe you for providing for me so beautifully. I am sorry that I wouldn't hear you at times, wouldn't feel where you were coming from. I'm sorry for the times that I didn't let you hug me, feed me, that I didn't want to have fun with you, didn't accept the love you were offering to me, but instead judged the way it was offered.

I'm ready to be an adult with you, to express what's true for me, ask everything, and to show up for you.

Thank you, Mom, for being the first place I ever knew. For my magnificent life, for the privilege of watching you work, and try, and cry, and thrive, so much of the time. For being so proud, for bragging about me, for sharing me and for forgiving me, time and again. Thank you for knowing me, and for growing up with me. And for reminding me that what I am will always be more than enough. As are you.

Love,

Stephanie

Until we can step back and see how invested we are in our sad narrative and all of the memories that come with it, we can't see our own fingerprints on the crime scene. We can't see the theories we're ever so married to when it comes to our parents and our childhood. We can't teach our parents to show up differently for us, to stop "drowning" before our eyes, when we're the ones sitting on their very life preserver, pretending we aren't.

The opportunity to bring the adult you to the table with the kid you to write and read these letters to your parents is molecule changing. It puts you in charge of who you always said you wanted to be, but weren't.

If you have kids, I swear, you could probably write their letters to you on their behalf. Most of us really do know what sucks about us as parents, what we wish we hadn't said, or done or behaved like. Even if we have forgotten the exact thing we said or did that we were taking to the grave with us that unintentionally hurt our child, there isn't one of us who, if asked, wouldn't apologize.

Okay. At least we all agree that's the right answer!

Especially if what we did as a parent that indeed sucked was presented in such a way by our kids, as these letters are, in a balanced and fair telling, with a sincere longing to resolve everything and to create a loving, honest, open relationship with us, between adults.

Here are some **helpful hints** for writing your parent letters:

1. **No surprises.** Letters should begin by explaining the context of the letter and a preview of what is to come in it. For example, "This letter is to account and apologize for things I have blamed you for and held over you. It is also to tell you how I felt about a few things, ask questions, and resolve some things I experienced growing up."

2. **No putting lipstick on a pig.** In other words, don't gloss over incidents to avoid feeling pain.

3. **No switch-hitting.** Beware of switch-hitting. This is when you give a compliment, but then undercut it in the next breath. Make sure you are genuine about the compliment, or don't write it at all.

4. **No mixing and matching.** Keep positives and negatives in separate sections. This way, the parent knows what they are getting at any point in time.

5. **No cramming.** Sometimes there is a lot to say. You need to go back over every incident. Don't cram a lot into one sentence. Give every feeling, thought, and experience its own line.

6. **No lying.** Always be on the lookout for inconsistencies in what you are writing. What doesn't seem true? What sounds as if a child wrote it? This is where we sort out fundamental character lies.

7. **No inconsistencies.** A letter should consist of both sharing your hurts and accounting for your role in the relationship. It is like a feng shui-ing of reality, and if it is too heavy on one side or the other, it is imbalanced and the truth is off-kilter. Keep it balanced.

8. **No making shit up.** Get knowledgeable about the story of your parents' life. Write it down. Find out what your parents have been through. Get the whole story about what made them who they are so you can understand them and have compassion for them.

Many of us think that bringing up what has long been buried will needlessly hurt our parents. Except, what if keeping these long-buried hurts buried is more hurtful than we know? Is meaner than we think? What if keeping these memories is what locks our own purgatory in place? Is what has us unable to get out of default when it comes to designing our own love life?

Here's what **Stephanie** had to say about her experience reading the letter to her mom:

> Reading my mom the letter was like sitting inside of the car as a kid when the car was going through the car wash. My entire world was washed clean. Each line of forgiveness and apology, all particles of dirt, long-held childish grudges swept away moment by moment. Watching her face fall into a gentle expression of disbelief as I owned my part in the play of our life was an unforgettable privilege.

Guess what was possible for Stephanie after writing and reading both of her folks their letters? A better Thanksgiving? Sure. But you know what else became possible when Stephanie was willing to lose her narrative's thirty-plus-year case against her parents?

Love.

ASSIGNMENT FOR CHAPTER NINE

1. If you're in a relationship or partnership with someone that has grown less intimate, follow the directions in this chapter on how to do a laundry list, and then do one.

2. To level the playing field, write up your own list of what you think the other person has on you too. In other words, write up what you think they think sucks about you.

3. With the same person (once you like them again), discuss all the departments the two of you have in your relationship. Together, divide up all the responsibilities so that the right person is in charge of the right department. Remember, use the criteria described in this chapter (i.e., who complains or who is best at it) to determine who manages the department.

4. Follow the instructions in this chapter and write a balanced, fair, and mature letter to your mother and father, separately. Make sure to include the following:
   - All the things you were hurt by or sad about.
   - All the things you need to account, clean up, and apologize for.
   - All of the things you've been hiding from him or her.
   - How you felt about growing up with him or her as a parent.
   - Ask questions about anything you still don't understand.
   - Write the most honest version of your experience that you can, without justifications or protecting yourself.

5. Follow every warning I have issued in this book. Use this assignment to grow up about your relationship with your loved ones, not blow them up. Use it to get closer, understood, and understanding of them. Find compassion, balls, your sense of humor, and your heart. Remember, you are here to teach *them*. Hell, if you wanna come on my ride, believe you picked them to learn all of this. Just as your kids picked you.

Okay, I think you've been through enough in this chapter, no **POP QUIZ**.

Just kidding.

Your [*fill in the blank*], whom you love but who you're pretty sure has a laundry list on you ever since you lost weight, quit drinking, and started telling the truth, is coming to town. They offer to bring pizza for dinner. You have no choice but to:

A. add pepperoni. Woo-hoo. You get to double-dip: eat pizza and blame them.

B. say, "Great!" but plan on eating before they arrive.

C. f*ck it. Tell them not to bring pizza. You were planning on chicken and salad and, um, you thought they were on a diet too. See if you can pep talk them past the pizza parlor. You remember how hard those days were for you.

D. over a skinless chicken breast and salad, have a heart-to-heart with them. Fess up about the laundry list you have been compiling in retaliation to the list you're sure they have on you. And, PS, question yourself too as to whether *maybe* it's you that likes them less now that you are soberer; and deal head-on, heart first, with that.

E. what the heck, add pineapple to the pizza too. What?! It's a fruit.

Answer: **C** and **D**, for care enough to deal. No one else is coming to save your flock. No one should. They are, after all, all yours.

CHAPTER TEN

Mission I'm Possible

Be You. Only Better.

Having discovered, through an uncritical observation of your reactions to life, a self that must be changed, you must now formulate an aim. That is, you must define the one you would like to be instead of the one you truly are in secret. With this aim clearly defined, you must, throughout your conscious waking day, notice your every reaction in regard to this aim.

—*Neville Goddard**

FULL DISCLOSURE

Designing your life is a lifelong process. We are always evolving, learning, and creating.

No doubt, if you've done a bunch of what I barked at you to do in this book, you can see your true mission, your master plan, and what you need to be doing that you're either doing or still reluctant about doing.

---

* As much as I love credit, and (clearly like to) quote Neville Goddard, I use him for one purpose only, his powerful lectures on using our imagination. When it comes to his opinion about religion and the Bible as purely allegorical, I advise clients to do as I do, duck and roll.

More than likely, you have mapped out how you're going to realize your dreams in the three areas you copped to caring about in this book. You've even made some promises and are keeping them (or most of them). You've got a whole to-do list. You've faced reality and you're dealing with it. You know what you've got to do. And someone other than you, for goodness' sake, is holding you to your promises!!

You've learned to dream and to understand what your inner dialogue has been up to all this time. You can show yourself how living with Personal Integrity has worked, whether you've been on three great dates, lost fifteen pounds, or have had the ten-minute conversation with your boss that you've put off for ten years. You asked for what you needed, and it makes you proud.

You feel very different.

You realize that you know how to beat your system that not that long ago felt unbeatable.

Turns out, you're not that tricky. You need to stay on a diet, you need to have drinking rules, you need to have a plan—not only for what you are going to do but how you are going to *be* about it all. And now you do.

You keep doing tune-ups to the dreams you wrote in Chapter One, like maintenance on a car. You understand that having really clear goose-bump-worthy goals—a specific trajectory, like wanting a promotion, a relationship, a certain amount of money, the body of your dreams, etc.—is the key. You take yourself seriously enough now to have a plan for it all and understand the *duh* factor in that too! You even get the joke that it took more effort to stay stuck than free. And the only things you are left haunted by now are my barkings.

Woo-f*cking-hoo, and whew!!

D-DAY

Well, since you've now gotten a taste (okay, a large mouthful) of designing your life, I'm thinking I should also teach you how to design each day of it too.

Every morning, yes, every, I personally write what I call a *daily design* (DD) and send it as an e-mail to a group of my closest friends, who hold me accountable for it. Not only does this practice of designing my day, each day, keep me connected to my nearest and dearest, it has *me* at the source of my day's creation, and not simply acting in response to it.

What you put in your daily design is an accounting of how you want your very best and most fun day to unfold, equipped with attitude and aspirations. Whether you had great sex, told the truth at a meeting and inspired everyone to do the same, completed all the work you set out to accomplish, had zero traffic, got the best gift ever from your mother-in-law, lost a pound, etc., *you* get to create excellence that is on point with your dreams in the twelve areas of your life. *You* get to manage and inspire yourself, keep your promises, and talk to your life, directing it and practicing the art of authoring it. I mean, after all, who else should be in charge of uh, *your* day?!!

So, for example, here's what one of my DDs could look like:

Monday DD
- The meeting went great! We discussed next steps and booked our follow-up meeting.
- I finished writing the book and sent it to Hachette.
- I had a great night with David. We were connected, loving, and snort-laughed twice.

You see. You are literally creating your day *before* it happens. Similar to how you wrote your dreams in Chapter One, you will also write your daily design in the past tense, as if it has already occurred. At the end of each day, you will close out your day by going back through the DD you sent in the morning, and telling the truth (yes, *that* truth thing again) about what actually happened in the day versus what you said would happen. So my *end of day* (EOD) to all my friends whom I cc'd in the morning would look something like this:

Monday EOD

- The meeting went great. We discussed next steps and booked our follow-up meeting. **YES.**
- I finished writing the book and sent it to Hachette. **NOPE. STILL ON CHAPTER 10.**
- I had a great night with David. We were connected, loving, and snort-laughed twice. **YES. BUT SNORT-LAUGHED THRICE.**

As the author of my life, I get to end my day, every day, powerfully.

I know what I did and didn't do so I can set myself up for the next day. Everyone who is reading my daily designs also knows *exactly* how I did, as I know exactly how they did. I'm in communication and get to feel connected with the people in my life, always. I mean, we are, after all, in it together! And how beautiful is that?! You get to design your day and hold your friends to account for theirs, as they lovingly hold you accountable for yours.

Now that's my kind of flock, no?

FREAK OUT

Clearly, you've done a massive amount of work here on yourself. You're proud. You're lighter. You're freer. You've never felt more present. You've pretty much got a direct line to your higher self, and, for f*ck's sake, can even giggle at how low your lower self is willing to stoop.

Right?

Except now, you might be left wondering about the few things that you are NOT going to change. Whether it's because you can't (ish) or just plain don't want to. Like, how you're always late or how you're hyper-organized or how you eat with your hands. Funky, funny, and annoying things about yourself that just aren't going away.

Yeah, Lauren, what about those?!

There really are things about you—traits, mannerisms, a style, which are wholly "you." Those idiosyncrasies, which are unique to you and possibly irksome and annoying to others, are what I call your *freak flag*. Most of us walk around either tripping on our own freak flag or hiding it. But by the very nature of a freak flag, I think, there is no flying one half-mast. We're here to either fly it, fix it, or fold it the f*ck up.

Can you imagine a world where everyone was free and proud to be their freaky selves?

The problem is most of us pretend we're going to change our ways, when we're really not. As a matter of fact, it's what upsets us about other people. They have freak flags that no one is talking about.

Flying your freak flag is about being true and honest with yourself and others about who you are. It's about being accountable for what you love, don't love, and are either changing about yourself or not. It's about not lying or feeling bad about yourself, ending your own two-facedness, and taking care of the people around you who simply might not be your freak's biggest fan.

So what's *your* freak flag?

Usually, it's a thing you're not super proud of, a habit, a quirky something about yourself that you may have thought you'd change one day, but you've lived long enough to know by now that it's not changing anytime soon. And, by soon, I mean, uh, *never*.

You know how to fix a freak flag?

Either own it and stop making excuses about it, or make the decision to fix it. Either way, making the decision to fix yourself *or* even making the decision to not fix something about yourself is a radical miracle in a person's life.

The key to owning and donning your freak flag proudly and responsibly is to make sure you fly it right at the beginning of a relationship, of any kind of relationship. This starts the relationship off with honesty and gives people a choice to accept it or not. Sure, it might be a deal breaker. Sure, your PR agent will think it something not to disclose.

That's why we fired the agent in Chapter Six, right?

Anyway. Since I'm calling you a possible freak, want to meet mine (or, yes, meet some more of mine)?

WALKS WITH FEATHERS

A few years ago, I discovered my own freak flag oddly folded.

It was a couple of days before Burning Man,* an art festival in the Nevada desert, where I run† a life coaching camp. Before heading there, a bunch of us got our hair done: wool dreadlocks, sparkles, beads—you name it, we donned it.

Giddily, I got feathers in mine. I loved them. My husband, as you know by now, far from a pushover, loved them too. I was totally tickled by my new look, until, that is, I remembered that I had to attend a friend's fiftieth birthday party, um, sporting 'em. The party was a sophisticated, semi-formal event with people I didn't know. Suddenly, I was worried. Worse, I was back in high school. Worser (if it were a word), I wasn't even self-conscious back then.

I considered not going to the party.

Of course, I went, but I spent most of the night explaining to everyone at the party about Burning Man and my feathers. Not because they asked, mind you. They didn't. They may or may not have had an issue with my feathers; I did. Once I got the joke that I was the one being a freak about my freak flag, I started to lighten up and make fun of myself for caring so much about what others (and I) thought.

It gets better.

I came back from Burning Man only to have to wait five more days for Dana, the woman who feathered me, to come and take them out. During those five days, those 120 hours, once again I had to get over caring what other people thought of me, and evolve my mom's trait that allows what other people think to style her. I got to, once and for f*ck's sake, get

---

* Yes, even the fact that I go to Burning Man is, yet another, freak flag of mine.

† By "run," I mean I invite everyone I love, and one of my best friends—gifted artist, marketing godsend to Handel Group, and Burning Man den mother with whom you *never* wanna mess—Linda Colletta, actually runs it. Bullhorn and all.

over my high-school-aged head noise and be the goofy person I honestly was and wanted to be, feathers and all.

The feathers have been in my hair for over four years now.

Obviously, there are many variations of freak flags. Some are equally as hairy as mine and some, well, not so much. In the business arena, there are some freak flags that people would rather you keep folded, permanently. Much to the dismay of some, I fly my freak flag there too. Perhaps my biggest one. Ready?

I don't read e-mails.

What the f*ck, Lauren?! How do you not read your e-mails?!

I know. But, unless you are a client and are sending me e-mails and homework, the odds aren't good that I'll read yours. However, if you need to speak with me, call me or come on over.

In case you were wondering which parent of mine this trait is reminiscent of—see my eighty-year-old dad, Joel, a corporate attorney who is still lawyering but who does a damn good rant on how people "in this day and age" expect responses as quickly as they hit send on their e-mail. So, yes, mystery solved. I get my preference and gift of gab, my retro (a.k.a. technologically lazy), my snarl, my stubbornness, and my bark from my dad.

Do people wish I were different? Most certainly. Except, here's the thing. I'm up-front with everyone *immediately* about this potentially annoying fact about me. And, because I honestly wave my freak flag, it frees me. It has integrity for me. And almost everyone I work with understands this about me and even finds it kind of, sort of endearing. It also saves us a lot of time and frustration. Rather than feeling bad about my freak or suffering over it, I own it and manage it with the people in my life. I don't hide it for one minute. I am up-front, honest, and accountable for it. I make sure everyone knows how to reach me. And, if you are ever put off or caught off guard by me, I explain immediately how I am this person, this jerk, and always try me by phone or text and never worry about following up with me; you might need to. And I'm sorry. This is me. But, boy, do I ever keep appointments, so get in my calendar and come to the Core Club (not too apropos a name for my NYC meeting spot). Come on. I dare you to get *that* daring about your freak flag and fly it, responsibly and proudly.

Here are some **steps on how to own your freak flag**:

1. **Make a list** of what you are simply not going to change about yourself.
2. **Accept your freak flag.** Make peace with it. Have a sense of humor about it. And, if it turns out your freak flag is something you can't sell to yourself or anyone else, then face that and change it. Lose the whine. Suffering about it is, after all, optional.
3. If you're keeping your freak flag, then **tell everyone about it.** Get it out in the open. And, if you need to manage it with the people in your life, do so. Fly your freak flag, but don't flap it in people's faces.
4. Once you see your own freak flag, **make a list of complaints** you may have about other people's freak flags that you need to accept. If you can't accept their quirks, then get honest about that too. Once and for all, face your two-facedness.

A CALL TO ARMS

Given all that you've learned, all the dots you connected, the traits you leashed, the theories you debunked, the hauntings you unraveled, and the code you cracked, you can now author what your life was *always* truly about, back then *and* now. You can now be accountable for how your autobiography is going down.

After all, you are who *you* say you are.

And it's up to you what you're going to be proving true about yourself from now on. I mean, you're the one who wrote your autobiography in the first place, right? You watched your family. You took notes. As did your folks take notes on their folks, as will your kids watch you.

Same pen.

But now you're well equipped to change the ink. Change what's going down on paper. Change from your current state to a newly designed state, by setting out to prove your new ideals. To care enough about yourself to honor your own truest ideals and visions for where you are in your life.

You get to go right/write who and how you are now going to be. To dare, stretch, and scare yourself big, as you did in Chapter One when you allowed yourself to dream. Only now, you are going to write your own *personal manifesto*, the truest of true pledge of allegiance to yourself. When you're writing your personal manifesto, make sure you include, in some shape or form, the following:

- Who are you?
- What are you putting an end to?
- What do you refuse to accept?
- What do you take responsibility for?
- What do you want your life to be about?
- What will you stand for?
- What are you taking on next?
- What are you promising?

I leave the directions for writing your own personal manifesto a bit loose here, on purpose, as this is an opportunity for you to let your own poetry happen. These manifestos, after all, are for you to inspire yourself, to be vulnerable, to be honest and so head over heels with what you wrote and for which you stand, that should a friend so much as cough during the reading of it (yes, you read that correctly) to them, you contemplate kicking them, which is a sure sign that you're in the right amount of in love with it.

Once again, *barking directions #1–12*: Hang in there. I will show you enough sample manifestos, so the writing of yours will be less debilitating than your former support staff (chicken, brat, and weather reporter) are trying to sell you at this very moment. And, if you're like me and binge watch Netflix shows because you hate cliff-hangers, it'll also allow me to catch you up on the evolution of the others who were on this ride with you.

Let's check out **Ethan**'s manifesto:

I am the ringmaster, and the three-ring circus of my life is my family, my career, and myself. I am taking charge of them all. No more blaming my crazy upbringing, no more sour moods and mopey head hanging. I chose it all and I make magic with it. I am fearless and fun with no time for staying stuck or just getting by. I romance Regina. We dine by candlelight, bathe in bubbles, and have hot foreplay and sex, at least twice (!) weekly. I have individual playtime with each of my kids every week and paint enthusiastically with my mom-in-law. Yes, totems and all! I get the raise and promotion that I no longer covet, I ask for. I demand excellence from myself and help others to achieve it in their lives. The busiest, most important asshole on earth has left the building to make room for more love, patience, joy, and inspiration. I happily take the chaos, craziness, fear, sadness, and struggle within and around me and transform it into thrilling, exuberant, fearless fun. My life is wild, beautiful, and amazing. I treat myself and those who join me with great love and care and respect and we all feel it. I entertain, lead, laugh, and get laughs. I keep the show rolling smoothly and take charge. No excuses, no blaming, no hiding, or playing small. I reach new levels of connection with my family and friends and new levels of performance and amazing results in my career. I have endless patience, overflowing optimism, and an amazing sense of humor that allows me to always get the joke (even when it is on me).

As you can see, Ethan is doing great. Almost unrecognizable from where he started, right? Clearly, he's got the right length harpoon line on his Mopey Dick and is no longer suffering the fate of his own Captain ~~Ahab~~hole.

And how about **Donna**? Here's her manifesto for the year. In it, she names the new sexy, mouthy trait she invented for herself, "La Femelle." Seems her higher self is part French.

Last year marked the last port for my swallowing martyr/save it for later/ and watch them hang until it is a mess. The year marks the end of making *Reine Donna* small. This is the year I captured my barefoot, carefree, humorous, sexy chick, who says it ALL and had outrageous fun! Our family dinners are not only healthy and Dr. Mark Hyman approved, they are fun-filled with laughter, storytelling, and sharing. I create a lovely balance between fun time on my own, either walking, reading, writing, or meditating; romantic time with John walking and talking; and fun adventures with the kids, hiking, biking, water sports, and exploring. This is the year I upgrade my friends to business class. And the year I *am* my own bestie!!! My best coach, teacher, cheerleader, and friend. This is the year I wake up each morning excited about spending the day with my best friend— *moi*. I am so proud of the love I have for myself. I love and embrace all of my humanity with a big heart and a sense of humor. I play the game of "Three Things for Me" each day with joie. The strategy is, "What cool things can I do for me that have me feeling ridiculously proud and super happy?" I love my "La Femelle"—the one who says everything and makes her man wild by speaking her truth with fire and passion—her Latin roots oozing from her pores as she speaks her truth. John falls madly in love with her and can't resist. He *melts* like the chocolate he feeds me.

Can you tell Donna is now at her marriage's helm and fighting the right fight—for finding her voice, for intimacy and honesty? For being in charge of the right departments in her marriage—from the children's department to housewares to, uh, bedding. For teaching her kids about their legacy, about ending her right (and subsequently their right) to be a victim in life, pretending to be the underdog and not the top dog of it, and, until now, not seeing the chicken in that. And guess what? Donna's IBS is in remission, as are her lying, shopping, and grumbling.

Okay. Now, let's see how **Stephanie** did with her manifesto:

I am a generous, compassionate, and loving leader. I use my style, my know-how, my sexy, and my savvy to make the world a hotter (not hellish) place! I have hereby fallen hard off my soapbox and have stood up, braver and kinder. I honor the meek and wounded. I am a leader in my community, my business, and my family. I have helped heal my family.

I have located my heart and rekindled my love for my big sister. I forgive myself and others with ease. I have ended my right to judge, hold grudges, and grumble. I happily follow the "three grumble rule" and clear up any mumbles I can't muzzle myself in twenty-four hours. I vow to never look down on myself or others again, and not see and show the way up. My joy and generosity flood everywhere and feed my body and career. I am sought after, and my work-life balance is impressive. I honor and respect time, my own and others'. I can do everything I need and play equally as hard as I work. I take wild vacations, yearly, and long weekends often. I talk to my mom once a week and am proud of the depth of our conversations. She feels my love and I hers. Jeff and I are hedonistically happy, and heroes in each other's eyes. Next year, I will have a baby and fall madly in love with her, healing all history. Never did I (clearly) think I'd ever be this at home with someone, but there's no place like this home. No ruby slippers required.

Seems, by dealing with her own narcissist, her own victimized blamer and finding her heart with her folks, that Stephanie thawed her own. That's right. Stephanie found love. The real deal. The whole package: a smart, hot author, professor, and—take a deep breath—surfer, no less.

They're engaged.

Clearly, the best "they" I've ever typed when talking about Stephanie!!

Okay. **Katie**'s turn. Let's see how she did with her manifesto:

I am a happy, healthy, confident, communicative, powerful, badass "A" player in my life and in the world. I am deeply connected to my heart, free and in my mission of making a difference on the planet through storytelling. I am an inspiration to those around me and help others find their voice, get healthy, and tell their story. I fully express myself and live an honest, balanced life in all areas. I embrace the real me and put an end to hiding, lying, and being self-destructive. No more victim, martyr, or being afraid to speak or stand up for what I believe. I am the author of my life moving forward and the source of everything in it. I deeply value my promises and realize they are the key to my happiness. I have finished and read my dad his letter and love speaking with him weekly. I have Lucy, my brat, on the right length leash (short) re: drinking and eating, forever and always. I have loving, fun, and honest relationships with my friends, family, and colleagues. I am deeply in love with "Mrs. Monday through Sunday." We support, honor, and lovingly push each other to greatness, always and obviously, communicating our truth. Our love story inspires others to freely be themselves. In my own mind and heart, I am free and proud to be gay and this much in love with the truth about my life. I will spend the rest of my life sharing my life story and being a positive role model for others, making the world a better place for future generations to come.

Can you see how, like Donna, Katie is also in the right battle for herself—speaking up. Katie has not only lost eighty pounds and bought her first home, she teaches people to write their own stories as she's in the process of writing her own, *Just Breathe.* She's committed to transforming lives and helping people get healthy by opening their mouths and speaking, instead of chewing. Katie and her ex-husband, Shaun, much to the shock of everyone who knew the two of them when they were divorcing, are friends. In fact, here's an e-mail Shaun wrote to Katie after she told him her whole truth and nothing but the truth.

Hi Katie,

You have been on my mind a lot recently. The world probably seems like a different place to you now. A new realm of unknown possibilities, both exciting and scary. I am sure you are filled with trepidation, and you may even have many doubts still lingering in the corners of your mind. You probably find yourself wondering what will this new future be for you, what will it bring. You know in life there are no guarantees, but you are now ready and willing to live that life on your own terms, and you will accept that whatever will be, will be. You are finding yourself all over again, but this time you are looking in the right places and I am sure you can feel the peacefulness settling in your soul.

I want to share something with you, and please know it's purely about me and is not intended to lay anything on your shoulders. For although it relates to you, it is in no way meant to be something for you to take on board or feel involved with somehow. It's just me sharing a piece of me with you, from one soul to another.

So first, let me start by saying thank you, Katie. Thank you for all that you brought to my life, the love and the tears, the joy and the pain. Even the heartbreak of losing you is something I thank you for, because it all contributes to who I am. The man I am today would not exist without the sum total of all my experiences. And you, Katie, were an integral part of so many of those experiences and life lessons, and for that I am forever truly grateful. I carry you in my very soul because you helped shape it in so many ways.

So, I want you to know, as a human being, how powerful you have been, how influential you have been, and how much you contributed to my life today. And that makes you pretty much the most amazing person that ever crossed my path. No one has affected me more than you. And I want you to know how deeply loved you are by me for that. A true and selfless love for everything you are, and everything you are not, a love that asks for nothing in return from you.

I love you, Katie. I am blessed that our Father in heaven filled my heart with love for you. And, although we are so far from where we once were, you were a gift to me that has never really left me because you are in my heart and soul forever, and that is a precious gift of joy that only God in all his grace could grant.

So travel well on this new journey, Katie. I wish so much love and happiness for you, and I will always be in awe of the incredible woman you are. And whatever the road may bring, know that I will always be here should you ever need a friend to talk to or turn to. You will never be alone as long as I walk this earth.

All my love,

Shaun

What's possible between two people, when they own up to every last thing about themselves, is an intimacy and connection they claimed to have always wanted, but were too invested in their own current reality to realize.

Once we get the joke that most of us are not nearly as nice as we claim, and are liars, chickens, brats, head cases, weather reporting about our lives as if we have no say-so, we can then actually have a say over what's so. We can create the relationship of our dreams, even the relationships with our exes of our dreams.

What was possible for Katie, once she finally, forty years later, told the truth about everything, from her drinking to her hiding to her hauntings to her traits to her sexuality and dealt with them all, was a freedom to just be herself. Katie, who never cared about love her entire life, got struck her first date *out* with a woman. No shit, she fell adorably, wildly, and deeply in love. Her girlfriend Kerri is moving in with her, practically as I type.

And on that note, here's your final assignment. Have fun with it, not just because compared to some of the others, it's an easy one, or the fact that it's your last one, but because it's the last one you'll need.

According to my GPS, you've made it. Your destination is on the right. Whichever right *you* want to author from this day forward.

ASSIGNMENT FOR CHAPTER TEN

1. Write a list of what you are not going to change about yourself (your freak flags). Once you're done, either choose to fly your freak flag(s) and tell everyone about it, or fix it. Quit the suffering either way.
2. Write your very own personal manifesto. Do it in your own flavor, but make sure to answer the following questions:
   - Who are you?
   - What are you putting an end to?
   - What do you refuse to accept?
   - What do you take responsibility for?
   - What do you want your life to be about?
   - What will you stand for?

- What are you taking on next?
- What are you promising?

3. When you're done with writing your manifesto and love it, read (yes, read) it to your most trusted friends. Be sure to follow the helpful hints in Chapter One on how to not kill your nearest and dearest when reading something that matters a ton to you.

4. Find a buddy or a few buddies who want to practice designing their days with you. Come up with a game plan that works for all involved. For example, the friends with whom I DD all have a rule that we must send our morning DDs out Monday to Friday before ten a.m. eastern time. If we forget or are late, we owe ten dollars. Same with ending our day, it's ten dollars if we forget. I highly recommend setting reminders, or if you're old-school, put a Post-it on your percolator. Figure out (the quicker the better) a way to not lose money. The idea, obviously, is to design your day, not go broke. Remember, when you are designing your day, write it in the past tense, and include how the day went, both physically and emotionally. You get to design it all.

Just to be fair, since I can be accused of a lot of things, but not equally outing myself is definitely not one of them, I thought the best way for me to end this short, light read of a first book is with my own manifesto:

I am a dreamer of a greater world. Of unfolding happiness into people's lives as we march through the method with fun and freedom. Of graceful and radical truth telling to an alarmingly, unexpected, and set-freeing degree. Here to help humanity love and understand themselves. Here to put an end to my own fear of not being ready, not being the right whatever I'd have to be, to get this job done. Here to refuse to accept that humanity doesn't want to get it, and that they and I can't have it all. And I mean *all*. *All* out of our love life, *all* with our kids, *all* with our family, *all* with our career, and *all* with our day-to-day life. I take responsibility for everything in my life and around me. I stand for the truth being told with love, and the dreams I hold for people, rocked and realized. On the docket, I get to bravely and unbrattily pick up my travel paint kit and hit the road, building more fun ways to impact the planet, all the while continuing to giddily chase my sex promise, exercise, snuggle with my kids, straighten my drawers (ish), have tea time with Marsha, build my business, create more and more content, and watch Netflix while eating baked apple chips with cinnamon. I hereby pledge to keep believing, dreaming, building, and barking. And slap you, me, and all who come with you, happy.

All right. It's time for your last **POP QUIZ**. Consider this your final exam. You finally finished this book. Plus, your hives have cleared up since the hauntings assignment. Sure, it was a long read and a bumpy road, but well worth it, you think. It's hard to tell. Except for the fact that:

A. you have magically lost the five pounds you have been complaining about for eight years.

B. it seems your metabolism somehow improved once you put the "cookie" down and went up the StairMaster.

C. you are getting laid again.

D. you and your tween daughter are getting along. An outcome you didn't fathom possible until maybe, one day, in the far, far, distant future, possibly, when she had a C-section of her own and was heavily medicated, she'd get how great you were. Okay, just maybe it was the promises you put in about ending your own eye rolling at her.

E. you fired your current social planner (you) and had an epiphany that you couldn't meet someone while hiding on your couch.

F. you found true love—you.

G. you didn't burp up as much bile as you used to from the likes of option F.

H. all of the above.

Answer: **H**, all of the above. But, particularly **F**, for from f*cked to FREE.

THE ~~END~~ BEGINNING

Notes

Epigraph

vii **Man, in his blindness:** Neville Goddard, "Fundamentals," *New Thought Bulletin*, Summer 1953.

Introduction

5 **A full 93.2 percent of them:** MIT student course evaluations for Living an Extraordinary Life, January 27, 2006.

Chapter Three: The Promise Land

69 **Newton's first law of motion:** Isaac Newton, *Mathematical Principles of Natural Philosophy* (London: 1687).

Chapter Five: Emotional DNA

104 *behavioral epigenetics:* Brian G. Dias and Kerry J. Ressler, "Parental Olfactory Experience Influences Behavior and Neural Structure in Subsequent Generations," *Nature Neuroscience* 17, no. 1 (January 2014): 89–96.

104 **Neuroscientists at Emory University taught:** Ibid.

106 **Phil, the weatherman (Bill Murray):** "Phil the Weatherman," *Groundhog Day*, directed by Harold Ramis (1993; Los Angeles, CA: Sony Pictures Home Entertainment, 2002), DVD.

Chapter Six: The Truth about Lying

111 **Most of us think that we are kind and loving:** Goddard, "Fundamentals."

113 *The Matrix's* **"red pill":** "The Red Pill or the Blue Pill," *The Matrix*, directed by The Wachowskis (1999; Los Angeles, CA: Warner Brothers Home Video 1999), DVD.

113 **"Fifty Ways to Leave Your ~~Lover~~ Liar":** Paul Simon, "50 Ways to Leave Your Lover" (Columbia, 1975), song.

120 *make a new plan, Stan. You don't need to be coy, Roy. Just get yourself free:* Ibid.

126 **Stepford Wife:** Ira Levin, *The Stepford Wives* (New York: Random House, 1972).

Chapter Seven: Hauntings

163 **Back to the Future:** "Changing Your Future," *Back to the Future*, directed by Robert Zemeckis (1985; Los Angeles, CA: Universal Home Entertainment, 1985), DVD.

Chapter Eight: Unstuck

176 **You get to see how your inner dialogue, your *pigeon*:** Mo Willems, *Don't Let the Pigeon Drive the Bus!* (New York: Hyperion Books for Children, 2003).

184 **Khaleesi won't even appear in tonight's episode:** David Benioff and D.B. Weiss, "Winter is Coming," *Game of Thrones*, directed by Timothy Van Patten, aired April 17, 2011 (Los Angeles, CA: HBO, 2011).

Chapter Nine: The Mother Load

186 **you're left in the land of "The Emperor's New Clothes":** Hans Christian Andersen, *Andersen's Fairy Tales*, trans. Jean Hersholt (New York: Heritage Press, 1942). Hans Christian Andersen, "The Emperor's New Clothes" (Copenhagen: C.A. Reitzel, 1837).

189 **playing *Candy Crush*:** King Digital Entertainment, *Candy Crush*, London: King Digital Entertainment, 2012, video game.

206 **Netflix documentary film:** "Parent Letter," *My Own Man*, directed by David Sampliner (New York, NY: Netflix, 2014).

Chapter Ten: Mission I'm Possible

220 **Having discovered, through an uncritical observation:** Goddard, "Fundamentals."

225 **a couple of days before Burning Man:** Burning Man is a weeklong festival that takes place every year before Labor Day in the Black Rock Desert in Nevada. The event is attended by tens of thousands of people who build a temporary city dedicated to community, art, self-expression, and self-reliance, www.burningman.org.

Great-Full

I am sure by now, you can imagine not only how many thank-yous I've gotten in my lifetime, but how many I owe.

To my family, who love me and have tolerated my freak flags long before I even named and waved them. To my Buckaroo Banzai–like hot husband, David, who holds the bar high for me to pole-vault over as a partner, wife, lover, and best friend. To my amazing kids, Kiya, Parker, and Daisy, who are not only here to raise, teach, and evolve me, but to spotlight the gap between who I am and who I want to be as their mom. To my parents, Marsha and Joel, for being the kind of folks I could practice on, tell the truth to, or tell the truth about, and who love and forgive me each time. To my older, wildly f*cking impressive sister Beth, who cofounded Handel Group with me; who always believed me bigger than I believed myself; and who, on a dime, is not only willing to change, but is hungry to. To my older, snarkier, brilliant, and closet-poet brother, Matt, who, because I so needed his love and approval, trained me to sit with anyone. To my middle (of four?) sister Marnie, who, because I had to double back and go get her to love me, my method of healing families exists; who shaped me in fun, style, and intimacy; who, if we were the last two people on earth, I'd be okay (not necessarily safe, but deeply, happily yakking until the very end); and who, it turns out, megillah magically (see: "volume II" of this book) was the only one who could have written this book with me. To Shir, a dreamer and believer, a wise and caring CEO, who can handle with heart all the hens in the house. To my wives and surrogate sisters, you really know who you are, who you have always been for me, and without whom I could not have gotten this far, thus far.

To my day husbands, Mark, Andy, and Jeff, among some amazing others, who love me, hold me to an impeccably high standard, and literally and figuratively feed me. To my executives, coaches, and coaches-in-training, holy shit, thank you for all you believe, teach, wait for, and give back. To Michelle Howry and everyone at Hachette Book Group for their honor and commitment to my dream. To my agent, Richard Pine at Inkwell Management whom I love, who needs to live forever so I can get everything I want done, whom I'd wish on anyone as their agent; and to Eliza, who had my back throughout the entire process. To every client present, past, and future who lets me bark, roll my eyes, place a napkin on my head, dub them (on top of calling them chickens, brats, liars, and pigeons) an odd, possibly grammatically incorrect name; and who not only lets me get away with it, trusts me enough to let me ride shotgun. For every story you generously told and entrusted to me, I promise you, I teach from. And, last but not least, to any of you that I obviously love, but may have forgotten to thank here, please reread Chapter Seven on hauntings and Chapter Ten on freak flags (mine, in particular) and call me; and for those of you who don't like me, once did, now don't, never did, e-mail me.

Resources

If you've made it this far and are *still* reading, you deserve not only a medal—a martini. Just kidding! How about a gift instead? Use the code **MAYBEITSYOU** at **InnerU.Coach** and get $100 off* of our kinder, gentler (but still kickass) digital course: Inner.U.

Go to **HGLife.Coach** to find out more about our many offerings, such as:

- Private Coaching: One-on-one sessions with a coach who has completed our rigorous personal development program. Schedule a consultation at coach@handelgroup.com.
- Design Your Life Weekend: An eye-opening weekend workshop when you will work in-depth and in-person on what matters most to you, or should: you.
- Free Workshops and Webinars: Heated and hot discussions on topics such as dating, managing your mind, mastering time, and more.
- Inner.U: A digital course to design your dream life online. It Includes 14+ hours of audio coaching with me, assignments, Q & A calls, a community forum, and prizes! (Yes, prizes!)
- Newsletter: Sign up for our weekly newsletter and get weekly hot tips, helpful hints, and how tos.
- Corporate Coaching: Find out more about bringing The Handel Method to your company at **HGCorp.Coach** or institute of learning at **HGEdu.Coach**.

---

* This offer may not be combined with any other offer.

You can also visit **MaybeItsYou.com** for links to special coaching videos and PDF downloads from this book, including the ever-important promise tracker. And please—send me your stories. As much as I curse, I care. Email me at **lauren@maybeitsyou.com**.

Love,
Lauren

@HGlifecoaching   @laurenzander

@HGlifecoaching   @laurenzander

@handelgroup